CONTENDING FOR THE FAITH

LEANDER S. KEYSER, D.D.

CONTENDING FOR THE FAITH

Essays in Constructive Criticism and Positive Apologetics

BY

LEANDER S. KEYSER, D.D.

PROFESSOR OF SYSTEMATIC THEOLOGY IN HAMMA DIVINITY SCHOOL,
WITTENBERG COLLEGE, SPRINGFIELD, OHIO

AUTHOR OF "A SYSTEM OF NATURAL THEISM," "A SYSTEM
OF GENERAL ETHICS," "THE RATIONAL TEST,"
"ELECTION AND CONVERSION," "IN THE
REDEEMER'S FOOTSTEPS," "IN THE
APOSTLES' FOOTSTEPS," ETC.

NEW YORK
GEORGE H. DORAN COMPANY

PRINTED IN THE UNITED STATES OF AMERICA

JUST A WORD HERE

The author desires to make grateful acknowledgment to the publishers of the following theological magazines for the privilege of reprinting in the present form the various articles that first appeared in their columns: *The Lutheran Quarterly*, Gettysburg, Pa.; *The Lutheran Church Review*, Philadelphia, Pa.; *The Theological Monthly*, Columbus, Ohio; *The Biblical Review*, New York, N. Y.

L. S. K.

Hamma Divinity School,
   Wittenberg College,
      Springfield, Ohio.

CONTENTS

CONTENDING FOR THE FAITH

CONTENDING FOR THE FAITH

CHAPTER I

THE NATURE AND NEED OF APOLOGETICS

THAT the truth should be both promoted and defended is a proposition that the author of this volume firmly believes. He has no sympathy with the lackadaisical and lazy motto which prevails in some quarters: "Do not concern yourself about the truth; the truth will take care of itself!" If that were a fact, the whole history of the world, and especially of Christianity, ought to be rewritten. Then all Christian people might as well lay down their arms and be "at ease in Zion." If the truth will take care of itself, why did Christ come into the world, incarnate the truth in His own person, and advocate and defend it on numerous occasions? If the truth will take care of itself, Peter and Paul and the rest of the apostles and evangelists did a vast amount of superfluous work, for much of their preaching and writing was devoted to the vindication of the truth. Now they were advocates; anon they were staunch defenders.

Dr. E. F. Scott has written a strong and valuable book on "The Apologetic Element in the New Testament" (1907), in which he proves that Christ and His apostles were often on the defensive as well as the aggressive, and

did not merely let "the truth take care of itself." **Again**
and again Christ defended His person, His mission and
His message against the Pharisees, Scribes and Sadducees.
Peter's Pentecost sermon was a defense against the false
charge, "These men are full of new wine," and a powerful
argument that Jesus, whom the Jews and Romans had crucified, was the Messiah of the Old Testament and the divine Son of God. Why did he not save himself the trouble and danger of bearing his testimony by simply reflect-
ing that "the truth will take care of itself"? The New
Testament tells us that Paul often "reasoned" with the
Jews in their synagogues. His speech on Mar's Hill was
an acutely relevant apologetic, as was also his classical defense before King Agrippa.

The inspired writers of the New Testament expressly
command Christ's disciples to use the apologetic method.
Read 1 Peter 3:15: "But sanctify in your hearts Christ
as Lord: being ready always to give an answer to every
man that asketh you a reason concerning the hope that is
in you, yet with meekness and fear." Nor is Jude less
emphatic (verse 3): "Beloved, while I was giving all dili-
gence to write unto you of our common salvation, I was
constrained to write unto you exhorting you to contend
earnestly for the faith once for all delivered unto the
saints." In the next verse he gives the reason why such
defense was necessary; because "certain men had crept in
privily" to destroy the doctrine of "our only Master and
Lord, Jesus Christ." The same reason for defense obtains
to-day, and has ever obtained in the history of the Christian religion.

There is only one way of propagating our holy faith, and
that is by testimony. We Christians cannot and should
not use force, but only persuasion and argument. "Ye
are my witnesses," said the Master to His disciples. Suppose they had refused to bear witness on the false notion

that "the truth will take care of itself," what would have become of the religion of Christ? When Jesus gave His great commission to His disciples, "Go ye into all the world and preach the gospel to the whole creation," He surely meant that the gospel should be proclaimed to gainsayers and opponents as well as to the ignorant and indifferent. Nor can we believe that all the noble army of defenders of the faith from Justin the Martyr, Arnobius and Irenæus to Luthardt, Orr and Green, have toiled in vain. When we turn to our library shelves, which are filled with the monumental works of the great apologists of the Christian faith, both ancient and modern, we cannot believe that all these scholarly investigations and self-sacrificing labors have gone for naught. Indeed, we are constrained to hold, from our study of church history, that Christianity would long ago have perished from the earth, had not brave, stalwart and competent defenders of the evangelical faith always arisen to stay the onslaughts of assailants. Why should not the Christian apologist, as well as any other teacher of religion, have a divine vocation?

The viewpoint of the unbeliever himself is also worth considering. Suppose no Christian scholar would ever enter the arena against him, surely he would think that Christians were cowards and knew they could not defend their cause. And would he not have a right to think so? It is both vain and wrong merely to sneer at the unbeliever or rationalist, or simply to aver that his arguments are not worth answering, or that he is dishonest and conceited. That is a cheap and easy way of dealing with doubters, and a lazy way, too; but it never convinces them; rather, it encourages and fortifies them in their skepticism. On the other hand, if the apologist can refute argument with stronger argument, can match scholarship with scholarship, and thus can vindicate the Christian faith at the bar of reason, he may succeed in convincing even the doubter and in leading him in the way of assurance and truth. If he cannot be won in that way, he surely can never be won by dogmatism, or browbeating, or contemptuous silence.

Let it be frankly admitted that not all preaching and teaching should be apologetic. In many cases the purely positive method is the better. It depends upon circumstances as to the proper plan to be pursued. If the preacher has no infidels nor rationalists in his congregation or no people who are troubled with doubt, he should not misspend his time in talking to people who are not present. Moreover, by saying too much about skepticism or radical criticism, he may even stir doubt in the minds of the innocent and unwary rather than fortify their faith. For the most part, the Christian preacher should simply take the truth of the Christian religion for granted.

However, such cases are very different from that of the writer who feels called to defend the faith against the prevailing and popular currents of unbelief, and to circulate his books among people who are inoculated with doubt, or distressed with difficulties which they cannot resolve. Surely it is some one's duty to come to the help and rescue of the people whose faith is being imperiled. If some men do not possess the gift or taste to enter the apologetic field, let them cultivate the gifts they have, and leave the field of argument, defense and vindication to those who feel that they have a divine vocation for such work. Let all evangelical believers encourage and abet one another in their several spheres of labor for Christ. It is merely a sign of narrowness for any one to scoff at every vocation save that to which he devotes himself. A good motto for all preachers and teachers of divine truth is found in 2 Cor. 4:1, 2: "Therefore, seeing we have this ministry, even as we have obtained mercy, we faint not: but we have renounced the hidden things of shame, not walking in craftiness, nor handling the Word of God deceitfully; but, by the manifestation of the truth, commending ourselves to every man's conscience in the sight of God.''

We must attend to another objection. Some years ago a correspondent (one who, by the way, was liberalistic in his theology) accused the writer of being unduly nervous about the truth, because, forsooth, we so frequently came to the defense of the orthodox faith. His allegation was that we could not ourself feel secure in our position, or we would not be so ''feverishly'' anxious to fly to its defense. That is, we were like the boy in the graveyard, ''whistling to keep our courage up.'' We were using the apologetic method to bolster up our own wavering faith.

Well, a suspicious mind, one given to ''judging,'' *might* read that ulterior motive into the conduct of a defender of the faith. But we most positively disclaim any such nervous anxiety on our own behalf. We are willing to admit, too, that, in God's all-wise economy and plan, His truth will finally prevail without our efforts. But that is not the point at all. First, the surer we are of the truth for ourselves, the more anxious we should be to win the erring to its standard. We regard it as wicked selfishness, utterly unworthy of a Christian believer, to rest ''at ease in Zion,'' on the ground that he feels secure in the saving truth of the gospel for himself. Is it not rather true that those who do *not* feel sure of the truth are the ones who keep silent?

Second, though God's cause will triumph in the end without our efforts, yet how many people may perish along the way if you and I fail to do our duty! *That* is the matter of paramount importance. God is able to bring good out of evil and make the wrath of man to praise Him— but how about the personal doom of those who do the evil? Yonder is a bright young man who is drifting into doubt through the perusal of some of the modern books of radical Biblical criticism. Are you simply going to let him drift, and lose his faith and perhaps his soul? Would it not be better to show him the errors of the men who are leading him astray, and thus try to reëstablish his faith? If you do save him, who knows but that he may become a flaming proclaimer of that faith which he had almost lost? For our part, we believe in trying to save the skeptical or rationalistic sinner as well as any other kind of a sinner. Perhaps you are best adapted to rescue one class of sinners; perhaps another man is best adapted to rescue another kind. "To every man his work." "To each according to his several ability." "But all these worketh one and the same Spirit, dividing to each one severally as He will." No; it is not a question of the final triumph of the truth, which is in God's hands; it is a question of saving and directing as many people as you can while life and opportunity last.

A few words should be said as to the kind of apologetics that the times demand. As the reader peruses this book, he will see that we believe in the positive method. For example, we do not believe in yielding so much to the disintegrating Biblical criticism as to endanger the divine authority and inspiration of the Holy Scriptures. Where we see danger, we have been free and frank to point it out. Our sincere conviction is that the orthodox faith, the faith that accepts the plenary inspiration of the Canonical Scriptures, is the faith that can best be vindicated at the bar of reason and that is based upon a sound, assuring and enduring religious experience; that it is easier by far to uphold this view by the rational process than to uphold a kind of *quasi,* half-and-half, pliant, fluid and compromising theology. We contend that, if half the effort were made by the rationalist to maintain the conservative position that he employs to undermine it, he would be a capable defender instead of a destructive critic. The thing that has amazed

us many a time has been the limping logic of the rationalist; the ease with which he can accept a theory that lacks
even a moderately rational basis. To put it in an epigram,
the credulity of rationalism is proverbial. At present we
admit that this is bare assertion; we hope to prove the
truth of the assertion in the body of this book.

We cannot agree with Professor C. W. E. Body, who,
in some parts of his valuable work, "The Permanent Value
of the Book of Genesis," maintains that there is no real
peril to the faith in the methods and conclusions of the so-
called "mediating" Biblical criticism of the Cheyne-Driver
school. We are compelled by the strictly logical process to
take a firmer position than that. If the Bible has been
composed in the way the aforesaid school of critics maintains, its divine inspiration is certainly invalidated, and
confidence in its teaching will surely be lost by those who
will insist on pushing the premises to their logical conclusion. We think we have proved this in the chapter entitled, "A Liberal Critic's View of Biblical Inspiration,"
the critic referred to being Driver. The reason some of
these critics, in spite of their destructively critical methods, still profess to hold to the evangelical faith is that they
fail to draw the legitimate inferences from their premises.
They stop short at the brink, and fall back on a forced
faith, a faith of mere feeling, a *naïve* faith, which is very
near akin to credulity. But most people will *not* stop
there; they will push on to the inevitable conclusion. And
this is the conclusion: If the Bible is made up of myths
and legends where it professes to recite history, and if it
contains many irreconcilable contradictions and scientific
blunders, as the said critics contend, then surely, surely it
cannot be divinely inspired in any sense in which men can
confide and upon which they can base their hope of salvation. If the critics themselves will not reason logically,
many of their readers and disciples will. A faith "that

trembles on the brink" is of little value in the stress of our earthly life.

Above we have referred to Dr. Body's excellent work. We hold that he makes some dangerous concessions to the Cheyne-Driver school of critics—concessions, too, that are entirely unnecessary, even on the ground of reason. In his discussion of the Bible and science he also takes a precarious position, which is evidenced by the very fact that he so often glides off into glittering generalities, and fails to state definitely and clearly just what he believes. Note his inconsistency. He holds that the first and second chapters of Genesis are of great and momentous religious value, and are vitally related to God's redemptive plan through Jesus Christ. But suppose, after all, that the Genetical narratives of creation are not true, but contain many mythological guesses and scientific errors—then, pray, how can they be of real religious value to the man who exercises his logical faculty? However, we are glad to acknowledge that Dr. Body, in the best chapters of his book, points out most effectively the untenable and irrational character of the literary analysis of the Pentateuch by the Driver school. On this account his work is a profitable apologetic. Our conundrum is this: How can he hold that the views of the critical school are so unreasonable and yet do no disservice to saving faith in the Bible? Surely a view that has no solid basis in fact and reason must imperil the evangelical position with people who draw logical conclusions.

But happily our author himself, inconsistent as his attitude may seem, points out in other places in his book the dangerous character of the critical methods and positions. For example, in his invaluable chapter on "The Creation and Paradise" (though there are some statements in it from which we must dissent), he gives many convincing reasons for the unity of the teaching of Genesis I and II, which the Cheyne-Driver school do their best to make contradictory. Dr. Body proves that they are not discrepant but harmonious and complementary accounts of the process of creation. Then, in the closing paragraph of this chapter (page 126), he sums up in this way: "In a word, to recognize the true relation between these accounts is to possess the necessary preparation alike for the deepest revelations of God and the highest conceptions of life. To tear them asunder is to inflict upon mankind serious spiritual loss. To lessen in any way their influence is to cut at the very root of true progress, either in the knowledge of God or the regeneration of man." In this paragraph Dr. Body has himself pointed out the deadly danger that comes from the critical methods of the school under consideration. Whatever inflicts on "mankind serious spiritual loss," and "cuts at the very root of all true progress either in the knowledge of God or the regeneration of man"—whatever does *that* surely must undermine the very foundations of Christian faith. In our author's excellent chapter on "The Fall and Its Immediate Results," he expresses fine and well-deserved indignation at the irreverent way with which President Harper and Professor Addis treat certain portions of the Biblical narrative (Gen. III), which, to Dr. Body himself, is as holy as a shrine. He should have remembered that Harper and Addis belonged to the so-called "mediating" school of critics, of which Driver was the dean. We do not blame Dr. Body in the least for his display of righteous indignation; but we are constrained to ask whether such treatment of the Genetical narrative as he rebukes so sternly does not imperil faith in the Bible as a divine revelation. Dr. Body shows effectually that the Biblical narrative of the Fall constitutes the basis of and reason for the redemptive work of Christ. If that is so, is not the very heart of evangelical and saving faith penetrated by those critics who treat the Fall narrative as if it were only a childish myth or a primitive human tradition? No; we must contend that the dissecting criticism which finds crudities, discrepancies, doctrinal and ethical errors in the Bible endangers faith in the Book as a God-given revelation. Those who hold otherwise are trying to cling to a very insecure position. Their faith—which they so loudly proclaim—is *naïve* rather than based on sound rational principles.

It is pertinent to show how stoutly Dr. Body stands for the Genetical narrative and how firmly he opposes the nullifying criticism of the Harper sort. Dr. Harper, in criticizing the narrative of the Fall, holds that our first parents, by eating of the forbidden fruit, "gained one superhuman attribute, viz., wisdom," and then hints—remember, *hints*—that God was "jealous" of the wisdom that man had thus acquired. This is more than Dr. Body can tolerate with patience. He breaks out thus: " 'Gained superhuman wisdom' indeed! Where, we may well ask, save in the lying sophistries of the Tempter, is there a vestige of such a conception?" Are not the positions of the critics dangerous to faith if they merit such a rebuke? Then our author adds, in commenting on the sentence, "Behold, the man is become as one of us, to know good and evil," that this statement, "when taken, as it should be, in the light of its context, is seen to refer, not to a real advance in wisdom, but to the rending of merciful limitations, which shielded the development of man's knowledge; to the premature and illicit acquisition of the knowledge of evil by experience, which, like every species of unlawful knowledge, does not really impart wisdom to the possessor, but rather destroys it. Surely we are entitled to protest against all this as not merely a grossly inaccurate, but as an utterly unjustifiable, method of dealing with Holy Scripture. As soon might one expect to hear the Sacred Volume branded as atheistic on account of the well-known utterance of the fool in the Psalter, as to find the merciful Creator suspected of an unworthy jealousy of the shame of His poor fallen creatures.''

This is robust defense of the faith; and, when you consider the momentous nature of the facts at issue, the lofty tone of indignation is seen to be justifiable. It proves our contention, namely, that the critical methods of the school in question do imperil the true faith.* So let us not capitulate to them; reason and facts do not warrant surrender.

As if to prove this contention by a concrete example, a notable instance has lately come to the fore. We refer to the publication of ''The Shorter Bible'' (only the New Testament as yet), translated and arranged by Charles Foster Kent, with the collaboration of a number of other critics of the same class. Dr. Kent is known as one of the most respected of the so-called ''mediating'' critics. In his introductory note he declares that this work is intended to include ''those parts of the Bible which are of vital interest and practical value to the present age.'' This certainly implies that what he has omitted is not regarded by him as of ''vital interest and practical value.'' But note some of the things deliberately, purposely omitted from this ''expurgated'' New Testament: 2 Tim. 3:16, 1 Pet. 1:21, 1 Pet. 1:25, Jude 3, Matt. 5:18, 19, and others, all of which teach the inspiration and divine authority of the Holy Scriptures. When such passages are actually eliminated by a critic, dare any one say that his methods do not eviscerate the integrity and inspiration of the Bible? Nearly all the passages teaching the doctrine of the atonement are cut out; so are many of those referring to sin, guilt, natural depravity, false teaching, and our Lord's second coming.

---

* Although we have ventured to pass some strictures on Dr. Body's work, yet it is of so much value that we have included it in the ''Selected Bibliography'' of conservative works at the end of this volume. It is too important to be omitted. Few books give a more demolishing refutation of the arguments of the Cheyne-Driver-Addis-Harper school of Biblical critics.

The great passage on the resurrection, 1 Thess. 4:13-18, is not included in "The Shorter Bible." It is significant, too, not to say pathetic, that Rev. 22:18, 19, relative to the danger of adding to and taking away from "the prophecy of this book," is left out. So is the great key passage, 1 Pet. 1:18-20: "Knowing this, that ye were redeemed, not with corruptible things, with silver and gold, from your vain manner of life, handed down from your fathers; but with precious blood, as of a lamb without blemish and without spot, even the blood of Christ; who was foreknown indeed before the foundations of the world, but was manifested at the end of the times for your sakes." Think, my brethren, of the theology of a critic who would elide that passage from the Bible as not being "of vital interest and practical value to the present age!" The whole epistle of Jude is omitted. Why? It contains the well-known exhortation to "contend earnestly for the faith once for all delivered unto the saints." Evidently that was too strong for this liberalist, who craves a more lackadaisical doctrine. Yet in his preface he declares that his book is intended to give "the true heart of the gospel."

Amazing it is, and distressing as well, to note how many people simply capitulate to the liberal criticism. At this very writing (July 22, 1919) an advertising circular from the publishers of "The Shorter Bible" comes through the mail to our desk.* It contains quite a number of "personal opinions and press notices" of the book. Many persons and periodicals of high rank commend the work, some of them almost fulsomely. The limpid and charming style of the translation seems to captivate them and dazzle the eyes of their judicial and critical faculties. Evidently they have failed to note the many vital excisions from God's in-

*A year later one of our religious periodicals informs us that the publishers are still "pushing" the book, and are making great claims for it.

spired Word, and, saddest of all, do not seem to have missed the elided portions. This fact proves the statement to be untrue that all one needs to do is to read the liberal books in order to be convinced of their weakness. The truth rather is that many people, even people of high standing in scholarly circles, are caught in the web of the insidious critical methods. Therefore the peril must be clearly pointed out. Had Dr. Kent simply given us a beautiful modern translation of the New Testament, without omissions or glosses, what a good and great service he might have done for the cause of evangelical Christianity!

No more need be said here about the sapping character of the critical methods of the liberals. We shall return to the subject more than once as we proceed with our analyses.

A thorough-going apologetic is needed to-day—one that gives cogent and convincing reasons for the orthodox positions. You cannot dismiss the liberalists and radical critics with a supercilious toss of the head or a scornful curl of the lip. That is never the right way to answer an opponent, nor the effective way. Ridicule seldom, if ever, is in place. The only ethical thing to do is to give sound reasons for the faith you hold and the hope you cherish. By all means try to treat your opponent fairly and respectfully. Sometimes you hear something like this: "You do not need to read a book in reply to the radical critics; just read their books yourself, and you will see at once how worthless they are!" That is what we would call "the high and mighty style." It is the dogmatic way. But it takes too much for granted, and does not coincide with the facts in the case. If it is true that the errors of the destructive critics are so easily seen and overcome, why do the critics believe themselves to be correct? And why do they command so large a following among scholarly and thinking people? If their works are so weak and unconvincing, why do so many publishers assume the risk of issuing them? A good many leading publishers within the last two or three decades have refused to publish any religious books except those of a liberal character, because conservative books could not be made to *pay*. There was not a sufficient demand for them to warrant the financial outlay. This condition of affairs is *prima facie* proof that many people are won over to the liberal side through the perusal of the critical productions. We have known young persons to be led astray by such reading, and it required not a little argument and persuasion to bring them back to the evangelical faith. Far too many people are caught by the plausibility with which the negative critics present their case. We know of no better remedy for their trouble than the perusal of cogently written rejoinders to the critics. And there are many such works, as the following pages will demonstrate. They are works written by competent scholars, who are able to match erudition with erudition, and to point out most effectively the weak points in the radical positions.

A word as to the proper spirit or temper of the modern apologetic. In the following writing, it is possible that sometimes a slight tone of scorn or indignation may be discernible, especially when a position seems to be utterly ill-taken; but we do not want any feeling of rancor to be read into or between the lines. We entertain no such emotion. Where some vigorous expressions are employed, they are to be attributed to earnestness, not to anger or contumely. Nor do we mean to call in question the sincerity of our opponents. We hold no brief for dealing with their motives; we have to do only with the positions they have taken on Biblical and theological questions. Surely we may try to prove their positions wrong and illogical without being called upon to pronounce a verdict on their standing before God.

Sometimes, when the bad logic of the critics is pointed

out, they raise the cry of "persecution." That is quite aside from the mark. Certainly, if they have a right to attack the evangelical positions, or undermine them surreptitiously, others have a right to defend them, and to set forth the rational grounds of their defense. It is only human that men who are in earnest should express themselves vigorously; but that is something far removed from the wish to persecute an opponent. The days of the thumbscrew in religion are happily gone. But it would be one-sided and unfair for the dissecting critics to be permitted to flood the market with their books, and then put an embargo on all replies to their attacks. If there is sometimes too much dogmatism on the conservative side, there often is no less on the liberal side, especially when that side claims all the "assured results" and "scholarship" of the day, and ignores the many scholarly works that have been written in response to the liberalistic output. Again and again we shall show in this work that the so-called liberals are often very illiberal; also that they are often ultra-conservative, while some of their views are old enough to be called "traditional." Let there be a free debate on both sides; only let us avoid the slashing, vituperative style of polemics.

Quite a number of the chapters of this volume deal with the problems of Biblical Criticism in their relation to Apologetics. It should be borne in mind that the two departments of theology, namely, Biblical Criticism and Apologetics, cannot be divorced. Whenever the former in any way affects the inspiration, integrity and authority of the Sacred Scriptures, it trenches on the territory of the latter. Indeed, all the branches of theological science stand in organic and reciprocal relations.

A few of the following chapters treat of certain doctrines that require defense, as we think, against the tendencies of so-called "modern thought." One of them discusses the much-vaunted theory of evolution, and another attempts to prove that the mysteries of physical science are no less insoluble than the mysteries of theological science.

The book is sent on its way with the prayer and hope that it may perform some part, even though humble, in extending the kingdom of Christ by emphasizing and inculcating a sturdy faith. It is the only kind of faith that will weather the storms and trials of our earthly life.

CHAPTER II

As has been shown in the preceding chapter, the position
is sometimes taken that the liberal criticism of the Bible,
especially that which wants to be known as the "mediating" criticism, does not annul or even endanger the inspiration of the Holy Scriptures, and that therefore conservative believers are wasting their energy in opposing
them. The following chapter, though only a fragment, is
intended to prove that the Bible as a divine book is not safe
in the hands of the said critics. While they may *profess*
to uphold the inspiration of the Bible, they virtually destroy it. They are illogical when they hold otherwise, but
many of their followers will carry their premises to their
legitimate conclusions, even when the critics themselves
do not realize the untenable character of their contentions.
So, in this chapter, we take as an illustration the work of
one of the best known of the liberal critics.

Before us lies a copy of Dr. S. R. Driver's "An Introduction to the Literature of the Old Testament," new edition, revised, 1913. This work was first published in
1891, and therefore might be regarded as almost out of
date; but, after running through seven editions, it was revised by the author in 1909, and brought up to date at that
time. In his addition to the preface of that edition the
author said (p. XIII): "Eighteen years have elapsed
since the first edition of the present work was published,
and the preceding preface written substantially as it still

stands." In the preface to the last edition (1913) the author says: "In the present edition the bibliography, and, where necessary, the references, have been brought up to date; the paragraph on Isa. 22:1-14, in view of recent exegesis, has been rewritten, and occasionally also a slight improvement has been introduced elsewhere; while some other matter (including a note on the value of the divine names as a criterion of authorship in the Pentateuch), for which space could not be found in the body of the volume, has been collected in the new *Addenda* (p. XXV ff.)."

Hence we have before us Dr. Driver's latest pronouncements on the criticism of the Old Testament. His death occurred since this edition was issued, and no statement has ever been made that he superintended a later revision. Anyway, a book published in 1913 ought not to be antiquated in 1920. If it were, all the critical labor bestowed upon it would surely be of small value, and would be labor lost. So we maintain that we have in this volume, wherever we may quote from it, Dr. Driver's latest views, his most matured decisions; therefore the liberal Biblical criticism brought up to date.

Now, Dr. Driver may be regarded as *facile princeps* among the more moderate of the liberal Biblical critics. He was not so radical as Robertson Smith and T. K. Cheyne, and contantly tried to mediate between the critical positions of the Graf-Wellhausen school and the evangelical faith. Admitting and defending the main positions (though differing on minor points) of that school, he was not willing to push on to all their naturalistic and anti-supernatural conclusions. Almost all the recent liberalistic critical writers on the Bible, such as Kent, Foster, Bade, Peritz and Sanders, depend on Driver to a greater or less extent for their material, and often parrot his teaching; and that frequently, it seems to us, without independent investigation or judicial weighing of the premises.

Our purpose now is to examine Dr. Driver's position on the doctrine of Biblical inspiration as we find it set forth in this latest edition of his work. We go directly to Driver's own book, because there are people who think that some of us who hold to the conservative position never read the works of the liberal critics, but confine our reading to the books that have been written on our own side. If such accusants were to come into our libraries, and see the shelves filled with the liberal output, they would at once have their minds disabused of their error. That aside, let us apply ourselves to Driver.

Looking in the index, we find only one reference to the inspiration of the Old Testament—pp. VIII-XI (it should be XIII) of the preface. In this whole book on the Old Testament, consisting of 577 pages, much of it in fine print, there is only this lone reference to divine inspiration, and that is in the preface! All the rest of it consists of criticism, hair-splitting refinements, discussions of human "sources," "traditions," "discrepancies," "variations," and so on and on. This is certainly not very encouraging, to start with. The very *atmosphere* of such a work is spiritually depressing. But we must be entirely fair to our author, and so will let him speak for himself. On p. VIII (preface) we find this statement:

"It is not the case that critical conclusions, such as those expressed in the present volume, are in conflict with the Christian creeds or with the articles of the Christian faith. Those conclusions affect not the *fact* of revelation, but only its *form*. They help to determine the stages through which it passed, the different phases which it assumed, and the process by which the record of it was built up. They do not touch either the authority or the inspiration of the Scriptures of the Old Testament. They imply no change in respect to the divine attributes revealed in the Old Testament; no change in tne lessons of human duty derived from it; no change as to the general position (apart from the interpretation of particular passages) that the Old Testament points forward prophetically to Christ.''

Here we must pause for a moment. How glad we would be if it could be made clear that the critical methods of Driver and his school actually do thus uphold the integrity and inspiration of the Bible! We conservatives are not anxious to discover that many scholars of the day undermine the authority of Scripture; it would be much more to our advantage if we could prove that the great body of them really uphold it in its integrity. However, respecting the foregoing quotation, we cannot help wondering why Dr. Driver was so persistent in advocating his views, spent so much time and effort, and used so much ink and paper in defending them, if, after all, they concern only the "form" of revelation, and in nowise affect the "fact." Is the mere "form" so important? Does it make the Bible so much more precious to the Christian to have his faith in it simply take another "form"? Anyway, what an immense amount of labor has been expended to establish merely a new "form"! Just look at the shelves on shelves of ponderous and erudite tomes that have been published merely in the interest of a "form of revelation." According to Dr. Driver, one would think the whole conflict is, after all, only a "tempest in a tea-pot," or "a mountain in labor bringing forth a mouse." But we turn to Driver again (p. IX):

"That both the religion of Israel itself, and the record of its history embodied in the Old Testament, are the work of men whose hearts have been touched, and minds illumined, in different degrees, by the Spirit of God, is manifest; but the recognition of this truth does not decide the question of the author by whom, or the date at which, particular parts of the Old Testament were committed to writing; nor does it determine the precise literary character of a given narrative or book. No part of the Bible, nor even the Bible as a whole, is a logically articulated system of theology: the Bible is a 'library,' showing how men, variously gifted by the Spirit of God, cast the truth which they received into many different literary forms, as genius permitted or occasion demanded,'' etc.

Many people will simply swallow and applaud the foregoing statement. It contains much truth, but it is only a partial, and therefore a specious, statement of the situation. It is true that divine inspiration will not, in some cases, decide the questions of authorship and date. However, in other cases these points are most intimately connected. For example, when the Bible declares that Moses wrote large portions of the Pentateuch, whereas the critics assert that he wrote none of it or very little, then are not the divine inspiration and veracity of the Bible endangered, nay, invalidated, by the critical process? Again, when the book of Genesis recites events as if they were actual history, and then the critics of the Driver school declare that they are not history, but mostly myth, legend, folk-lore and tradition, invented and composed by writers living centuries afterward, will not the question of date and authorship affect the "fact," as well as the "form," of revelation? Therefore our author's statement, quoted above, will not bear critical analysis; it is more adroit than accurate.

Often have we remarked that it is next to impossible for a liberal critic to be logical and consistent. After saying (p. VIII) that his critical methods "do not touch either the authority or inspiration of the Scriptures of the Old Testament," Dr. Driver remarks on page X: "None of the historians of the Bible claim supernatural enlightenment for the *materials* of their narrative: it is reasonable, therefore, to conclude that these were derived by them

from such human sources as were at the disposal of each
particular writer; in some cases from a writer's own personal knowledge; in others from early documentary
sources; in others, especially those relating to a distant
past, from popular tradition."

We are not overlooking Dr. Driver's next remarks, but
will come to them later. Let us now stop and analyze the
above. "None of the historians of the Bible claim supernatural enlightenment for the *materials* of their narrative." The italics are Driver's. Moses was a historian.
He certainly claimed "supernatural enlightenment" again
and again, and that, too, for the "materials" of his narrative. Just drop down almost at random in the book of
Exodus—12:43-49, beginning, "And Jehovah said unto
Moses and Aaron, This is the ordinance of the passover;"
13:1: "And Jehovah spake unto Moses, saying, Sanctify
unto me all the first-born," etc.;" 14:1: "And Jehovah
spake unto Moses, Speak unto the children of Israel that
they turn back and camp before Pi-hahiroth," etc.; 20:1:
"And God spake all these words, saying," etc.; and so on
through chapter after chapter. Now, if the critics teach
that God did *not* give Moses all this material, and the Bible
says He *did,* how can Dr. Driver hold that his critical
methods do not affect the authority and inspiration of the
Bible? To show our author's inconsistency with himself
again, we quote a footnote, taken from Sanday's "Oracles
of God," which Driver cites approvingly (p. X):

"In all that relates to the revelation of God and His
will, the writers (of the Bible) assert for themselves a
definite inspiration; they claim to speak with an authority
higher than their own. But in regard to the narrative of
events, and to processes of literary composition, there is
nothing so exceptional about them as to exempt them from
the conditions to which *other works would be exposed* at

the same place and time." (Italics ours for emphasis.)

Note this well. It means that some parts of the Bible are divinely inspired, while other parts are only human compositions, subject to the same conditions as "other works"; yes, even "exposed" to the same kind of liability to error. If it does not means that, it has no meaning; it is mere beating of the empty air. Yet Driver had said on a previous page that his critical theories "do not touch either the authority or the inspiration" of the Scriptures! If the writers in narrating historical events were "exposed" to the same conditions as other writers, and hence liable to error, what becomes of their authority and inspiration? Hear Driver again (p. X):

"It was the function of inspiration to guide the individual writer in the choice and disposition of his material, and in his use of it for the inculcation of special lessons."

That certainly is good; it sounds almost as if the writer believed in *verbal* inspiration; it certainly would spell *plenary* inspiration; yes, and *infallible* inspiration. If only the author could have held fast to such principles in the rest of his book! Note again how orthodox he was: "The whole is subordinated to the controlling agency of the Spirit of God,. causing the Scriptures of the Old Testament to be profitable 'for teaching, for reproof, for correction, for instruction which is in righteousness.' "

Why, that is almost rashly orthodox and conservative. It must have been Dr. Driver's heart, and not his head, that indited that statement. Nor can any conservative theologian object to the following discriminating remark: "But, under this presiding influence (that of the Holy Spirit), scope is left for the exercise, in different modes and ways, of the faculties ordinarily employed in literary composition. There is a human factor in the Bible, which, though quickened and sustained by the informing Spirit, is never wholly absorbed or neutralized by it."

Who ever said it was? Here Driver is stating a commonplace truth, which no conservative scholar has ever questioned. Why should he assume a polemical tone in stating it? He is fighting a man of straw. What he says in the next sentence, spite of its challenging air, is so trite and generally accepted that it is not worth quoting. Let us now see how consistently our would-be champion of Biblical inspiration stands by his principles. On page XI he inserts a long footnote, which we must now scrutinize.

There are "two principles," he says, "that will be found to solve nearly all the difficulties," which "are insuperable" according to "the traditional view." And what are those principles? The first is, "that in many parts of these books (of the Old Testament) we have before us *traditions,* in which the original representation has been insensibly modified, and sometimes (especially in the later books) colored, by the associations of the age in which the author recording it lived."

Logical inconsistency is the chronic malady of the rationalist. Compare the above with what the author had just said on p. X: "It was the function of inspiration to guide the individual writer in the choice and disposition of his material, and in his use of it for the inculcation of special lessons." Here inspiration is claimed for the Biblical writers. But how does that comport with the statement (p. XI) that in many parts of the Old Testament books "we have before us *traditions,*" and that "the original representation has been *insensibly modified,* and sometimes *colored,* by the associations of" the writer's age? How could the writer be under "the controlling agency of the Spirit of God," and yet "modify" and "color" the "original representation"? If the "original representation" was true, and the writer modified and colored it, he turned it into error, and therefore could not have been guided "in the choice and disposition of his material" by the Holy

Spirit. If the "original representation" was wrong, and the writer corrected it, why are there any "difficulties" in the Biblical text which, according to the traditional view, are "insuperable"? The simple fact is, Driver means in this passage to say that the Biblical writers were themselves responsible for creating the "difficulties," because they "insensibly modified, and sometimes colored" the facts. Would they have glossed them thus if they had been guided by the Holy Spirit? Cannot the reader see why, in spite of the protests of Driver and his followers, their views annul the authority, trustworthiness and inspiration of the Sacred Scriptures? Their chief proponent cannot hold his head steady on two consecutive pages! We will not call in question their motives, but we confess that we have no confidence in their logical processes. To prove it further, we are going to convict our author from this same footnote of disloyalty to his own claim that the Old Testament writers were divinely inspired. He says (still on page XI):

"Should it be feared that the first of these principles, if admitted, might imperil the foundations of the Christian faith, it is to be pointed out that the records of the New Testament were produced under very different historical conditions; that, while in the Old Testament, for example, there are instances in which we can have no assurance that an event was recorded until many centuries after its occurrence, in the New Testament the interval at most is not more than 30-50 years." Then he claims that the facts of our Lord's life could not "have been the growth of mere tradition, or anything else than strictly historical." Then: "The same canon of historical criticism which authorizes the assumption of tradition in the Old Testament forbids it—except within the narrowest limits, as in some of the divergencies apparent in the parallel narratives of the Gospels—in the case of the New Testament."

Now note: he puts the Old Testament and the New on

different bases. While arguing that the New Testament is historically reliable, he admits that the Old is not, because it is made up largely of "tradition." Yet on the preceding page he had said of the Old Testament: "The whole is subordinated to the controlling agency of the Spirit of God." That is a fair specimen of the logic of rationalism. Do you wonder that we cannot allow the major premises of these liberal critics?

On p. XII our author tries to show that his critical view of the Old Testament does not invalidate the authority of our Lord. We can take the space to quote only what is relevant:

"He accepted, as the basis of His teaching, the opinions respecting the Old Testament current around Him; He assumed, in His allusions to it, the premises which His opponents recognized, and which could not have been questioned (even if it had been necessary to question them) without raising issues for which the time was not yet ripe; and which, had they been raised, would have interfered seriously with the paramount purpose of His life."

Such arguments have frequently been answered; see Orr, "The Problem of the Old Testament," pp. 3, 38, 370, 523; Lias, "Principles of Biblical Criticism," Chap. VII; Smith, "The Integrity of Scripture," Chap. III; Beattie, "Radical Criticism," Chapters XIV, XV; Urquhart, "The Inspiration and Accuracy of Holy Scripture," Book I, Chap. VI; Burrell, "The Teaching of Jesus Concerning the Scriptures"; Wright, "Scientific Confirmations of the Old Testament History," Chap. I; Blanchard, "Visions and Voices," Chap. IX; McGarvey, "The Authorship of Deuteronomy," pp. 264-297 (very acute), and many others. We will simply say here that, if Jesus accepted the current views of the Old Testament, which were wrong, according to the critics, then He either knew they were wrong, in which case He connived at and encouraged error, and became an opportunist; or else He did not know they were wrong, in which case He was not divine. In either case our confidence in Him would be undermined. Let us add that we have read a good many of the liberals who hold Driver's views, and nearly, if not quite, all of them have inadequate ideas of the person and work of Christ. Here is another remarkable quotation from Driver's book (p. XIII):

"Criticism in the hands of Christian scholars does not banish or destroy the inspiration of the Old Testament; it *presupposes* it; it seeks only to determine the conditions under which it operates and the literary forms through which it manifests itself; and it thus helps us to frame truer conceptions of the methods which it has pleased God to employ in revealing Himself to the ancient people of Israel, and in preparing the way for the fuller manifestation of Himself in Christ Jesus."

That sounds well, and if it were consistently carried out by Driver's critical method, all of us would hail him as an evangelical scholar and paladin; but, alas! like the previous professions we have noted, it is scarcely uttered before it is forgotten. Already in 1893 Dr. James Robertson, in his great work, "The Early Religion of Israel," criticized this sentence, and declared that Dr. Driver ought to give a definition of inspiration, and say wherein his view differed from the defective and naturalistic views of the Graf-Wellhausen school. In remarking on Driver's claim for the "inspired authority" of the Scriptures, Dr. S. C. Bartlett, in "The Veracity of the Hexateuch," acutely says: "But when we are informed by the same writer that we have but 'traditions modified and colored by the associations of the age in which the author lived,' and that the author used his 'freedom in placing speeches in the mouths' of the several characters, such as 'he deemed to be consonant,' . . . what becomes of the 'inspired authority' and religious lessons of such a book?''

Verily the liberal critics have a hard time keeping ·in their possession the jewel of consistency. It is with them as it was with the idolators of old of whom the Psalmist wrote: "Their sorrows shall be multiplied that exchange the Lord for another God" (Ps. 16:4).

We have another fault to find with Dr. Driver's *dictum*, namely, that he *presupposes* the inspiration of the Old Testament. While we believe in conservative methods, we do not believe in being so *ultra* conservative as to *presuppose* one of the chief things to be investigated. If the critic is going to be unbiased, he cannot enter upon his investigations by presupposing the main proposition. Let us imagine a conservative critic making such a statement as Driver makes, and what an ado the liberals would raise about "preconceptions," "predilections," "hide-bound prejudices," and so forth! Drs. William Henry Green, James Robertson, James Orr and J. J. Lias—all of them staunch conservatives—never began their work with any presuppositions like that; but, on the contrary, taking nothing for granted, they endeavored to prove each proposition as they proceeded.

It remains now to see how faithfully and consistently Dr. Driver held to his "presupposition," in the body of his work. Turn to p. 8. Here our author contends that Genesis is "composed of distinct documents or sources, which have been welded together by a later compiler or redactor into a continuous whole." What are the proofs he adduces? They are mainly·two: "(1) the same event is doubly recorded; (2) the language, and frequently the *representation* as well, varies in different sections." Then he proceeds to give examples of variance. Thus the first and second chapters of Genesis "contain a double narrative of the origin of man upon the earth." Of course, he ad-

mits, it might be argued that the second chapter gives "a
more detailed account of what is described summarily in
1:26-30;" but he will not allow that interpretation; for
he says: "But upon closer examination, differences reveal
themselves which preclude the supposition that both sections are the work of the same hand." In proof, he says
that in 2:4bff. the order of creation is this: man, vegetation, animals, woman, which he say is "*evidently opposed to*
the order indicated in Chapter I"—vegetation, animals,
man. In the next sentence he calls these differences "*material* differences" (italics his own). Now turn back to
page XIII of his preface, and note what he says there:
"Criticism, in the hands of Christian scholars, does not
banish or destroy the inspiration of the Old Testament; it
presupposes it;" also page X: "The whole is subordinated
to the controlling agency of the Spirit of God." Yet the
Spirit led one Genetical writer to give one account of the
creation in the first chapter, and another writer to give another and *contradictory* account in the second! Now we
submit the question to any logical mind whether Driver's
critical procedure does not, after all, "banish or destroy
the inspiration of the Old Testament." Would the Holy
Spirit contradict Himself? One cannot help wondering
what was Driver's idea of divine inspiration. Even a
sensible redactor would not have permitted his narrative
to contain evident contradictions, if he expected it to be
believed. As to whether the first and second chapters of
Genesis are really discrepant or not, is not the question we
are dealing with now. They have been proven to be harmonious so often, the second being merely a more detailed
narrative of man's genesis and relations, that we need not
tarry, but simply refer the reader to the works of Green,
Orr, Cave, Body, Wright, *et al.*

On p. 9 Dr. Driver insists that there are many
"differences of representation" in the book of Genesis: for

instance, in the narrative of the flood one document says that "of every clean beast *seven* are to be taken into the ark," while the other says "*two* of every sort without distinction." There are two accounts of the promise of a son to Sarah, "with an accompanying double explanation of the origin of the name *Isaac*." In one place Rebekah urges Jacob to depart from Canaan "to escape his brother's anger," and in another "to procure a wife agreeable to his parents' wishes"—that is, different motives are assigned. Two explanations are given of "the origin of the name *Bethel*"; "two of *Israel*." In 32:3 and 33:16 "Esau is described as already resident in Edom, while in 36:6f. his migration thither is attributed to causes which could have come into operation only after Jacob's return to Canaan." Then in a footnote he says: "Keil's explanation of this discrepancy is insufficient."

What becomes of the doctrine of divine inspiration in these cases? Would the Holy Spirit, under whose "controlling agency" "the whole is subordinated" (p. X), and who guided "the individual writer in the choice and disposition of his material"—would *He* have led men to commit such puerile contradictions and discrepancies? *

Thus we might go through Driver's whole book; but we drop down almost at random on page 137, near the bottom, where he shows up the contradictions between Dt. and P: "Thus (*a*) in Dt. the centralization of worship at one sanctuary is *enjoined*; it is insisted on with much emphasis as an end aimed at, but not yet realized; in P it is *presupposed* as already existing. (*b*) In Dt. any member of the tribe of Levi possesses the right to exercise priestly functions, contingent only upon his residence at the Central Sanctuary; in P this right is strictly limited to the descend-

---

* All these apparent discrepancies are effectively dealt with by many of the authors named in our "Selected Bibliography" near the end of this volume. *Cf.* especially Keil's great commentary; also the special works of Orr, Green, Tuck, Haley, Torrey, etc.

ants of Aaron.''* Then he goes on to point out with great
elaboration two more contradictions between Dt. and P.
What about ''the controlling agency'' (p. X) of the Holy
Spirit in these cases? Would the Holy Spirit have con-
tradicted Himself?

Just one more sample of Driver's remarkable conception of divine guidance and inspiration. On pages 140-142
he points out a number of variant representations between
P and JE, D, and Ez. ''Contrast,'' he says, ''the geneal-
ogies in JE (Gen. 4) with those in P (Gen. 5).'' JE and
P give variant explanations of ''the growth of sin.'' In
P ''there is also a tendency to treat the history theoretically.'' ''Dillman and Kittel seek to explain the contradiction, or silence, of Dt., etc., by the hypothesis that P was
originally a 'private document,' '' etc. On page 142: ''The
contradiction of the pre-exilic literature does not extend
to the *whole* of the priests' code indiscriminately. The
priests' code embodies *some* elements with which the earlier
literature is in harmony, and which indeed it presupposes;
it embodies *other* elements with which the same literature
is *in conflict,* and the *existence* of which it *even seems to
preclude.*'' (The italics are ours.)

We have not aimed to answer Dr. Driver's contentions about contradictions and discrepancies; that has
been done with ample scholarship and effectiveness by Robertson, Green, Orr, Bartlett, Redpath, Watson, Lias, Moeller, Wiener, and many others. But we believe that we have
made good our primary contention, namely, that Dr.
Driver's critical methods do, in spite of his assertions to
the contrary, nullify the inspiration of the Old Testament.
That is the reason, and the chief reason, why we are opposed to those methods; by a logical process they would
practically destroy the evangelical faith.

* For an effective answer, see Baxter's fine work, ''Sanctuary and
Sacrifice.''

CHAPTER III

Was it a Revelation or an Evolution?

WE have been moved to write this chapter by the reading and re-reading of Frederick William Bade's book, "The Old Testament in the Light of To-day." The book belongs to the class of the radical criticism, and is one of the most negative works we have ever read. Dr. Bade is the professor of Old Testament Literature and Semitic Languages in Pacific Theological Seminary, Berkeley, California.* After reading all his slashing criticisms of the Old Testament, its moral teaching, its theology and its history, we could not help wondering why a man holding such views should want to be a teacher in a theological school founded by Christian people (it was founded by the Congregationalists, though now it is non-d____inational), and especially why he should want to be a teacher of the Old Testament. Students trained for the ministry under such a régime surely cannot go out in the world with much of a message. The author not only represents the Old Testament as a very defective book morally and religiously, even a very wicked book in some ways, but also thinks that Christ's disciples corrupted the teachings of their Master after His departure from them. Thus it would seem that there is not much of the Bible left for the student who graduates from the

---

*This chapter was first published in *The Lutheran Quarterly* for October, 1916.

Pacific Seminary, if he accepts the teaching of Professor Bade.

The author's liberalism is also made obvious from the men who have commended his work and to whom he refers with "grateful acknowledgments" in his preface. Among them are Karl Marti, Dr. Charles F. Aked and Winston Churchill, the last the author of "The Inside of the Cup." Besides, a circular from the publishers contains an enthusiastic endorsement of the book by Mr. Churchill. This writer of fiction with a theological coloring displays his critical depth and intelligence by saying of Dr. Bade's book, "Above all, it is constructive." We wonder what Mr. Churchill's ideas of "constructive" teaching are, anyway; for after reading through the book, we are moved to say that, according to the author, the Old Testament is about as worthless a production as was ever foisted upon a long-suffering world.

The author's position may also be seen from the list of authorities he cites, especially in a footnote on page 88. Among them are the following: Budde, Cornill, Kuenen, Marti, Oort, Smend, W. R. Smith, H. P. Smith, Stade, Steuernagel and Wellhausen. Even though Kuenen's and Stade's works were published away back in 1877-1887, Dr. Bade still cites them as authorities. But throughout his whole work he never makes a single allusion to such conservative authors as Keil, Delitzsch, Hengstenberg, Klostermann, Orelli, Moeller, Cave, Orr, Girdlestone, Urquhart, Green, McGarvey, Robertson, Wiener, Wilson, et al. So completely does he ignore the conservative and evangelical Old Testament scholars (except to scoff at their views and misrepresent them) that the reader would think there were so few of them as to be a negligible quantity. Compare with this studied avoidance of evangelical writers the method of Dr. William Henry Green in his great work, "The Unity of the Book of Genesis," who uses over two pages in citing the books referred to in his volume; among them are nearly all the liberal authors from Astruc to Kuenen; and, of course, to be fair, he also cites a fine list of evangelical scholars. Note also the extensive bibliography on pages 543-547, over four pages of fine print, in Dr. James Orr's "The Problem of the Old Testament." We simply make these comparisons to show the difference between the methods of a radical and a conservative critic. Dr. Orr's list contains nearly every author, conservative and liberal, who, up to 1905, had ever done anything noteworthy in Old Testament research.* No wonder Dr. Bade goes on repeating the old, threadbare objections to the Old Testament as if they had not been answered by evangelical scholars again and again.

Our purpose, however, is not to give a general critique of Dr. Bade's work, but to call attention to his main viewpoint, which forms the keystone to the whole structure he has erected. Nowhere does he accept the Old Testament at its own estimate, or from its own point of view, but reconstructs its whole history to fit it into his own scheme of evolution. A number of citations will indicate both the spirit and the viewpoint of the author. As we proceed, we shall offer some remarks on the quotations.

In beginning his preface he says that the "one thing of supreme importance, actually and historically, is the idea of God." It is tautological to say "actually and historically," for when a thing is historical, it is actual. Then he adds concerning the idea of God: "This idea did not come in full feather, nor fall as a bolt from the blue." Both these expressions are slangy, and therefore are not in good taste, especially right at the beginning of a work on so serious and important a subject. Besides, they are in-

* Here it might be well to call attention to the great list of conservative Biblical scholars who have written for "The International Standard Bible Encyclopedia," edited by Dr. Orr and others and published in 1915.

tended as a gibe at the orthodox view. But, as is almost
always the case with the girds of the liberalist, it is an
untrue representation of the convictions held by conservative scholars. Not one of them that we know of has ever
held that the idea of God "came in full feather." An
outstanding principle of conservative historical criticism
is that the revelation of God in the Bible was progressive; that God led His people along from point to
point, making His revelation fuller and fuller all
the way. Everybody knows, even those who make no pretense to scholarship, that the Old Testament was preparatory, and that God unfolded His plan by degrees until the
"fullness of time" came. So in the second sentence of his
book Dr. Bade has misrepresented the orthodox position,
and has set up a man of straw. Not a very promising beginning for a book which, according to Winston Churchill,
is "above all constructive."

A few sentences further on the author says: "The
helpful teacher of the Old Testament now employs the
higher achievements of Israel's religion as grave-diggers
for the defunct moral crudities that have dropped by the
way. The usual procedure has been to embalm them with
a 'Thus saith the Lord,' and to carry them along until the
living expire under the dead."

Here is another fling at both the Bible and orthodoxy.
Yes, a fling at the Bible, because it contains the expression, "Thus saith the Lord," many times, and Dr. Bade
will simply have to cast aside all such Biblical announce-
ments as delusions or impostures. Of course he does
this without conscience, for wherever the Biblical teaching contravenes his theory, he simply throws the Biblical
teaching incontinently overboard. Note, too, how disre-
spectfully he speaks of some portions of the religion of
Israel as "defunct moral crudities." No wonder, for afterward he surely does represent the Old Testament mo-

rality as woefully distorted. His fling at orthodoxy consists in his saying: "The usual procedure has been to embalm those moral crudities." That is scorn, not argument. Conservative scholars embalm no moral crudities. They teach that God adapted both His revelation and His leading to the unfolding mental and moral capacities of His people during their progressive development.

In the author's "Introduction" he says: "Two views of the Old Testament still contend for mastery among the adherents of Christianity. The one regards it as a sort of talisman, miraculously given and divinely authoritative on the subject of God, religion and morals in every part. The other regards it as a growth, in which the moral sanctions in each stage of development were succeeded and displaced by the next higher one."

Let us pause a moment to consider this. Wherever the author can use a word to cast discredit on the conservative view he does not fail to do so. Note the word "talisman" above. Did men like Keil, Hengstenberg, Orr, Cave and Green look upon the Bible as a sort of "talisman"? Is it to be supposed that all the living evangelical theologians and ministers and scholarly laymen in our evangelical churches use the Bible in that way? No; every one should know, if every one does not, that they see nothing magical in the Bible, nor do they use it for purposes of superstition. They regard it as a special divine revelation—one that the good and holy God gave to mankind for their enlightenment in the way of salvation. To impute superstition to such people is to advertise one's lack of acquaintance with them. He also girds at the view that the Old Testament was "miraculously given and divinely authoritative." Well, that is what the Book claims for itself. If its claim from beginning to end is put on a false basis, why does not Dr. Bade simply come out as an infidel like Voltaire, Paine or Ingersoll, and reject it *in toto?* Why stand up for a Book that is fundamentally false throughout?

This author will not tolerate the view that any part of the Old Testament was given by direct divine revelation and inspiration. No, it is a "growth," a "human growth," a "development of human thought." Let us quote (p. 18 of the "Introduction"): "With respect to much in Hebrew religion the student has done his full duty when he has traced its origin and assigned it a place in the development of human thought. There are intellectual conceptions, moral ideals, motives and rites, which, in spite of their divine sanctions, have fortunately forever fallen below our moral horizon." Page 19: "Since religion in primitive times was not a body of abstract beliefs, but concretely a part of almost all that we would class as general culture in the form of tribal institutions and customs, and since primitive culture undeniably has, by a long process of evolution, developed into modern civilization, it follows inevitably that religion has shared this process of progressive development. It passed by stages from the crudest expressions of religious instinct, in nature, ancestor and fetish worship, to the exalted form in which it has expressed itself in the teachings of Jesus." Page 20: "No less is the history of morality in Hebrew religion a history of human growth, which exhibits, on the one hand, a process in man; on the other, a progress in idea and institution. The process is the growing fitness of the vehicle of revelation. The progress is the growing moral perfection of the religion. Needless to say, the conception of revelation that underlies this study regards it as an illumination from within, not as a communication from without; as an educative, not an instructional, process." On page 21 he regards the literary analysis of the partition critics as having settled the dates of the various books of the Old Testament and also the view of their composite character. Then he adds: "This knowledge naturally has become the basis for a reinterpretation of Hebrew morals and religion in terms of development."

On pages 12 and 13 the author gives his ideas of revelation. He quotes Trench's definition, which is as follows: "God's revelation of Himself is a drawing back of the veil or curtain which concealed Him from men; not man finding out God, but God discovering Himself to man." Then Dr. Bade says: "Against the word 'revelation' so understood we wish to enter an early protest. Thoughtful men everywhere are abandoning this old conception, which came in as a correlate to the transcendent idea of God, and to a world-view that has been outgrown. A God apart from the world was necessarily believed to reveal Himself from without, objectively. . . . It is a different world of thought in which men are now living. . . . The change from transcendence to immanence in our thought of God has involved the corresponding transition from an objective to a subjective theory of revelation. . . . Not through the medium of external agencies, but in and through personality does God reveal Himself to men."

Enough quotations have been given to show how utterly the author is committed to the theory of evolution, and that to him the idea of a direct divine revelation is intolerable. What is to be said respecting this hypothesis?

The first thing we note is that the whole Old Testament history must be manipulated, reversed and reconstructed to suit the theory. Instead of accepting the history as it stands in the Bible, as tradition has believed it to be through all the centuries, and as Josephus substantially narrated it, with Genesis leading and the rest of the books following in the natural order to make a consecutive narrative, Dr. Bade, following the dissecting critics, turns the whole history about. Of Moses (1300-1200 B. C.)

there are "no authentic literary remains" (p. 22 of the Introduction). "Probably few Old Testament scholars would now venture to claim a genuinely Mosaic origin for even the smallest literary fragments of the Pentateuch" (p. 18). "Early traditions and songs" are assigned to 1200 to 1000 B. C., and these fragments are part of the song of Deborah, David's lament over Saul, parts of Jacob's blessing, Jotham's fable, and the speeches of Balaam. The J document, consisting of "materials scattered through the Pentateuch and Joshua," was written in 850; the E document is dated 750 B. C.; Amos, Hosea, Isaiah (Chapters 1-39) and J and E compiled into a single document 650; Micah comes next; D (Deuteronomy), *circa* 650-621; JE combined with D, 560; P (Priest code), 550-450; Pentateuch completed (JEDP) 420; Daniel 165; Esther 150. We have given only a part of this critical program, for the author assigns to each book of the Old Testament what he regards as its proper place.

From the foregoing it will be seen that the whole Old Testament history is transposed. Instead of treating it as it stands in the Bible, each event falling in its proper place in consecutive historical order, he splits up the narrative, assigning one section or paragraph to one date and another to another date perhaps centuries later. The whole Biblical narrative is thus treated as if it were a mosaic, a hodgepodge, instead of an organism. Is there in all the world another piece of history or literature that has been composed in this way? What would we think of an author who would accord such treatment to the history of Egypt, Greece, Rome or Mohammedanism? And why is all this confusion wrought in the Biblical history? Solely in the interest of the author's pet theory of evolution. According to that theory, the exalted teaching about God in the opening chapter of Genesis, His unity, His creation of the universe, etc., could not have been conceived in the primitive times; therefore that narrative must be brought down to a late date in order to fit into the evolutionary program. Is that historical criticism? Is it not rather manipulating the historical data in order to make it fit into a preconceived and subjective theory? Whatever may be said of this method, it is not scientific, for the inductive method, which is the scientific method, first takes into account all the facts as it finds them, and then formulates its theory. We accuse Dr. Bade, and the whole Wellhausen school to which he belongs, of using the *a priori* method, in spite of all their pretensions to using the inductive or *a posteriori* method. It is a clear case of what the Greeks would have called a *hysteron proteron* —of putting the conclusion before the premises.

We wish here to emphasize the fact that Dr. Bade's mode of treatment means a decisive rejection of the testimony of the Bible itself. He will not have it that God ever directly manifested Himself to any of the Old Testament characters. Everything, according to Bade, is simply the evolution of subjective human ideas. If God ever made any revelation of Himself or His will, He did it merely through the imperfect subjective impressions of men, who made many mistakes of a very serious nature. By the way, that would be a queer kind of divine revelation! But what is the testimony of the Bible on this point? Does it teach that God revealed Himself directly or only by means of subjective experiences? Every Bible reader will tell you the former. The Bible says God spoke directly to Adam and Eve, to Cain, to Noah, Abraham, Isaac, Jacob, Moses, Samuel, and all the prophets. If there is anything plain and outstanding in the Bible, it is that God gave special objective revelations of Himself at intervals throughout the whole Old Testament history.

"Oh! but that is all a mistake of the writers of the various documents!" asserts the critic. "Either they credulously accepted the traditions and myths of the primitive times or else they purposely colored the narratives.''

All right, then. That indicates the precise position of the critic. He pointedly rejects the explicit testimony of the Bible. His quarrel, then, is with the Bible. Why not just come out and say so? Why turn upon orthodox theologians, as if they were responsible for putting the Bible in its present form? Whether such a critic has the truth on his side or not, he ought to be classified as an unbeliever rather than as an evangelical theologian.

However, what is the bearing of the critic's own theory on the doctrine of evolution? It eviscerates it, and for this reason: Suppose, as the critic maintains, the view of a direct revelation of God belongs to a very crude and primitive age, the age of mythology; and suppose, again, that the Pentateuch was not completed until *circa* 420 B. C.; then we want to ask why, in the name of reason and common sense, the advanced editors, whoever they were, did not eliminate the narratives of direct revelations and miracles, and tell the people that the whole history of the world and of Israel was merely the result of "the development of human thought?" Either they knew that the history they were giving the people was untrue, or they did not know it. If they thought they were writing the truth, when it was not the truth, what becomes of the theory of evolution? At so late a date evolution should have had a more enlightening effect upon them. Instead of that, they actually thought they were reciting a true narrative of God's direct revelations to His people. If they knew that the traditional belief was not true, they imposed a mendacious history and world-view upon their fellow-Jews; and the people accepted their representation as a special revelation from God! Again we ask why evolution did not clear the minds of the people at so late a date as 420 B. C. of those simple and primitive ideas of a

God who made a direct revelation? Surely evolution proved itself to be a very deficient teacher. But that is not all. Even in the time of Christ, the Jews and Christ Himself believed that the Old Testament contained a true narrative of a special divine revelation. And even to-day there are millions of Jews and Christians who hold firmly to the view of a special divine revelation in the Old Testament. If this is all that evolution can do, its effectiveness is surely very questionable.

Yet it is on account of this very theory of evolution that the critics assign most of the Old Testament composition to a late date, so that they can give development plenty of time to develop! We insist on knowing why the editors and redactors of 600-420 B. C. did not construct the history and religion of the Pentateuch and the other Biblical books prior to their time according to the theory of evolution instead of according to the primitive and traditional view. We will tell you just why: The theory of evolution is not the true view. It is illogical. It is built on the wrong foundation. It is based on false premises and *non sequitur* modes of reasoning.

Now, this is the main proposition to be proved—that evolution is a futile theory, is not adequate to its task, and is disproved by history, science and religion. Suppose we look at the history of nations. Go back in the annals of almost all the nations of the earth—those that have any annals and have left any archeological remains —and what do you find? Evidences of a high civilization. Note what is being found in Egypt, Babylonia, Palestine, Greece, Rome. Pyramids, palaces, aqueducts, towers, monuments, cuneiform tablets, legal codes—all these bear testimony that nations long before the historic period began outside of the Bible were wonderfully advanced in the arts of enlightenment. Even in Turkestan recent explorations have unearthed the remains of great cities, with their telltale evidences of a marvelous ancient civilization. The same kind of discoveries have been made among the ruins of the Aztecs of Mexico, the Toltecs of Central America and the Incas of Peru. Some of us can remember how Wendell Phillips was wont to thrill us with his lecture on "The Lost Arts." Some of the arts of these ancient civilizations are "lost" even to the present day. Therefore we maintain that the story of nations, so far as it can be traced by both history and archeology, does not point to a period of primeval savagery, but the reverse. And that fact invalidates the theory of evolution.

The like is true of the history of religion. It is a well known fact, brought out by Max Müller, Orr, Fairbairn and many other writers, that the further back you trace most of the ethnic religions, the more nearly they approach to pure monotheism. The discovery of the Egyptian "Book of the Dead," the most ancient bit of Egyptian literature yet found, corroborates this statement, for it shows that the most ancient ritual of that nation asserted the view of only one God. A similar claim can be upheld for the religions of India, China and Persia. The evolutionists often aver that the primitive religion of mankind was fetichism or animism. This cannot be proved. There is *not one example* on record of a nation that has evolved by its own efforts from animism through polytheism to monotheism. On this point we quote from Principal Fairbairn, who, in speaking of the evolutionists, says: "They assume a theory of development that has not a single historical instance to verify it. Examples are wanted of people who have grown, without foreign influence, from atheism to Fetichism, and from it through the intermediate stages into Monotheism; and until such examples be given, hypotheses claiming to be 'Natural

Histories of Religion' must be judged as hypotheses still''*

Here is also a relevant passage from Dr. James Orr's "The Christian View of God and the World," page 75: "Volkmar has remarked that of monotheistic religions there are only three in the world—the Israelitish, the Christian and the Mohammedan; and the last named is derived from the other two. . . . This limitation of Monotheism in religion to the peoples who have benefited by the Biblical teaching on this subject suggests its origin from a higher than human source; and refutes the contention of those who would persuade us that the monotheistic idea is the result of a long process of development through which the race necessarily passes, beginning with Fetichism, or perhaps Ghost-worship, mounting to Polytheism, and ultimately subsuming the multitude of divine powers under one all-controlling will. It will be time enough to accept this theory when, outside the line of the Biblical development, a single nation can be pointed to which has gone through these stages and reached this goal." We would also refer the reader to Dr. Orr's pertinent notes on pages 409-414; also to Dr. Tisdall's two scholarly books, "Christianity and Other Faiths" and "Comparative Religion"; Valentine's "Natural Theology" is very good on this thesis.

Let us look at the facts without prejudice. There is plenty of evidence in history and archeology of the degeneration of both civilization and religion. The decay and disappearance of nations afford abundant proof. There is not one instance of any people advancing by its own efforts from the lower forms of religion to the higher. On the other hand, the evidence all points to the fact that the further back we pursue our historical study of religions, the more nearly they approach the monotheistic conception. These things being true, what is the most adequate

* "Studies in the Philosophy of Religion," p. 12.

theory to account for all the facts? It would be that the original idea of God was monotheism, and that the lower and baser religious conceptions are decadent forms. We do not need to have the Bible to prove that sin, superstition and spiritual darkness are in the world, and these would account for the human tendency to degeneration in religion. At all events, such a tendency is an outstanding empirical fact. Even in Christian lands there are periods of religious decline. All forms and ideas, however pure at first, are liable to become perverted and perfunctory. By simply accepting facts as we find them in all the world, we see that the conception of primitive monotheism and the tendency to deterioration afford the most adequate theory. And with this empirical fact the teaching of the Bible agrees fully. In the beginning God revealed Himself as the one true God; but sin came into the world, and men degenerated, and fell into lower and lower forms of superstition. To this tendency to idolatry the Jews were also subject, and it was only by special revelations of Himself that God was able to keep alive in the world the true original monotheistic religion. Here is a view that is adequate, that tallies with the facts, and that therefore is the only scientific hypothesis.*

In the next place, we will proceed to convict Dr. Bade out of his writings of disloyalty to his own theory of evolution. He calls Amos and Hosea "pioneers of a new era" and Isaiah (Chapters 1-39) "the prophet of holiness." The first two came very near, at times at least, to preaching true monotheism, and both they and Isaiah proclaimed a very high type of morality. Of course, according to the modern critic, they had not thrown off the shackles entirely; yet they were comparatively free from the monola-

---

* This is not a mere argument *deus ex machina,* but is a conclusion based on the legitimate induction of facts, as above indicated. Such induction cannot rightly be scoffed at as a "cutting of the Gordian knot."

try and ritualism of the rest of the Jews. Now note: According to Bade, Amos and Hosea prophesied 750-735 B. C. and Isaiah 740-700. However, the Priests' Code (P), including Leviticus, etc., was not written until 550-450—that is, from 200 to 300 years after the prophets named above. Yet the Priest's Code was a reversion to the ritualism that had been so severely condemned by those prophets! Here, according to Bade himself, there was deterioration instead of evolution. If evolution did not hold its own in the times of Amos, Hosea, Isaiah and Ezra, what good reason have the critics for insisting on its having been the dominating law in the composition of Genesis and the rest of the Pentateuch? The whole theory seems to be lacking in empirical support.

In another way our critic invalidates his development theory. He holds that the later prophets got away from the idea of a direct revelation of God, and held to the view which Bade himself champions, namely, that God operates only immanently through the conceptions of men. Well, those prophets wrote from 750 to 460 B. C. (*circa*, of course, for everything is guess work). But, lo and behold! the Pentateuch was not completed until (*circa*) 420 B. C., 40 years after the last of the prophets. And now these final editors and redactors of the Pentateuch, writing nearly a half century after the last of the prophets and more than three centuries after the first, did not construct it according to the high ideals of immanent revelation held by the prophets, but actually throughout the whole book represented God as given direct and objective manifestations. Worse yet for the theory of evolution, the conceptions of the Pentateuchal redactors prevailed in Israel. Here is surely an acute case of degeneration. According to Bade's own representation, therefore, the evolution theory did not work in the history of the Israelitish nation.

Bade also argues that Amos and Hosea came very near

teaching pure monotheism, and denounced the narrow
Jahvism (the idea that Jehovah was only a national god)
of the Israelites prior to that time. But these prophets
flourished 750-735 B. C. Two hundred years later the
Priests' Code was written, and was accepted by Israel;
yet this code inculcated the old crude Jahvism or monolatry instead of the advanced theism of the prophets.
Another case of reversion instead of evolution. If evolution does not serve the disintegrating critics better than
this, what advantage has it over the evangelical view?

But we convict our author once more out of his own
book of being untrue to his favorite hypothesis. On pages
7-10 he tries to prove that Christ Himself was a critic of
the Old Testament, rejecting portions of its teaching, and
substituting a higher and truer view. We think he mis-
represents Christ here, but that is not the point just now.*
Then on page 10 Dr. Bade adds: "Passing on to the
apostles, one finds, strangely enough, that they narrowed
the scope of criticism, if they did not deny it altogether.
They apparently accepted the moral criticism applied to
the Old Testament by Jesus, but they also believed in the
literal inspiration of the text. A thorough comprehension
and acceptance of Jesus' principles would have prevented
the apostles from binding themselves and their converts
once more to the letter of the Jewish Scriptures. They did
not, could not, fully comprehend."

That is, here again evolution would not work. It should
have enabled the apostles to go right forward developing
Christ's higher critical ideas and principles. Instead
of evolution, there was reversion here once more. The
apostles went back to the Old Testament conception of an
objective revelation instead of the nebulous "immanent"
unfolding of "human thought." The apostles should not

* This subject is dealt with in Chapter IX of this volume:
"Christ's Witness to the Old Testament."

have been so stubborn. More than that, they proved Christ (whom Bade seems to want to accept as a true teacher) to be a false prophet, for He promised that the Holy Spirit would "lead them into all truth." Why did not the immanent Spirit of God lead them immanently in the right and the promised way, the all-prevailing way of evolution? Even the Holy Spirit became obstinate!

We have shown that the history of nations, their civilizations and religions disprove the hypothesis of evolution. So does human biography. Here we need not take the Bible as our guide, but need only to glance at the pages of secular history. In Greece most of the truly great men came too soon for the theory of evolution. Homer, who flourished about 1000 B. C., had no contemporaries or successors who were his equals in epic poetry. He should have been obliging enough to wait for evolution to develop him at the proper psychological moment. And there are Pericles, the greatest in statesmanship; Euripides, in tragic poetry; Phidias, in sculpture; Demosthenes, in oratory, and that triumvirate of philosophers, Socrates, Plato and Aristotle—all of them came prematurely, and so do not fit into the evolution hypothesis; for they were born, lived, wrought and died, without leaving successors who were their equals. The same may be said of Rome with her Cicero, Seneca and Marcus Aurelius. Other nations gave the world its Shakespeare, Milton, Goethe, Schiller, Washington and Lincoln long before the strategic moment had come to prove the pet theory of the day to be a verified hypothesis. Human history is a rather recalcitrant pupil in the school of evolution.

It is interesting to note that Biblical history follows in this respect the same *régime* as secular history. Here and there recur conspicuous characters as beacon lights for the rest of the world, standing almost alone in the sphere of spirituality—Enoch, Noah, Abraham, Moses, David, Isaiah;

then in the New Testament Christ came "in the fullness of time" according to the divine plan, but, if evolution is true, very much out of season. In this respect Biblical and secular history coincide—they do not display a uniform progressive process, but exhibit individuals who stand head and shoulders above their contemporaries and describe alternating periods of civil and religious advance and decline.

Thus we think we have shown that the religion of Israel cannot be accounted for on the theory of mere psychological evolution. That hypothesis is not adequate, and is therefore unscientific. If evolution must be given up, what view shall we accept? We know of only one view that is adequate, and that is, the Bible is a divine revelation, as it claims to be. Since evolution has proved itself insufficient, it is no longer necessary to rearrange the books of the Old Testament or reconstruct its history, but we can simply let everything stand as we find it in the Bible.

Suppose now, instead of being atomistic and picayunish in our criticism, we take the large, the comprehensive view of the Biblical system as a *Weltanschauung,* and see whether it is not rational, and at the same time so wonderful a scheme as to afford a presumption that it must be an especially revealed plan. First, there is the idea of God as the personal Creator as set forth in the first and second chapters of Genesis. How marvelous it is that any one living in that remote age should be able to get such a conception! There is not another cosmogony in the world that begins with God as a personal Being and the Creator of the cosmos. All heathen cosmogonies represent the gods as coming from the world or the primordial impersonal essence of things. How does it happen that the Bible alone of all ancient books gives us this clear monotheistic conception, and the view of God as the Creator? Even the wisest philosophers of Greece and Rome did not rise to this exalted conception. The only sufficient way to account for the amazing fact is that God Himself revealed the truth to some one; and that is what the Bible teaches.

The creation of man in the divine image is another wonderful idea that man could not have discovered by his own thinking. Remarkable, too, is the conception that he was created a free moral agent, with power to choose between good and evil. Here is an ethical view of man that will account for all the facts of history. When man fell into sin by his own volition, what human ingenuity could have devised or discovered a plan by which he might be rescued by divine love and mercy, without setting aside and dishonoring the divine and eternal law of justice? Yet we find all the Old Testament history and symbolism leading up to "the fullness of time" when God sent His Son, "born of a woman, born under the law, that He might redeem them that were under the law." Thus, according to this profound world-view, God was "able to be just and the justifier of every one that believeth on His Son." The Old Testament begins with Paradise formed and lost; the New Testament ends with Paradise restored and regained. So the Bible is all one great unified plan, comprehending all facts, all needs, all aspirations, all moral and spiritual imperatives. Could so marvelous and profound a scheme ever have been the mere evolution of human thinking? We do not believe it. It has been divinely revealed. In this connection we would reëcho the inspired conception of the prophet (Isa. 55:8, 9): "For my thoughts are not your thoughts, neither are your ways my ways, saith Jehovah. For as the heavens are higher than the earth, so are my ways higher than your ways, and my thoughts than your thoughts."

CHAPTER IV

THE MORAL CHARACTER OF THE OLD TESTAMENT JEHOVAH

A Defense of It Against an Assailant

"A FORMER generation called into question chiefly the historical difficulties presented by the traditional view," of the Old Testament. "The present generation is troubled by the crudities of its moral implications, and by what Matthew Arnold rather severely characterized as 'its insane license of affirmation about God.'"

The above is a quotation from one of the latest books belonging to the class of the radical Biblical criticism. We again refer to William Frederick Bade's "The Old Testament in the Light of To-day," some features of which we reviewed in the preceding chapter. The book is of the most negative sort. What its author says by way of criticism of the religion and morality of the Old Testament amounts to an arraignment. If the Old Testament is such a book as Dr. Bade represents it to be, it surely is unfit.

However, the trouble, we believe, is with the author, not with the Bible. His destructive criticism of the Old Testament is due to several preconceptions that are fundamentally wrong. First, he looks at the Bible purely from the secular viewpoint, and is lacking in spiritual appreciation of its character; second, he will not interpret the Bible from its own point of view and in its own light, but solely from the ethnic viewpoint; third, he is so obsessed with the theory of evolution that he twists, distorts and reconstructs

63

the Biblical history and teaching to fit his theory; fourth, he seems to be afflicted with a feeling of resentment against orthodoxy and traditional views. For these reasons he simply goes through the Bible with his rationalistic blade, picks out what he thinks objectionable, magnifies and mis-construes it, and then proceeds to hack it to pieces.

Now, had we the space, we might take the book section by section, and show its illogical character, its specious reasoning, and its harmful teaching. But in this article we shall confine our remarks to Chapter III, in which the author tries to portray the moral character of Jahveh (which is the same as Jehovah in our English versions) as he finds it set forth in the "early literature"—that is, the JE "material scattered through the Pentateuch and Joshua." Of the "JE traditions" he says (p. 54): "We shall now use them as direct sources for the period which extends from the time of Deborah to that of Amos, from 1200 to 750 B. C." It should be remembered that, according to Bade's dissecting criticism, this is the earliest Hebrew literature, and even this, especially that of the tenth and eleventh centuries, is far from reliable. Of Moses he says there are "no authentic literary remains," though he does not say why, but depends on the say-so of his critical masters, Kuenen, Stade, Budde, Wellhausen and Marti. So it is from these so-called "JE traditions" that our analyst tries to glean a true portrait of the moral character of Jahveh.

And who was Jahveh, according to Bade? A mere national deity, a tribal God, a clan-deity. He was "the God of Palestine alone, being more or less localized at sanctuaries within its borders, and consequently an *intramundane* deity." He "was the God of Israel alone, being concerned solely about the welfare of his Israelite worshipers and the retention of their exclusive homage." "He is, therefore, a national deity—an ardent partisan on behalf of his clients when they are loyal, and destructively resentful when they pay homage to rival deities. Within the boundaries established by these two controlling ideas practically the entire religious thought of the period moves.''

These quotations are literal, and are found on page 56. From one who holds such ideas of the theological and ethical teaching of the Old Testament you may know what to expect. Sometime we may be able to consider Dr. Bade's absurd representations of Jahvism and Monojahvism, which he sets forth in other chapters of his books;* but just now we shall confine our observations to his assault on the moral character of the Jehovah of the Old Testament. We must also limit ourself to his presentations in Chapter III. We begin with statements on page 65: ''Apparently it was the physical limitations of Jahveh which, in the thought of ancient Israel, sometimes made him act from unworthy motives. We find in the early traditions no assured conviction that God uses his power *only for moral ends*. The self-regarding motives with which the early writers endow him often betray him into unethical actions. Hence the possession of great power on his part was to them a source of fear rather than comfort, for they thought he used it more often to avenge personal affronts than to enforce obedience to the moral customs of the time.''

This quotation is a fair sample of Dr. Bade's way of representing Jehovah. Whenever He punishes the sinner, Dr. Bade thinks He does it out of petty personal resentment. In this way Dr. Bade simply reads his own ideas of Jehovah into the sacred narrative. A specious method he employs is to attribute the people's wrong notions of God to God Himself; therefore he fails to distinguish between what God Himself commands and sanctions and what imperfect men attribute to Him. This confusion vitiates his

* This has been at least partly done in Chapter V of this volume.

whole book. Let us see whether God does not act from purely moral ends. According to Dr. Bade, one of the "JE traditions" is the history of Cain and Abel. When Cain's offering was not accepted, he became wroth. Now note what Jehovah said to Cain: "Why art thou wroth? and why is thy countenance fallen? If thou doest well, shall it not be lifted up? and if thou doest not well, sin coucheth at the door, and unto thee shall be its desire; but do thou rule over it." This is according to the American revised version. If this narrative, and particularly the part of the conversation attributed to Jehovah, does not show true and deep ethical insight, we do not know where genuine ethics is to be found. It proves that God was not satisfied with mere outward forms of worship, and that the secret of Cain's ethical failure was sin couching at the door, like a panther ready to leap upon its victim and destroy it. Then comes the deeply ethical injunction, "But do thou rule over it." Which means, "You should be master of yourself; you should conquer the sin that seeks the rule over you." Why did not this critic call attention to this ethical passage? Because it did not fit in with the case he wanted to make out against "Jahveh."

Take one of the earliest J documents. (We do not believe in the partition theory of the radical critics, but we use their own terminology now and then for the sake of brevity, and to convict them out of their own mouths, as it were.) The passage we refer to is Gen. 6:5, which reads: "And Jehovah saw that the wickedness of man was great in the earth, and that every imagination of the thoughts of his heart was only evil continually." Then, on account of this very wickedness, and not for arbitrary reasons, He decided to destroy mankind with a flood. Does not this passage indicate deep and penetrating ethical insight? There could be no way of expressing real inner moral obliquity more incisively than the clause, "Every imagina-

tion of the thoughts of his heart was only evil continually.''
It goes as deep as Ps. 51: 6, Prov. 21: 2, Jer. 31: 33, Matt.
5: 8, or Heb. 4: 12.   Yet it is found away back there in
the "J document."   Why did not our critic cite this
passage?   It did not suit his purpose.

Our author has no reverence for the sacred Scriptures.
On the margin of our copy of his book we have felt compelled to write the word "sacrilege" a number of times.
Wherever he can use an ugly word he does so—almost any
word to cast derogation and contumely on the Biblical
records.   For instance, he calls the people of Jahveh His
"clients," as if He were a sort of petty lawyer.   Reverent
folk call the Israelites "God's chosen people."   Something
which Jehovah had forbidden this irreverent critic says
was "tabooed."   He knows well enough that the word
"taboo" carries the idea of crass superstition and paganism.   Note this (p. 47): "More often than not the
offense consisted in the breaking of some taboo like that of
the tree in the garden of Eden."   What does the reverent
believer think of such handling of Biblical material?   The
forbidden things in the ceremonial law were "ceremonial
taboos."   Uzzah, when he touched the ark, had "violated
a taboo" (both of these on p. 66).   But what does the
reader think of this (p. 65), referring to Jehovah's expressed fear lest Adam and Eve, after the fall, should eat
of the tree of life?   "In other words," says our lampooner,
"the tree possesses a *magical* virtue which is independent
of Jahveh's will or power."   (The Italics ours.)   Instead
of seeing the profound ethical and spiritual depth of
Jehovah's language, this shallow author can do nothing but
put such a miserable construction upon it.   We cannot help
feeling that this writer affords a clear illustration of what
is written in Prov. 8: 36: "But he that sinneth against
me wrongeth his own soul."   The "me" in this text means

that true spiritual wisdom whose beginning is "the fear of the Lord."

Wherever this professor of Old Testament literature in a theological seminary can cast a slur at the Biblical representations of God, he does not hesitate to do so. He is a past master at reading a bad or an absurd meaning into the language of the Bible. Here are some examples on page 64: "But even these expressions do not disguise the fact that the ancient Hebrew thought of God as overcoming resistance with effort, and as feeling exasperation over the thwarting of his plans." Notice that he represents God as a petulant being. A reverent scholar would call God's anger at sin righteous indignation. Not so Bade; with him it is "feeling exasperation." Then he goes on: "The latter was due in part to the assumed limitations of his knowledge. In order to find a mate for Adam he first engaged in a futile experiment with animals." Here we cannot help exclaiming, For shame! for shame! This is the same calumny that Mr. Ingersoll used to proclaim. A small and cavilling spirit *might* read such a purpose into the brief narrative in Gen. 2:18-20; but no one who is able to take a comprehensive view of the whole Biblical system would ever do so. The Genetical story says that God brought the animals "unto man to see what he would call them," not to see whether he could find a mate for man among them. Then it says that "the man gave names to all the cattle, and to the birds of the heavens, and to every beast of the field." To this it adds, "But for man there was not found a helpmate for him." A mean, petty, carping spirit might read into the language what Dr. Bade does, but the subsequent narrative shows that the transaction was not an "experiment" with God. Far from it; the purpose was to show man that he belonged to a higher order of creatures than the non-rational animals gathered around him; to prove to him that the evolutionary theory is not correct—that he was not a monkey nor the relative of a monkey! Then what did Jehovah do? Precisely what was worthy of Himself and the man who had been made in His own image. He proceeded to make a helpmate for man; a being who was rational and human like himself; and, beautiful to contemplate, instead of forming her out of another portion of the ground, he took her from the physical and psychical being of man himself, so that the congenitality and solidarity of the human race might be preserved, and man might know forever that woman was "bone of his bone and flesh of his flesh." Who that has a true human heart pulsing in him would want to have it otherwise? In biology the cell divides itself, and the cell that comes from it is like it because it is organically a part of it. So with man and woman. Ah, yes! when God brought the animals to Adam to be named, and thus to prove to him his superiority over the animal creation, He knew precisely what He was going to do. When the man waked up from his "deep sleep," and saw the woman standing before him, he saw that God had done right. But the evolutionist, who thinks that man descended from the animal creation, ought to be the last man in the world to find fault with the God of the Bible, even if He had tried an "experiment"; for, according to that view, both man and woman were once animals.

Bade again: "Disappointment over the corruption of mankind 'grieved him at his heart' (Gen. 6:6 (J)); so that he resolved upon the destruction of his handiwork." Note the constant innuendoes. The critic seems to think the expression, "grieved Him at His heart," a crude and anthropomorphic mode of representing God. We do not see why. How does Dr. Bade want God to feel over the sins of His rational creatures? Does he want Him to sit coldly upon His throne, unmoved by sin and its havoc? Christ represented God as so loving the world as to give

His only begotten Son. Is not such love akin to grief. Did not Christ "feel compassion" toward the multitude? Did He not weep at the grave of Lazarus and over stricken Jerusalem? And whatever Dr. Bade thinks of the doctrine of Christ's person, he certainly must believe that He manifested the heart and love of God to the world. So God must have feeling. He is not a mere cold Monad. He made man in His own image, according to the Scriptures, and since man is moved by feelings of grief, indignation and love, God must have kindred emotions, only in infinite degree and perfection. Therefore, in spite of the infidel sneer, we maintain that the God of feeling in the Old Testament is the same as the God of feeling portrayed in the New.

Notice the keen rapier-like thrust of the critic: "so that he resolved upon the destruction of his handiwork." Now what does the Bible teach? As clearly as day that it was on account of the *extreme wickedness* of the people that He determined to destroy them. It was not because He took "pleasure in the death of the wicked," for He wants them to "turn unto Him and live." The fact of the matter is, the wickedness of his people "grieved Him at His heart." And why did He destroy them? The only remedy for desperate and diabolic corruption is destruction. In the long run their sins by natural processes would have destroyed them, anyway. In one way or another sin will always destroy its votaries. "And sin, when it is full-grown, bringeth forth death" (Jas. 1: 15). See also Isa. 59: 1, 2.

The old infidel objection, exploited by Paine and Ingersoll, about Uzzah and the ark of the covenant is brought forward by this critic (p. 66). Observe how he puts it: "Uzzah, with the best intention, put forth his hand to keep it (the ark) from falling off the cart at a point where the oxen became restive." "With the best intention" is cunningly thrust in to show that Uzzah was not to blame, and therefore that the Jehovah of Israel acted unjustly in slaying Uzzah. "Whether the realization that he had violated a taboo induced heart-failure or a stroke of apoplexy, is impossible to tell," the critic pursues. "In any case sudden death overtook him, and this fact required explanation. The one which the Biblical writer offers is surprisingly unethical, but quite in accord with contemporary superstitions about Jahveh and the ark." Similarly, David was afraid of Jahveh that day. "He distrusted his mood," says this critic. Therefore, David did not take the ark to Jerusalem, but elsewhere, and awaited "a change in Jahveh's temper." In this way Dr. Bade goes on and on, casting contempt on Jahveh by sly innuendoes.

However, we must be patient, and try once more to "vindicate the ways of God to man," as has been done so often in the past by evangelical apologists and commentators, whose masterly works should have been read and heeded before a professor in a theological school wrote so destructive a work as the one in question. According to the Scriptures, the ark was a sacred vessel, a symbol of God's presence, holiness and grace. Its form, arrangement and contents typified deep spiritual realities. In those days more symbols were needed than to-day, for it was the childhood of the race and the period of preparation for the clearer revelation that was to be made "in the fullness of time." Even now the most advanced Christians are helped in their conceptions of God by object teaching and in their worship by sacred symbolism. For this reason we have Baptism and the Eucharist in the New Testament dispensation. (Of course, Lutherans hold that the sacraments are not mere symbols, but chiefly means of grace.) Our churches have the cross, the altar, the chancel arrangement, pictures, and all of them are suggestive of spiritual realities while we are here in the flesh, subject to local limitations and the perceptions of the sense. If all this typology is helpful to-day, why was not the typology divinely commanded in the Old Testament helpful to God's ancient people in a dimmer age? They surely could not think of God as the absolute Being, for no one even to-day has a clear conception of such a Being. God could not have accommodated Himself more graciously, fittingly and pedagogically than by using earthly objects as types of heavenly and abstract realities. This He did in the Old Testament dispensation.

Of all the sacred symbols the most holy was the ark of the covenant in the Holy of Holies. Here God, as it were, condescendingly localized Himself. He had to do so, if He desired to reveal Himself at all. Even to-day, if He reveals Himself in our hearts, there is a true sense in which He must put Himself in relation with time and space. Why then should we be so hypercritical when the Bible represents Him in the same way? We speak to-day about God "coming and going." If a man is given up to apostasy we say, "God has forsaken him." We do not mean that God has withdrawn His essence from him, but His saving grace. Somehow, we *sense* the true meaning in all such figurative language.

Now, the ark was not a "taboo." Shame on the man who has such crude, unspiritual ideas! It was a sacred symbol of God's holy presence. That is the way the Bible represents it. Being sacred, it was to be held so; it was to be treated with veneration. God had to teach His people the spirit of reverence and awe. Is it not right that people should have such feelings inculcated in them, and especially toward God? Or does our critic think it would be better for people to have no reverence for sacred things? Our observation has been that reverent people are not wicked and base, but irreverent people usually are. Perhaps Dr. Bade thinks one place just as much holy ground as an-

other; yet we are disposed to think that he does a good
many things outside of the sanctuary that he would not do
within it. Or does he not believe in churches that are dedi-
cated to the worship of God? Judging him by his book,
it is very difficult to form any idea of what he does believe,
but we certainly think that a professor in a Christian seminary ought to believe in temples set apart for worship.
Then, if it is now good for us spiritually to have sacred
places and objects, was not Jehovah pursuing the normal
method when He disciplined His ancient people in the
same manner? As the ark was a sacred vessel, its handling
was regulated in a special way. Only the priests were to
touch it, and even they must bear it from one place to
another by a peculiar method. No unconsecrated hands
were to touch it. Uzzah surely must have known this sacred
law. At that particular time it was necessary for God to
teach His people a stern and impressive lesson of reverence. When Uzzah, from whatever motive, stretched out a
desecrating hand and touched the holy vessel, God by con-
dign punishment taught the people then, and all people
since that day, that He wants holy things to be treated in a
reverent way. Not all irreverent people are stricken down
so summarily. If they were, some critics of the Bible would
have little chance to repent. But by this outstanding and
impressive example God taught the world that all desecra-
tion will sometime be punished if unrepented of. God has
various ways of punishing, and uses various methods of
education. Sometimes he punishes quickly; sometimes He
delays. But let the sinner be sure his sin will find him
out. "Because sentence against an evil work is not ex-
ecuted speedily, therefore the heart of the sons of men is
fully set in them to do evil" (Eccles, 8:11). "Though
hand join in hand, the evil man shall not be unpunished"
(Prov. 11:21). When a certain worldling and infidel
declared that he had plowed most of his field, planted his

corn, tended it and husked it, all on Sunday, and then boasted to a religious editor that he had the best corn in the neighborhood, the editor replied, "The Almighty doesn't settle all his accounts in October!"

Did space permit, we would examine all the charges that our critic brings against the Jahveh of the Old Testament, but we can deal with only a few. All the rest will yield to a similar treatment, if one can only get the right viewpoint, which is that of the Bible itself. Says our author (p. 69): "A peculiarly primitive conception of Jahveh's personality comes to expression in the Jahvistic stratum of Ex. 32 and 33. The jealous wrath of Jahveh is aroused by the worship of the 'golden calf,' and he resolves to destroy the faithless Israelites."

Note what a vicious twist this writer gives to every incident. "The jealous wrath of Jahveh," etc. Let it be remembered that God had led the Israelites out of bondage that He might have a peculiar people, who should be the bearers of His plan and message of salvation to the world. While God was giving the law to Moses on the mountain, the people, helped by Aaron, made a golden calf, and fell into idolatry. This was the very sin from which He desired to save them, because they could be good and happy only by the worship and service of the one true God. Therefore God's wrath was not petty jealousy of a golden calf, but righteous indignation against sin, which would be ruinous to His people. Does the critic want a God who is indifferent to idolatry? Suppose God would have said: "I am not a jealous God; it makes no difference to me how many idols, golden calves and all, you worship," what would you think then of His moral character? If a man were to say, "I am not the least bit jealous of my wife; no difference to me how many other men she makes love to!" you would have your opinion of his moral character, and would be likely to express it freely. The faithful pastor teaches his catechumens, who are still only children, that the word "jealous" is used sometimes in a good sense and sometimes in a bad sense.

Then our critic proceeds: "Moses intervenes by reminding him (Jahveh) of his oath, and by recalling him, as it were, to his own better self, so that he is led to 'repent of the evil which he would do unto his people.' By comparison Moses appears more just and humane than God, who, like a quick-tempered monarch, is protected by his vizier from the consequences of his own ill-considered actions."

You will take note of all those running innuendoes. Dr. Bade interprets this passage in the crass and ugly way. Let us look at it in the evangelical way—the way that the teaching of the Bible as a whole would lead Christian people to construe it. God, being the true God, and loving His people with a true divine love, was justly angry when they forsook Him and fell into idolatry. His justice would lead Him to destroy them. But Moses intercedes for them, and they are spared. Does not the Bible teach us to pray to God for the things we want and need? Did not Christ Himself teach men to pray; always to pray and not to faint? Did He not offer intercessory prayer for His disciples? While hanging on the cross, He cried, "Father, forgive them, for they know not what they do." So it must be part of God's plan that men shall pray, and not only for themselves, but for others. "I will be inquired of concerning this thing," He said. Now, when Moses interceded for Israel, it was not because Moses was more merciful than God, but because God had ordained that His just punishment should be averted by Moses' prayer. If Moses' prayer here was foolish, then all prayer is foolish. If Moses' prayer was availing, then all true prayer will be availing.

On page 70 Bade calls God a "partisan deity" and on

page 72 a "clan-god!" These accusations are made because Jahveh gave special aid and comfort to Abraham, Isaac, Jacob, Moses, etc. This is an amazing criticism to make on the Bible, for the whole plan of redemption through Christ is based on the postulate that God had a "chosen people," to whom He revealed Himself and whom He led in a peculiar way. One wonders how He could have had such a people if He did not in some ways bestow upon them His special guardian care. That was God's way. For reasons of His own He seems to have elected it. He might have revealed Himself equally to all nations and to all men; but, speculate about it as you will, He did not choose to do so. That is also His way with science and invention. He might have led all men to discover the Copernican theory of the universe at the same time—but he didn't. He might have brought about the universal discovery of the power of steam and electricity—but he didn't. He has always led a few men to make the great discoveries and inventions, and then give them to the world. Critics may not like that way, but they will have to put up with it. That God had a chosen people, and that He bestowed upon them special favors (and at the same time laid upon them special responsibilities) is a patent fact; for everybody knows that we get the best religion in the world from the Hebrews. Whether God wrought this by direct or immanent revelation makes not a particle of difference so far as the ethics of it is concerned. As has been said so often, the Greeks had a genius for art, the Romans for law, and the Hebrews for religion. We have never yet heard a critic, however radical, call God a "partisan deity" or a "clan-god," because He endued the Greeks with superior artistic spirit and skill, and the Romans with a predilection for law. No; it is only the God of the Bible, the most spiritual book in the world, who is faulted thus by the critics!

But it must be borne in mind always that God did not choose Israel for selfish purposes. They were to pass through a period of tutelage and discipline, till "the fullness of time" should come; then they were to proclaim the gospel to all the world. Even away back there in Abraham's day the universal promise was given: "In thy seed shall all the nations of the earth be blessed." Why cannot the critics see God's vast and beneficent plan? It is because they are dissectors, and cannot view an organism in its entirety. They lack spiritual vision.

Obsessed with the idea that Jahveh was only a henotheistic or tribal god, our critic, in allusion to Abraham's adventures with Pharaoh and Abimelech, says (p. 72): "Thus the clan-god secures to Abraham the practical advantages of his own deception. . . . The action of Jahveh exhibits this moral defect, for he helps Abraham, not because he is right, but because he is his client."

This disposition to pervert everything in the Bible certainly tries one's patience; it all comes from a low point of view. Drs. Keil, Green, Orr, and many other evangelical scholars have dealt amply with all these objections of infidels and critics (for both of them raise the same difficulties); but Dr. Bade gives not the slightest proof in his book that he has ever read a first-class book of an apologetic character. In Abraham's case, why, pray, did God choose *him* for His "client"? Was it not because He saw that Abraham, with all his imperfections, was morally and spiritually the best fitted instrument for His purpose? He did not select Abraham without a profound spiritual reason, nor merely as a matter of caprice; nor does the Bible ever "idealize" Abraham and the other patriarchs, but tells their story in the frankest possible way, never glozing over their moral obliquities. When they got into trouble by wrong-doing, God did not sanction their conduct, but led them patiently to higher ideals.

The study of good evangelical commentaries like Keil's and Lange's and apologetic works like Orr's, Green's and Urquhart's, which Dr. Bade would not think worth while, might have spared him from finding fault with Jehovah on account of Jacob's duplicity. Let it be understood that Jehovah never commanded nor sanctioned Jacob's deceptions, but, on the contrary, permitted them to bear their natural punishment in the trouble they brought upon him. Jacob had to flee for his life before Esau. But while Dr. Bade finds fault with God for slaying Uzzah, he seems to think that He should have knocked Jacob in the head for wrong-doing. However, the subsequent history of God's redemptive plan through Israel and the Christ who came from Israel, proves that God chose wisely when He selected Jacob rather than Esau as the ancestor of the world's Redeemer. But why did not God choose better men for His purposes? complains the caviler. We reply, God had to use such instruments as He could get, just as He has to use imperfect men to-day, if He is going to accomplish the world's evangelization. Of course, God might have destroyed the free moral agency of those Bible characters, and made them mere lamb-like automata; but we know well enough that God never did that, and does not do that now. If men will read the Bible as a whole, instead of atomistically, they will see that His plans are large and organic. Of all the Bible characters, and of all God's instruments to-day, Paul's profound words are true: "But we have this treasure in earthen vessels, that the exceeding greatness of the power may be of God and not from ourselves" (2 Cor. 4:7). Oh, if Bade and his class could only see this divine method in the Bible, how much good they might do for the cause of religion!

Mr. Ingersoll used to vent his wrath against the Bible because, in the old version, it said that the Israelites "borrowed" from the Egyptians, with no intention of bringing back what they borrowed, and they did this by Jehovah's direction! What was our amazement to find Dr. Bade, a professed Hebrew scholar, repeating this charge (pp. 73 and 124)! If he had even read the American revised version of the Bible, he would have seen that the Hebrew word is translated "ask," not "borrow." We wish that the reader would turn to Keil's "Commentary on the Books of Moses," Vol. II, page 446, and read the whole explanation. Keil says: "But the only meaning of *sha-al* is, *to ask* or *beg*." Again further on: "No proof can be brought that *hish-eel* means to *lend,* as is commonly supposed; the word occurs again in 1 Sam. 1:28, and there it means to *grant* or *give.*" The last statement is quoted by Keil from Knobel. See Haley in his "Alleged Discrepancies of the Bible" (pp. 300-302) for a lengthy explanation. He says that Hengstenberg, Rosenmueller, Lilienthal, Tholuck, Winer, Lange, Murphy, Keil, Wordsworth, and a host of critics, understand "that the Hebrews asked and received these things simply as *gifts.*" He quotes Josephus as corroborating this view, for he says of the Egyptians: "They also honored the Hebrews with gifts; some in order to secure their speedy departure, and others on account of neighborly intimacy with them." See Robert Tuck in his scholarly "Handbook of Biblical Difficulties" (pp. 79, 80): "But the revisers have now sealed the very satisfactory explanation that has often been given, that the word translated 'borrow' really means 'ask' or 'beg'; and so the Israelites, in fact, received these jewels as gifts, not as loans; the matter being perfectly honorable and straightforward on both sides." Read Dr. Tuck's whole article, which is very illuminating. Says Murphy ("Commentary on Exodus," p. 33): "*Shall ask*, as a gift, if not for compensation for long unrequited services. The word cannot mean 'borrow' here, when the Egyptians were perfectly aware that the Israelites would not return." So we might quote authorities without number, all of whom have been ignored by Dr. Bade.

But we cannot tarry over these details, much as we are tempted to do so. Just one more criticism (pp. 82, 83): "Many a pious soul has been troubled by such questions as, Why did God destroy, not only adults in the flood, but all the children and animals? They surely deserved a better fate!" Then he slashes at the idea of "collective guilt, collective responsibilities," and debates that "righteousness, sin and punishment can concern only the individual." He is also much concerned over "the smiling babes," as Paine used to call them, that were slain by the Israelites in their conquest of Canaan.

We reply: The same fault that Dr. Bade and his fellow-unbelievers find with the God of the Bible can be found with the "immanent" God whom they advocate. He certainly permits the innocent to suffer with the guilty, and often for the guilty. When a flood, an earthquake, or a cyclone occurs, does it spare the good people and destroy only the wicked? Does it save the innocent babies, and kill off only the adults? Figure it as you will, the "immanent" God does and permits some very mysterious things. In the great world-war did Dr. Bade's "immanent" God see to it that only the guilty were made to suffer? No; strange as it may seem, the principle of "collectivism" prevails largely in the *régime* of the world, and, whether we accept it by faith or grumble about it, we must put up with the constitution of the world as it is. After all, in this world of sin, we cannot expect even-handed justice always to be done. Perhaps even some of the Biblical critics will think that they have to suffer injustice at the hands of *their* critics; yet the "immanent" God permits them to suffer such unjust persecution! "Many a pious soul has been troubled by such questions."

Really, however, if God were to do what the Biblical

critics want Him to do, He would have to destroy the organism of the cosmos, in which all living things are united into a living whole Besides, their idealistic scheme would banish all suffering from the earth, for if all people saw that righteousness always "paid" in the coin of the realm and in the economy of nature, how good they would strive to be! Perhaps, after all, when we look at things fundamentally and not superficially, we shall find that the present regimen is the best one for the discipline and development of real, true and sterling moral character. Besides, if God had spared all the children at the time of the flood, and drowned only the adults, we are in a quandary as to how Noah and his family would have taken care of all those babies! They certainly would have had their hands full! Perhaps most of them would have starved, and that would have been more cruel than quick and painless death by immersion. Moreover, we are glad to say that we have more faith in Jehovah than the critics have, seeing that He "so loved the world that He gave His only-begotten Son," and so we do not believe that innocent children, no matter how they may pass out of the world, are lost. Christ said of little children: "Suffer them to come unto me; for of such is the kingdom of heaven." And the God whom Christ represented was the God of the Old Testament. Who knows but all those antediluvian infants, had they and their wicked parents been spared, would have fallen into the same universal corruption?

Here, in closing, we come upon a remarkable passage from Dr. Bade's book (p. 85). After his terrific indictment against the moral character of Jahveh, he says: "It would be easy to brighten the picture which we have drawn by citing those instances in which the higher conceptions of God and duty came to expression." Then, in the name of justice, why did he not "brighten the picture" if it would have been "easy" to do so? Would not fairness and honesty have compelled him to give the *whole* picture? Instead, he has represented Jahveh as little better than a moral monster, and that is the picture that will remain indelibly fixed on the minds of his readers and students. One would think that a seminary professor of Old Testament literature would feel in conscience bound to limn the true and whole picture of Jahveh, and not merely admit grudgingly that the black sketch he has drawn might have been easily "brightened." Let us have positive teaching and apologetics in our theological schools, and no more of this Biblical nihilism.

CHAPTER V

Was He the Universal God or Only a National God?

THE modern radical critics of the Old Testament contend that the religion of Israel was an evolution, not a direct revelation. It was simply the product of human thought, of human development. If God had anything to do with Israel's religion, it was only in an indirect "immanent" way. According to this view, the religion of Israel started with fetichism and animism, gradually developed into polytheism, then into henotheism, and finally into monotheism. Therefore, at a certain point in this evolutionary process Israel regarded Jehovah as merely a national God, and it was only in the time of the prophets that they began to look upon Him as the God of the universe and of all nations.

Dr. William Frederick Bade, in his book, "The Old Testament in the Light of To-day" (1915, second impression, 1916), champions this view. On page 56 he says: "Jahveh is the God of Palestine only," "the God of Israel alone, being concerned solely about the welfare of his Israelite worshipers and the retention of their exclusive homage. He is, therefore, a national deity—an ardent partisan on behalf of his clients when they are loyal, and destructively resentful when they pay homage to rival deities." On page 57 he declares that "the Hebrews, during the cruder stage of the national-god period of their

83

religion, believed Jahveh's presence and power to be limited to the territory inhabited by the Israelites." Page 70: "A national deity is a partisan deity, and Jahveh is no exception in this respect." On page 72 he calls Jahveh "a clan-god." Page 96: "The prohibition of the worship of other gods obviously does not constitute monotheism, but monolatry. The framers of this decalogue did not question the actual existence of other gods." Again, on the same page: "Monotheism, even in Hebrew thought, came by stages, and not as a flash from the blue." Compare also page 187. Even Deuteronomy did not reach a higher conception than "monojahvism" (pp. 187-217).

These quotations are enough to indicate Dr. Bade's position and that of the school of critics to which he belongs—Kuenen, Wellhausen, Stade, Cornill, Budde, Marti, W. R. Smith, H. P. Smith, etc., whom he cites as his authorities (see p. 88, foot-note). It is not our purpose to follow this author in detail, but rather to present a positive argument in favor of the conservative view, namely, that the Jehovah of Israel was the God of the universe, and not a mere local or tribal deity. Our aim shall be to consider the Bible as it is, and carefully note its real teaching; then to show that this teaching is consistent, unitary, and rational; whereas the opposing theories of the destructive critics do violence to the Holy Scriptures and nullify their value and religious authority. We shall confine our discussion to the *theology* of the Old Testament, the doctrine of God.

Instead of "Jahveh," we shall chiefly use the form "Jehovah," which is the form used in the American revised version of the Bible. We shall also use the name "Elohim" in most of the cases where that name is used in the original Hebrew. Suppose we begin at once with the passage which has been the *crux* with the radical critics, and which has caused them no end of confusion—Exodus

6:2, 3: "And Elohim spake unto Moses, and said unto him, I am Jehovah: and I appeared unto Abraham, unto Isaac, and unto Jacob, as God Almighty (El Shaddai); but by my name Jehovah I was not known to them."

Here, it is said, is a direct contradiction of the many passages in Genesis in which Jehovah is represented as revealing Himself to the patriarchs. Therefore, it is contended, Genesis must be divided between at least two authors, the Elohist and the Jehovist, each of whom wrote a history from the creation to the close of Joseph's life. But their accounts did not agree; they contained evident contradictions, not all of which were removed by the redactors who welded the two documents together. Of course, other contradictions in the Pentateuch are cited, but this is one of the most palpable ones.

Suppose we scrutinize the moot question of discrepancies and contradictions in the early books of the Old Testament. One thing is certain—at some time in the world's history these books were composed and written; some time these wonderful conceptions came in some way to a human mind; some time an author or redactor wrote the first verse of Genesis: "In the beginning God created the heavens and the earth." This is one of the noblest and sublimest conceptions ever registered by human thought. No other ancient religion ever rose to the lofty idea of a personal God as the Creator of the universe. All other religious systems fail to attain to the idea of creation. In the ethnic cosmogonies the gods did not *create* the universe, but were *evolved* from it. Note the Babylonian conception of Tiamat and Marduk—how crude, crass, and puerile in comparison with the majestic statement of the first verse of the Bible! Now, suppose for the sake of argument that this conception first came to a writer—the "great unknown" of the critics—in the days of Josiah or Nehemiah or Ezra or even later, is it likely that an editor capable of a theistic conception that far transcends the greatest conceptions of Socrates, Plato, and Aristotle would have pieced together a history that was full of palpable contradictions, and then would expect his own people to receive it as a direct revelation from God and the norm of their religious life? Suppose he was piecing together various documents and traditions, is it probable that he would have permitted Genesis to state that Jehovah appeared to the patriarchs again and again under that title, and then would have declared, in diametrical contradiction: "By my name Jehovah I was not known to them"? Here was an author who could conceive the thought of Genesis 1:1, and yet was too dense or too careless to note a plain contradiction on the surface of the writing he was trying to impose on his people! The book which gives us so many of the great religious and theological conceptions we have to-day ought to be capable of a more rational interpretation. This may impress some men as an *a priori* presentation of the case, but we submit whether it is not reasonable.

Let us see now how beautifully the opposite view resolves the apparent difficulty respecting Jehovah. That view is that Moses himself composed the Pentateuch. On the ground of its unity of plan, doctrine, and historical unfolding this is a reasonable hypothesis. Some years ago Dr. Alfred Cave, in his cogent book, "The Inspiration of the Old Testament," contended that Moses was himself the Jehovist writer of Genesis. Moses may have had before him the Elohist document or tradition, which had been handed down to him from the fathers. Now, when God appeared to him at the burning bush and subsequently, He may have revealed Himself for the first time by the name Jehovah, whereas prior to that time He had made Himself known to the fathers as Elohim, El, and El Shaddai. Note, now, what God said to Moses in Exodus 3:6, at the burning bush: "I am the Elohe of thy father, the

Elohe of Abraham, the Elohe of Isaac, and the Elohe of Jacob.'' Then in verse 15: ''And Elohim said moreover unto Moses, Thus shalt thou say unto the children of Israel, Jehovah, the Elohe of your fathers, the Elohe of Abraham, the Elohe of Isaac, and the Elohe of Jacob, hath sent me unto you.'' This is repeated almost verbatim in the next verse. In verse 18 Moses and the elders are instructed to speak in this way to the King of Egypt: ''Jehovah, the Elohe of the Hebrews, hath met with us; and now let us go, we pray thee, three days' journey into the wilderness, that we may sacrifice to Jehovah, our Elohe.'' In chapters 4 and 5 the same statement is made a number of times. In 6:5 Jehovah says: ''I have remembered my covenant,'' and in verse 8: ''And I will bring you in unto the land which I sware to give to Abraham, to Isaac, and to Jacob; and I will give it you for a heritage: I am Jehovah.''

How significant are all these passages and others that might be cited with just as much relevancy! Here God assures Moses again and again that He, Jehovah, is the very Elohim who appeared to the fathers and covenanted with them. Jehovah and Elohim are identical—the same Divine Being, known by different names to designate His varied characteristics. Line upon line God impresses this fact on the consciousness of Moses and the people of Israel. How beautifully this view preserves the unity and consistency of the Old Testament theology, and also its historical continuity! Why break the Pentateuch up into inconsequential fragments, when its solidarity and organic oneness can be seen by the simplest interpretation?

We are coming now to the crucial point. Suppose that God revealed Himself to Moses as the Elohim of the fathers, but under a new and tenderer name, Jehovah. Suppose again that, with this knowledge, Moses wrote the book of Genesis, using as his guide such documents or traditions, or both, as may have come down to him from preceding generations.* Under these circumstances would he not have inserted the name Jehovah in the Genetical narrative in many places? God may not have revealed His name Jehovah to the patriarchs, but Moses, who knew that Jehovah and Elohim were identical, would, in reciting the history, use both cognomens interchangeably.

On this presumption how rational is the use of the divine appellations in the first and second chapters of Genesis! When Moses recited the general history of creation, he naturally used the name Elohim, by which God had been known as the Creator from the earliest time. However, when he came to record the more detailed account of creation (Gen. 2), and especially the creation of man, the chief creature of God's love and care, Moses introduced the name Jehovah. But if he had employed that name only, his readers might have thought that a different God was now making man and dealing with him; besides, God had said to Moses: I, Jehovah, am the Elohe of thy fathers, Abraham, Isaac and Jacob. So what was more natural and consistent than for Moses, in Genesis 2, to link together the two divine names, and say: "And Jehovah Elohim formed man of the dust of the ground," "And Jehovah Elohim planted a garden eastward, in Eden," "And Jehovah Elohim said, It is not good that the man should be alone"? Thus, just as Jehovah and Elohim were identified in Moses' vision at the burning bush, so they were identified by Moses in the wonderful creation history in the first two chapters of Genesis.

As Dr. Cave has shown in his brilliant and logical way, Moses used the divine names with scientific precision throughout the entire history in Genesis, never putting the

---

* Our own view is that, while Moses may have had before him such "documents," or "traditions," or both, he was inspired by the Holy Spirit in a *special* way in his editorial use of them, as well as in the additions he made to them. This view agrees with and conserves the teaching of 2 Timothy 3:16, 2 Peter 1:19-21, and of the New Testament generally.

name Jehovah more than once or twice into the mouths of the ante-diluvian and post-diluvian patriarchs. In the narrative portions, which were the writing of Moses, both names are used as suited the narrator's purpose, but in the conversational parts the name Elohim, with very few exceptions, alone is used. This is just as it should be if Moses was the writer and compiler of Genesis. Then after Exodus 3-6 the two names are employed largely without distinction. This hypothesis preserves the unity and integrity of the Pentateuch, whereas the divisive critical theories convert the Bible into historical, literary, moral, and religious chaos.*

Turning from mere minutiæ and superficies, and looking at the Biblical system as a whole, one may see what a wonderfully rational and unified *Weltanschauung* (worldview) it presents. First, Elohim created the heavens and the earth; therefore He is the universal God, not a mere tribal deity. Then Jehovah Elohim (the same God, the God revealed to Moses in Exodus 3-6) created man and woman, and watched over them and *all* their posterity, as is shown by the history of the ante-diluvians, the flood, the tower of Babel, and the dispersion of the tribes after the confusion of tongues. Then, without withdrawing His

* Since the foregoing was printed in *The Biblical Review*, New York, we have read with much interest and profit Dr. A. Troelstra's excellent monograph, ''The Name of God in the Pentateuch'' (1912, translated by Edmund McClure). We recommend it most heartily. It is published by the Society for Promoting Christian Knowledge, London, most of whose publications are here commended as safe and valuable. Dr. Troelstra presents a different method of explaining Exodus 6:2, 3. It is ingenious and plausible, and, if true, preserves the integrity and organic unity of the Pentateuch, just as our own view does; but we cannot help thinking that his treatment is roundabout and over-complicated; whereas the view we have presented is simple and clear, and meets all the exigencies of the case. Here it is, put in its most condensed form:

Moses was the inspired compiler of Genesis; to Moses God revealed Himself for the first time under the name Jehovah; hence Moses in writing Genesis would use the various names of God almost interchangeably, proving that the same Supreme Being was meant throughout.

general presence and providence from the other nations of the earth, He selected Abraham to be the father of His chosen people. With him and his descendants He covenanted and dealt in a special way, made special revelations to them as need required, delivered to them the Sacred Oracles as a sacred trust, carried them for centuries through a special course of moral and spiritual discipline; then at last, in "the fullness of time," He gave, through them according to the flesh, His only-begotten Son to be the Redeemer of the world. Is it not throughout a coherent plan? The Hebrews were not elected as the chosen people merely for their own sakes. God did not become their "partisan" and they His "clients." That is a *slur* on the teaching of the Bible. God chose the people of Israel in order that, at the proper epoch, they might fulfill the divine commission to go "into all the world and preach the Gospel to every creature." Thus, after all the centuries of patience and discipline, the promise to Abraham was made good: "In thy seed shall all the nations of the earth be blessed" (Gen. 22:18; *cf.* 26:4; 28:14; Acts 3:25). The unity of Biblical doctrine is also seen in the New Testament passage: "For as in Adam all die, so also in Christ shall all be made alive" (1 Cor. 15:22; *cf.* Gen. 3:1-21). So also the Paradise that was lost in the first book of the Bible is regained in the last (*cf.* Gen. 3: 22-24; Rev. 2:7; 21:1-5).

Our point is this: If the Biblical teaching is taken just as it is, and in its historical order, it will be found to be characterized by a divine unity, a wonderful organic consistency and completeness. On the other hand, if the partition view is held, the Bible becomes a moral and religious medley, a chaos of indeterminateness. The former view affords an adequate explanation of the salutary influence of the Bible upon the world; the latter does not.

Which view, then, is the more scientific, the adequate or the inadequate one?

By a general survey we have now shown that Jehovah was the Creator and Preserver of the universe and the God of all nations. Our next object shall be to ascertain whether He sustained this universal character after the call of Abraham. Note first Genesis 11:9: "Therefore was the name of it called Babel; because Jehovah did there confound the language of all the earth: and from thence did Jehovah scatter them abroad upon the face of all the earth." Does that sound as if God were only a "clan" deity? How could universalism and monotheism be made more pronounced? Then follows the recital of the "generations of Shem" to Terah and Abram, their removal from Ur of the Chaldees to Haran, the death of Terah, and the call of Abram. The last event is given in the opening verses of Genesis 12. Note how the record begins: "And Jehovah said 'unto Abram." It is Jehovah, the same Jehovah who ruled all the world and its peoples up to that time—not a tribal god. Abram's call is recorded in Genesis 12:1-3, and ends in this way: "And I will bless them that bless thee, and him that curseth thee will I curse; and in thee shall all the families of the earth be blessed." Here Jehovah is most certainly exhibited as the God of all nations. In choosing Abram He did not abdicate His care and rulership of the rest of the world. When God converts an individual, and calls him His son, that does not mean that He forsakes and forgets all the rest of the human family—surely, surely not!

Immediately Abram and his retinue journeyed to the land of Canaan, where Jehovah—the same Jehovah, remember—appeared to him again, and said: "Unto thy seed will I give this land" (Gen. 12:7). How could a mere clan deity presume to make such a promise to Abram when that very country was then denizened by another nation, the Canaanites (v. 6)? When famine arose in Canaan, Jehovah went with Abram down into Egypt, and saved him and his wife Sarai from the hand of Pharaoh. There is not the least hint in the Biblical account that Jehovah came into conflict with any "rival" gods in Egypt, whom He overcame with difficulty. On coming back from the slaughter of the kings (Gen. 14), Abram met Melchizedek, King of Salem, who "was priest of God Most High" (Hebrew, *El Elyon*). Then: "And he [Melchizedek] blessed him, and said, Blessed be Abram of God Most High, possessor [margin, *maker*] of heaven and earth: and blessed be God Most High, who hath delivered thine enemies into thy hands." This ancient worthy, Melchizedek, was able to hold in mind the idea that God could be the God of Abram and at the same time the supreme God. He could see that there was no inconsistency between the two ideas.

In Genesis 16 the angel of Jehovah appears to Hagar, and says to her: "I will greatly multiply thy seed, that it shall not be numbered for multitude" (v. 10). "And she called the name of Jehovah that spake unto her, Thou art a God that seeth" (v. 13, Hebrew, *El Roi*). Here the Bible teaches that Jehovah, instead of confining His providence to Abram and his seed, would also exercise oversight over the Ishmaelites. No doctrine of henotheism taught here. Advance into chapter 17: "And when Abram was ninety and nine years old, Jehovah appeared to Abram, and said unto him, I am God Almightly" (*El Shaddai*). Here it is significant that the Biblical history identifies Jehovah with El Shaddai, showing that all these names are simply the appellations of the one Supreme Being. This was verse 1; then verse 3, continuing the incident: "And Abram fell on his face: and Elohim talked with him." How interesting to note that in this brief passage Jehovah, El Shaddai, and Elohim are identified as the same God. Then (v. 5) God changed the patriarch's name to Abraham, "for the father of a multitude of nations have I made thee.'' Not merely of one nation, but ''a multitude of nations.'' What becomes of the assumption that Jehovah was merely a provincial deity? The destruction of Sodom and Gomorrah proves that God had not abandoned the rest of the world to bestow all His attention on Abraham. He took cognizance of their wickedness, saying: ''Their sin is very grievous'' (Gen. 18:20). If Jehovah was only a tribal god, how could He bring utter destruction on the cities of the plain which were under the jurisdiction of another deity? Where were Jehovah's ''rival deities''? The theory of a tribal god will not hold together. In 18:25 Abraham prayed thus to Jehovah: ''Shall not the Judge of all the earth do right?'' So it would appear that Abraham did not cherish crass and narrow ideas of Jehovah. Chapter 20 recites Abraham's adventures in Gerar with King Abimelech. Note this (v. 17): ''And Abraham prayed unto Elohim: and Elohim healed Abimelech, and his wife, and his maid-servants; and they bare children.'' Was God only a tribal god here?

After Isaac's birth and Abraham's compact with King Abimelech, the record says (21:33): ''And Abraham planted a tamarisk tree in Beersheba, and called there on the name of Jehovah, the Everlasting God'' (*El Olam*). With the idea of the Everlasting God in this passage correspond all the marginal references, namely, Exodus 15: 18; Deuteronomy 32:40; Psalm 90:2; Isaiah 40:28; Jeremiah 10:10, showing that the identical conception of God prevailed throughout Israel's whole history. In Genesis 22:18 Jehovah renewed His covenant with Abraham, saying: ''In thy seed shall all the nations of the earth be blessed; because thou hast obeyed my voice.'' In 24:3 Abraham calls Jehovah ''the Elohim of heaven and the Elohim of the earth,'' and in verse 7 ''the Elohim of heaven.'' The romantic story of Isaac and Rebekah is told in chapter 24, and here again the case is diametrically against the rad-

ical view, for Abraham's kindred, away in Haran or Meso-
potamia, replied thus to the entreaty of Abraham's servant:
"The thing proceedeth from Jehovah; we cannot speak
unto thee bad or good. Behold, Rebekah is before thee,
take her, and go, and let her be thy master's son's wife,
as Jehovah hath spoken."

The same God renewed His covenant with Isaac and
Jacob. To the latter Jehovah appeared in a vision, and said
(Gen. 28:13, 14): "I am Jehovah, the Elohe of Abraham thy father, and the Elohe of Isaac: the land whereon
thou liest, to thee will I give it, and to thy seed; and thy
seed shall be as the dust of the earth . . . and in thee and
thy seed shall all the families of the earth be blessed."
God keeps up His cosmical interest throughout the whole
thrilling narrative. Through all Joseph's career in Egypt
"Jehovah was with him" and "the spirit of Elohim" was
in him. God also proved that He had control of natural
and national affairs in Egypt, bringing plentiful harvests
for seven years and then a distressing drought for the same
length of time, and making Joseph the second in rule over
all the land. If Jehovah was only a tribal deity, it is remarkable that He did not encounter any successful opposition from the national gods of Egypt. There is not a
syllable in the entire history giving a hint of even the
existence of other gods. Even the Pharaoh acknowledged
the sovereignty of Elohim (41:37-40). Many more similar
passages might be cited from Genesis, but these are ample
to prove that God is everywhere represented as the one and
only God. It is only by inverting and subverting the history that this concurrent testimony can be overcome. The
difference, therefore, between the two views is simply this:
The former accepts the Biblical history; the latter does not.
Hence the issue is clearly defined.

Does the teaching of the rest of the Pentateuch agree
with the pure monotheism of Genesis? We shall see that

it does. Our examination of Exodus 3 and 4 has shown that Jehovah revealed Himself to Moses as the God (Elohim) of the fathers. In the whole contest of Moses with Pharaoh, Jehovah certainly proved Himself not only the God of the Hebrews, as He frequently called Himself, but also the sovereign over Egypt and her people as well. It was Jehovah who brought all the plagues upon Pharaoh and the Egyptians (Ex. 7:20, 21; 8:6, 16-18, etc.), who hardened Pharaoh's heart (ch. 10), who discomfited the hosts of Egypt in the Red Sea (14:27; 15:19). Even the magicians of Pharaoh were compelled to admit: "This is the finger of Elohim" (8:19).

Naturally there are many passages in the Pentateuch in which Jehovah is called "the God of Israel." But there are also many direct teachings which show that the revealing God of Israel was none other than the God of the universe and of all nations. The question to be settled is not: What did Israel think of God? but: In what character did God *reveal Himself to Israel,* according to the clear teaching of the Bible? To mix up the two, and especially to make God responsible for the defective thinking and conduct of Israel, as is so often done, is to violate every principle of Biblical hermeneutics. Such a method would make chaos of any historical book.

"Now therefore, if ye will obey my voice indeed, and keep my covenant, then ye shall be mine own possession from among all peoples, for all the earth is mine" (Ex. 19:5). The very basis of His choice of Israel is that all the earth is His, and therefore He has the right and the power to choose whom He will. How beautifully this teaching coördinates with that of Psalm 24:1: "The earth is Jehovah's, and the fullness thereof; the world, and they that dwell therein." Exodus 20:8-11: "Remember the sabbath day, to keep it holy. Six days shalt thou labor, and do all thy work; but the seventh day is a sabbath unto Jehovah thy God . . . for in six days Jehovah made heaven and earth, the sea, and all that in them is, and rested the seventh day; wherefor Jehovah blessed the sabbath day, and hallowed it." Interpreted naturally, this commandment of the decalogue involves the following significant points: That Moses and Israel were conversant with the creation story of Genesis 1; that Jehovah and Elohim were one and the same, for Genesis 1 attributes the creation to Elohim and this passage attributes it to Jehovah; that Jehovah is the universal God, not merely a tribal deity. Exodus 34:10, 11, Jehovah said to Moses on the mountain: "Behold, I make a covenant: before all thy people I will do marvels, such as have not been wrought in all the earth, nor in any nation; and all the people among which thou art shall see the work of Jehovah . . . behold, I drive out before thee the Amorite, and the Canaanite, and the Hittite, and the Perizzite, and the Hivite, and the Jebusite." This passage, like a number of others containing the same promise, proves that Jehovah's domain and power extended far beyond Israel. It would hardly have been safe for a mere "clan-god" to make such sweeping promises. He might not have been able to overcome His "rival deities."

Numbers 16:22 (the prayer of Moses and Aaron in relation to Korah's rebellion): "O God [El], the God [Elohe] of the spirits of all flesh." Ever and anon the idea of Elohim as the universal God comes to the fore; it is always a latent thought; it breathes through the whole history. Chapters 22-24 of Numbers tell the story of Balak and his prophet Balaam, who were Moabites. All through this story Balaam, though a Moabite, recognizes Jehovah and Elohim as God, and can prophesy only what He reveals to him. Take one example among many. Balaam said (Num. 22:8, 12): "I will bring you word again, as Jehovah shall speak unto me." "And Elohim said unto Balaam, Thou shalt not go with them." Plainly Jehovah's rule extended beyond Israel. Why did not the gods of Moab inspire Balaam to curse Israel to please his king?

Deuteronomy 4:32 (the words of Moses to Israel: "For ask now of the days that are past, which were before thee, since the day that God [*Elohim*] created man upon the earth, and from the one end of the heaven unto the other," etc. Verse 35: "Unto thee it was showed, that thou mightest know that Jehovah he is Elohim; there is none else besides him." Verse 39: "Know therefore this day, and lay it to thy heart, that Jehovah he is God in heaven above and upon the earth beneath; there is none else." Much more than a "clan deity" here. Deuteronomy 5:26: "For who is there of all flesh, that hath heard the voice of the living God speaking out of the midst of the fire, as we have heard, and lived?" The phrases, "all flesh" and "living God," connote the universal theistic conception. Deuteronomy 6:4: "Hear, O Israel: Jehovah our God is one Jehovah: and thou shalt love Jehovah thy God with all thy heart," etc. This famous passage, with other passages, teaches much more than monolatry; it teaches the divine unity and universality—that God is *unus et unicus*. Deuteronomy 7:6: "Jehovah thy God hath chosen thee to be a people for his own possession, above all peoples that are upon the face of the earth." Is it not clear that the Bible teaches that God is both the God of His people Israel and the Ruler over all the earth? Read the whole of chapter 7 in proof of this conception. Chapter 8:20: "As the nations which Jehovah maketh to perish before you, so shall ye perish; because ye would not hearken unto the voice of Jehovah your God." Chapter 32:39 (all of Moses' song in this chapter should be read): "See now that I, even I, am He, and there is no god with me: I kill, and I make alive; I wound, and I heal; and there is none that can deliver out of my hand." This teaches pure monotheism—"there is no god with me"—and divine omnipotence. Chapter 33:26, 27 (from Moses' parting benediction): "There is none like unto God, O Jeshurun, who rideth upon the heavens for thy help, and his excellency is on the skies. The eternal God is thy dwelling-place, and underneath are the everlasting arms." No doctrine of a circumscribed deity is taught here. Compare 2 Samuel 7:22-24; Isaiah 46:9; and Jeremiah 10:6-10 to see how easily the inspired writers could carry the double conception that God is at the same time the only God and also the God of His peculiar people. They had no difficulty, as the radical critics seem to have, in mastering that simple thought.

A few citations from Joshua. In 2:11 Rahab the harlot said to the spies in Jericho: "For Jehovah your God, He is God in heaven above, and on earth beneath." Where did Rahab get her lofty conception of Jehovah? It must have been communicated to her from an Israelitish source and from the reports of Jehovah's wonderful works. Wonderful that this pagan woman could master a higher theistic idea than that of a mere provincial god! Chapter 4:23, 24: "For Jehovah your God dried up the waters of the Jordan . . . as Jehovah your God did to the Red Sea . . . that all the peoples of the earth may know the hand of Jehovah, that it is mighty; that ye may fear Jehovah your God forever." Joshua did not have a provincial view. Whatever men may think of Joshua's command to the sun and the moon to stand still (10: 12-14), whether it was an actual occurrence or only a poetical representation, it shows that Joshua and Israel regarded Jehovah as the omnipotent one, and not merely as a limited tribal deity. The 24th chapter goes back in Israel's history to Terah, the father of Abraham, when "your fathers dwelt of old time beyond the River . . . and they served other gods," and traces God's dealings with them amid all the idolatrous nations, proving Himself the only true and victorious God.

Most consistently does the Bible sustain the historical continuity.

We might continue our study through all the remaining books of the Old Testament, and prove its consistent and persistent monotheistic teaching. Wherever this conception is not expressly set forth, it is clearly implied. We need not pursue the question further along this line. We shall now treat of two matters that seem to trouble those holding the tribal-god theory.

The first is that the Old Testament so often calls Jehovah the God of Abraham, Isaac, Jacob, and Israel. Such langauge strikes the critics as the language of henotheism, making God only a tribal god. But why not also ponder the many passages which represent Jehovah as the God of the heavens and the earth and of all nations? Does not the Bible, right on its surface, mean to inculcate the conception that the God of Israel is also the true, living, and universal God? For His own wise purposes He selected a "peculiar people" to train and discipline, to receive and bear His oracles, and finally to bring forth the world's Redeemer. If one believes in the Christian religion at all, if he believes that Christ is the Savior of the world, he must admit that, whether God wrought directly or only immanently with Israel, He pursued the plan of using a chosen people. The "immanent" God did not give the world's Messiah through the people of India or China or Japan. So *per se* the "immanent" God acted just as partially as the true God of the Old Testament did.

But the difficulty comes solely from a stiff, contracted interpretation which does not give a large Biblical conception of God, and does not make clear distinctions. There is a broad sense in which God is the God of the universe and of all nations; there is also a peculiar sense in which He is the God of His people. God does not stand in the same relation to the true Christian and the wicked unbeliever. His general care is over all; His special care and grace are bestowed on those who accept Christ and do His will. He is *essentially* present and active everywhere, but He *functions* differently under different circumstances. There is no contradiction between the two conceptions. And this is the plain, simple teaching of the Bible from beginning to end. It ought never to have been mistaken by any student of the Divine Word.

Another point raised is that the Old Testament frequently speaks of idols as if they were real gods; for instance: "Thou shalt have no other gods before me" (Ex. 20:3); "and worship other gods, and serve them" (Deut. 30:17); "and they served other gods" (Josh. 24:2). Do not these expressions prove that Israel and even their supposed Jehovah regarded the idols of the heathen as real beings, real gods? "The prohibition of the worship of other gods obviously does not constitute monotheism, but monolatry" (Bade, p. 96). Even an untrained reader should see that the word "gods" is employed in such places according to a common usage of speech. The heathen people regarded their idols as gods. So the Biblical writers simply made use of their own term. We do the same to-day. We speak of the "gods" of the heathen. Do we mean to convey the impression that their gods are real gods—that they have a real existence? We simply mean that they are the gods of their imaginative superstition. The same intelligence should be accredited to the Jehovah of the Bible and to His inspired prophets. The stumbling-stone of Dr. Bade should have been removed by reading on in Exodus 20 to the 23d verse, for there Jehovah said: "Gods of silver, or gods of gold, ye shall not make unto you." In 32:31 Moses said to God: "Oh, this people have sinned a great sin, and have made them gods of gold." This agrees with Isaiah 44:10: "Who hath fashioned a god, or molten an image that is profitable for nothing?"

Also verse 15: "Yea, he maketh a god, and worshipeth it; he maketh it a graven image, and falleth down thereto." Chapter 42:17: "They shall be turned back, they shall be utterly put to shame, that trust in graven images, that say unto molten images, Ye are our gods." Thus the Bible uses the word "gods" in the sense of idols.

But there is express teaching in the Bible that the gods of the heathen are "nothings" (*elilim*). Leviticus 19:4: "Turn ye not unto idols [Hebrew, *elilim*, things of naught], nor make to yourselves molten gods: I am Jehovah your God." Also 26:1. With this agrees the later teaching of the Bible, which is still more pronounced and explicit, showing that the Old Testament religion is not a mere natural evolution; it is a progressive revelation from Jehovah. In Psalm 96:4,5: "For great is Jehovah, and greatly to be praised: He is to be feared above all gods. For all the gods of the peoples are idols [*elilim*]; but Jehovah made the heavens." Here even the Psalmist, who calls them *nothings*, calls the idols "gods." 1 Chronicles 16:26: "For all the gods of the peoples are idols [*elilim*]; but Jehovah made the heavens." Note Hezekiah's prayer (2 Kings 19:17, 18): "Of a truth, Jehovah, the kings of Assyria have laid waste the nations and their lands, and have cast their gods into the fire; for they were no gods, but the work of men's hands, wood and stone; therefore they have destroyed them." Perhaps it will be said that this is a contradiction, due to "variant" documents; for Hezekiah called them "gods" in one sentence, and in the next declared that "they were no gods." Perhaps the redactor is to blame here for not noticing the contradiction in his JEDP documents. Poor Jeremiah also committed a crude contradiction when he wrote (2:11): "Hath a nation changed its gods, which yet are no gods?" How could they be "gods" and "no gods" at the same time? We believe that the whole Old Testament conception of heathen deities is summed up in the words of Psalm 115:4-8: "Their idols are silver and gold, the work of men's hands. They have mouths, but they speak not; eyes have they, but they see not. . . . They that make them are like unto them; yea, every one that trusteth in them."

No doubt many of the people of Israel had crude ideas of Jehovah and of the heathen gods. It would be no wonder if they had, surrounded by idolatrous nations as they were, and held in bondage for four hundred years. Their many relapses into idolatry furnish proof of their idolatrous tendencies. But their crass conceptions should not be accredited to Jehovah, or to His inspired writers and prophets who constantly rebuked the idol worship of the people. It is this very tendency in human nature to fall into idolatry that makes a divine and authoritative revelation, such as we have in the Bible, a positive necessity. Otherwise we would all perhaps still be bowing down to idols to-day.

Anent this point, Dr. James Orr ("Problem of the Old Testament," p. 123) has a good sentence: "That the religion of Abraham, and Moses, and other great leaders of the nation was at heart the worship of the one true God, recognized by them to be the Creator, Ruler, and Lord in providence of the whole world, we see not the smallest reason to doubt." We also venture to quote the closing paragraph of an acute section of Dr. Orr's book (p. 133).

"We conclude that no good ground has been shown for the view that 'ethical monotheism' was first introduced by the prophets, beginning with Amos. We have found monotheism already imbedded in the narratives in Genesis, which, in their J and E parts, are, on the critic's own showing, 'pre-prophetic.' So far from monotheism being the creation of the prophets—with perhaps Elijah as a precursor—these prophets, without exception, found upon and presuppose an older knowledge of the true God. They bring no new doctrine, still less dream of the evolution from a Moloch or a Kenite storm-god—as much the product of men's fancies as Chemosh or Dagon—of the living, holy, all-powerful, all-gracious Being to whose service the people were bound by every tie of gratitude, but from whom they had basely apostatized. They could not have understood such evolution from an unreality into a reality. They were in continuity with the past, not innovators upon it. Dillmann speaks for a large class of scholars when he says, in decisively rejecting this theory: 'No prophet is conscious of proclaiming for the first time this higher divine principle: each reproaches the people for an apostasy from a much better past and better knowledge: God has a controversy with His people.' "

And we may add, it is because some students do not see this "controversy," cannot distinguish between God's progressive revelation and the sinful subjective tendencies and crude views of the stiff-necked people of Israel—it is for this reason that they make such a sorry jumble of the history and doctrines of the Bible. Thus they fail to see its divine unity. On account of their extreme subjectivism, they have lost the key to its interpretation. That key is this: Jehovah Elohim reveals Himself in the Bible as the one true and living God, the Creator, Preserver, and Redeemer of the whole cosmos.

CHAPTER VI

SEVERAL times we had seen and heard recommendations of Dr. Frank Knight Sanders' "History of the Hebrews," and had come to the conclusion that it must be a useful and evangelical book, but had not found time to give it a personal examination. However, when we saw it meeting with the approval of the liberalistic writers (particularly of Dr. Bade in his "The Old Testament in the Light of To-day," p. x of the preface), we decided that it would be well to give the book a personal examination. A good deal of suspicion was stirred in our mind on noting that Dr. Bade claimed Dr. Sanders as one of his "former teachers at Yale." If Dr. Sanders' teaching resulted in the production of such a book as Bade's, or did not prevent such a production, then Dr. Sanders' teaching, by that very token, could not have had very much evangelical virility and effectiveness; for Bade's work is by all odds one of the most rationalistic and destructive works that has yet come from the American press. We may say here that, while Dr. Sanders' book is much better than Bade's, the latter is simply the legitimate fruit and logical outcome of the teaching of the former. Dr. Sanders accepts the premises, but declines to push on to the inevitable conclusion; while Dr. Bade has more courage and logic, and hence does not halt midway. However, this assertion awaits its proof at the proper place.

Dr. Sanders' book was published in 1914. At that time

he was the president of Washburn College, Topeka, Kansas, which was founded by the Congregationalists, "but is non-sectarian in policy and government." The "Foreword" of Dr. Sanders' book would indicate that the volume is intended mainly for a college text-book (p. vi). This is also implied in his very gracious formula of dedication, which is as follows: "To the Students and Faculty of Washburn College, for whom and with whom we have spent five happy years." The title and sub-title of the book are as follows: "History of the Hebrews: Their Political, Social and Religious Development and Their Contribution to World Betterment."

To mention some of the commendable features of the book first, we are glad to say it is comparatively reverent in its attitude toward the Old Testament. In this respect it differs widely from the slashing treatment in Bade's book. Dr. Sanders does not directly criticize the ethics of the Old Testament, and never holds it up to ridicule and scorn, but usually gives it a mild kind of defense; that is, he explains the situations in such a way as to make a fair apologetic for some apparent ethical defects and discrepancies. Indeed, in some respects he offers quite a satisfactory defense of the Bible. The spirit and tone of the book are excellent. Much credit is given to the Old Testament for its pure religious teaching and powerful influence in the world. In many ways the book may seem to be an answer—without the least hint, however, that it is meant to be so—to the extreme positions of the radical critics. In this respect the book may be somewhat useful, serving as a kind of foil to the ultra-radicals. Indeed, it is about the most successful attempt at maintaining the "mediating" position that we have yet seen among the smaller contributions to Biblical criticism. The temper of the book would certainly lead to the conclusion that its author is a man of a cordial and winsome disposition.

Having said so much in the book's favor, it is not pleasant to have to turn to finding flaws; but we must follow our conscience and reason. Such a book ought not to pass uncensored. The very fact that the writer exhibits so fine a spirit, and holds so many evangelical principles, makes his book all the more dangerous; all the better calculated to undermine the faith of young men and women in the Bible as an inspired and trustworthy revelation. The more truth a writer embodies in the midst of fundamental error, the more insidious will be the peril; for in such a case many minds will not be able to separate the truth from the error. Well does Shakespeare warn us of the peril of craft in the lines:

> "And oftentimes to win us to our harm
> The instruments of darkness tell us truths."

A man who approaches you with a concealed dirk is more dangerous than the man who comes flourishing his weapon in the open, announcing his intentions. So where Bade's open and frank assault will at once put the student on his guard, the suave, subtle, disguised method of the writer in question will be apt first to win the student's confidence, disarm his suspicion, and then, ere he knows it, convert him to the rationalistic view. We have actually known young men who thought Dr. Sanders' book was sound and evangelical, not being able to detect its subtle method of destroying the historical character of the Old Testament.

However, the foregoing assertions must now be made good. So let us look frankly at the book itself. We must be as brief as possible. We shall deal with the author's main positions, going into detail only in a few cases where necessity requires. First, here is a professed "History of the Hebrews," drawn mostly from the Old Testament itself, and yet it contains not one word about *divine inspiration*. The word "inspiration" does not occur in the index, and we cannot find it in the text. The word "inspirational" occurs (p. 13), but has no reference to the doctrine of Biblical inspiration. It may be said that the author was not discussing the subject of inspiration, but writing a history of the Hebrew people; therefore such a discussion would have been irrelevant. But that is only an evasion, or at least a very lame apology. Where did Dr. Sanders get most of his material for his so-called "history"? From the Old Testament, which is an integral part of our Christian Bible. But Moses and the prophets all claimed to receive their messages directly from God —so the Bible declares again and again. Would that not connote just what we mean to-day by the doctrine of inspiration? Is it dealing adequately with the "history of the Hebrews" to ignore that claim, which lies at the very basis of their religion? Moreover, the New Testament, referring expressly to the Old Testament, as is evident from the context, says (2 Tim. 3:16): "Every Scripture is inspired of God," etc. (We are convinced that this is the correct translation, though others may not agree.) Also 2 Pet. 1:20, 21: "Knowing this first, that no prophecy of Scripture is of private interpretation; for no prophecy ever came by the will of man; but men spake from God, being moved by the Holy Spirit." Now to write a professed history of the Hebrew people, and draw upon their sacred books as the main source of material, and yet never even mention the claim of divine inspiration, is a manifest evasion of the most vital point in that history. No man would try to write a history of Mohammedanism without at least recognizing Mohammed's claim to a divine revelation, and endeavoring in some way to give an account of it. Read Irving's history, and see whether he side-steps this claim. Would an evangelical writer who truly believed in the divine inspiration of the Holy Scriptures have written a history of the Hebrews without saying something about its claim to a divine origin? Remember, too, that the author in his sub-title announces that his book is to be, among other things, a history of the *"religious* development" of the Hebrews. A part of that history, lying right there on the surface, is the claim of a direct divine revelation.

Next, we call attention to the critical authorities cited by our author (pp. 337-353). He calls them "references for the teacher and student." He wants to encourage the habit of looking up these more extended works. He says: "Attention is called below to some of the best untechnical literature available to-day." Who are the writers cited? With all our searching we can find only two really conservative authors in the long list. One of them is Dr. James Orr, whose monumental work, "The Problem of the Old Testament," is once alluded to; but even here the reference is a very casual and unimportant one. The other conservative book, once cited, is Sir William Ramsay's "Cities of St. Paul"—a work which, we are sorry to say, we have not yet had time to read carefully, but which, if we may judge from his other and more recent books, is likely to be conservative. However, it must be remembered that Ramsay was once a liberal critic, but more thorough investigation converted him to the conservative position. See his book, 1916, on "Archæology and the New Testament."

Among the critical authors cited by Dr. Sanders are the following: Cheyne, Driver, Kent, George Adam Smith, Gray (T. B.), Skinner, Ryle, Cornill, Wade, Mc-Fadyen, Mitchell, Hastings, Budde, Jastrow, Kennedy and Riggs. This is certainly a liberal list of *liberals*. These works are not only cited, but a number of them receive special commendation. For instance: "For a scholarly and helpful discussion of the origin of the ideas of these chapters (Gen. I-XI), see Jastrow, 'Hebrew and Babylonian Traditions,' 1914; Ryle, 'The Early Narratives of Genesis,' 1890, etc." Also: "The most helpful commentary is that by Driver (Westminster Comm.)"

This list is as remarkable for what it excludes as for what it includes. As we have said, with possibly two exceptions (and those cited relative to nothing vital), all the authors belong to the "liberal" camp. All of them go on the assumption that much of the Old Testament is composed of myth, legend, folk-lore and tradition, even where the Bible, at least on the surface, gives plain historical narratives. All of them tell us that the Old Testament contains many historical and scientific errors and contradictions, and that little or none of it can properly lay claim to direct divine revelation and inspiration. Practically all of these authors accept the "documentary" hypothesis, which cuts up the historical portions of the Bible into many discrepant parts. All of them, as does Dr. Sanders himself, reconstruct the Biblical history to fit it into their subjective critical views.

Here, we are compelled to say, is where this book will prove harmful in its effects upon young minds. The conclusions of these "advanced" disintegrating critics are set forth as if they were absolutely proved; as if all modern scholarship held them; as if there could be no question about their correctness. There is not even a hint, so far as we can see, that many of the so-called "assured results" of the liberal critics are mere hypotheses, with only a slender basis of truth, if any, and that conservative scholars have again and again questioned and discredited them, and that with powerful arguments. The following great conservative writers are never even mentioned by Dr. Sanders, but are treated as if they were *non ens*:

Hengstenberg, Havernick, Klostermann, Orelli, Oettli, Hommel, Moeller, Koehler, Bissell, Robertson (James), Cave, Girdlestone, Urquhart, Sayce, Watson, Lias, Blomfield, the authors of "Lex Mosaica," Redpath, Green, McGarvey, Hilprecht, Clay, Warfield, McKim, Wilson, Wiener, and many more. We mention this long list of great names only to show the culpability of an author who ignores them, and presents as veritable truth only one side of the question in a college text-book. Is it fair, we ask in all kindness, to young collegians for an instructor in our holy religion to set forth only the liberal positions as if nothing had ever been said against them? Is that the way to arrive at the truth? Would a fair-minded, wholehearted, and truly scientific teacher give only one side of a mooted question, and utterly ignore everything that has been said on the other side? Worse than all, not even hint that there *is* another side? *

Let us give instances of the unfairness of such a procedure. Dr. Sanders says of Driver's work on Genesis that it is "the most helpful commentary," and constantly treats its positions as established. Is it frank for him never even to hint that Dr. Orr, in his "The Problem of the Old Testament," has called in question most of Driver's positions, and has shown again and again that other critics just as learned do not agree with Driver? Why

---

* We have another object in giving the above rather formidable list of conservatives. In the last few years in this country there has been a veritable propaganda of liberal views. These views have been popularized by a number of rather spicy writers who have simply accepted offhand the views of Graf, Kuenen, Wellhausen, Driver and Cheyne, and a special effort has been made to get these books into circulation. Many persons have become more or less acquainted with this liberal output, but have not seen or read or even heard of the deeper, solider, more finely argued works that have been published on the conservative side. We wish to call attention to these scholarly works, so that men may study both sides of the question. Note also what is said anent this matter in our remarks introductory to the "Selected Bibliography" at the close of this volume.

did not Dr. Sanders tell his readers that Dr. Henry A. Redpath has written a compact (and to our mind a convincing) rejoinder to Driver in his little book, "Modern Criticism and Genesis," second and revised edition, 1906? When our author recommends Skinner's commentary on Genesis, is he treating his readers and students squarely not to tell them that Harold M. Wiener has, in the opinion of many scholars, effectually demolished Skinner? Why does not Dr. Sanders let his readers know that President Samuel C. Bartlett, D.D., in his "The Veracity of the Hexateuch," has presented a crushing answer to all of Driver's works published up to 1895? When Dr. Sanders, following his masters, Kent, Riggs, Bevan, and McFadyen, assigns the book of Daniel to 166 B. C., centuries after the Bible Daniel's time, why does he not have the grace and frankness to say that Dr. John Urquhart, in his "The Inspiration and Accuracy of the Holy Scriptures," offered a most powerful argument for the traditional view of the book in question? Nor is it right for Dr. Sanders to overlook what Dr. Wilson, of Princeton, has done in defending the conservative view of Daniel.* While Dr. Sanders himself accepts offhand the fragmentary theory of the Pentateuch, is it right for him never to tell his readers that great scholars like William Henry Green did not, and many others do not now, hold that hypothesis? When he avers without proof that Moses could not have put the Hexateuch (he means the Pentateuch) into its present form (p. 13), we think he ought to tell his students that great scholars like Orr, Cave, Moeller, Green, Urquhart, Lias, Watson, Robertson, and McGarvey, do believe that Moses was the author of the

* The above was written before Dr. Robert Dick Wilson's monumental book, "Studies in Book of Daniel" (1917), was published, but while chapters of that work were running serially in *The Princeton Theological Review.* No one hereafter has a right to deal with the Daniel controversy and ignore Dr. Wilson's work.

first *five* books of the Bible (except, of course, the last chapter of Deuteronomy, which may have been added by Joshua). Dr. Sanders seemed to be utterly unconscious of Dr. Johannes Dahse's epoch-making article, "Is a Revolution in Pentateuchal Criticism at Hand?" which was published in 1912, and shortly afterward translated into English by Edmund McClure, with a telling preface by Prof. A. H. Sayce.

We venture to ask, Is this habit of ignoring the works of conservative scholars ethical? We have acquaintance with quite a number of conservative teachers of the Bible in various colleges and seminaries, but we do not know of one who ignores the works of the radical critics. Their method is to present both sides of the question, and then to try to prove what they honestly believe to be the true position. Just so our conservative writers never ignore the arguments of the radicals, but examine them critically to see whether they are sound or not. Therefore we maintain that conservative scholars are broader and fairer than their opponents, and are, at the same time, their peers in scholarship.

Our next duty will be to show Dr. Sanders' fundamental position on the doctrine of the Bible itself (the science of Bibliology). Does his view of the Bible agree with what the Bible claims for itself and with the well-known evangelical view? Here we shall quote, beginning on page 4: "The most important contribution made by the Hebrew nation to the world was *its interpretation* of religion. More clearly than any other known people in the centuries preceding the Christian era the Hebrews *thought of God* as a moral being, a Character, the Father of mankind, who rules the world in righteousness and wishes to have it pervaded by goodness and friendliness." In our quotations we shall italicize the words that are significant and that afford a clew to the more or less disguised unevangelical views of the author. The above sentence has its good points, and is very different from the assaults of Bade. However, it does not express the Biblical view nor the evangelical view. The Bible nowhere indicates that it sets forth the Hebraic "interpretation" of religion, but always God's *revelation* of religion. This is also the evangelical view. The Bible does not teach what the "Hebrews *thought* of God," but what God *revealed* Himself to them to be; which is also the evangelical position.

On page 23, section 32, our author says: "In the first eleven chapters of Genesis we find a group of *stories* which convey the *ideas* of the Hebrew people concerning the creation of the world, the beginnings of human life, the conditions of primitive humanity," etc. "These *ideas* for the most part they evidently *inherited* from their Semitic forefathers and adopted without serious question. Such *ideas* have their proper place in the Bible, *not because God wished to make a special revelation* concerning such facts, but because, through these *beliefs* of the people, correct *ideas* regarding God, man, the universe, and their mutual relations could be established."

Here again the evangelical view is different, holding that these chapters contain special divine revelations, and not merely the "beliefs" and "ideas" of the Hebrew people. If the first chapter of Genesis contains only a record of Semitic "beliefs" and "ideas," how can we be sure that "in the beginning God created the heavens and the earth?" If it does not correctly describe "the process of creation," as Dr. Sanders intimates on page 24, why should we accept its statement about the creation itself? Could it state a profound and infallible truth in the first verse, and then drop into crude error in the verses that immediately follow? How are you going to know which statements are true and which are not? "Oh! reason teaches us that the first verse is true, but that the rest cannot be," the critic replies. But that is rationalism, not Biblical and Evangelical Christianity. In view of the innumerable egregious and harmful blunders that human reason has made in the past, and is making to-day, does it beget much confidence in itself as a sure guide? The reason of Democritus, Epicurus, Lucretius, Plato, Aristotle, Spinoza, Tyndal, Huxley, and Spencer did not lead them to believe in the doctrine of divine creation. Nor did the reason of Haeckel, Vogt and Feuerbach convince them of such a conception. The difficulty with such views is that they simply destroy the inspiration and infallibility of the Bible in any and all of its parts.

Here, then, is our author's fundamental conception of the Bible—it is a record of human "ideas" and "beliefs," many of them wrong, some of them right. Sometimes the author uses the word "revelation"—but very sparingly— never, though, in the objective and infallible sense, but only in the subjective sense, which permits of almost any amount of the admixture of human error. To our mind, such a revelation is little better than none at all, and is only that of natural theology. Without arguing the question now, we submit to the Christian people of the land whether they want their sons and daughters to receive such teaching when they send them to college. If they do, that is their option; this is a free country; but they should at least be apprised of the real inner character of the instruction.

Next we must investigate Dr. Sanders' teaching on the historicity of the Bible. The threads of truth and error are so closely and deftly woven together that it is difficult to separate them. Many objectionable sentences and phrases might be cited from the "Introductory Studies," but we shall begin with page 23, where the author comes out a little more in the open. He says: "The history of the Hebrew people *really begins* with the crossing of the Jordan River and the conquest and settlement of Canaan as a permanent home." Yes, according to Cheyne, Driver, Skinner, Gray, Kent, McFadyen, etc., but not according to the Bible. According to the Bible, the history of the Hebrew people began with the call of Abraham, who was separated by the Almighty from the rest of mankind to become the father of His "chosen people." The record of events from Abraham to the crossing of the Jordan bears just as distinct a historical atmosphere, just as much an impression of verisimilitude, as does the record afterward. Note the *aplomb* of the author. He is simply cocksure. He gives no clew to the fact that the following great scholars are against his opinion that Israelitish history began when he says it did: Keil, Delitsch, Klostermann, Orelli, Moeller, Orr, Cave, Green, Lias, Watson, and scores of others. An author has no right to pretend that there is unanimity of opinion among scholars on such a mooted point.

Our author continues (note the adroitness of his language): "For hundreds of years before the entrance into Canaan, however, the Hebrew people were in making. Our knowledge of this period is *very scanty.*" We hope one of Dr. Sanders' innocent students will ask him why it is so "scanty." There is a pretty full and detailed history given in the Pentateuch; in fact, by far the greater part of the Pentateuch is occupied with a recital of the history of the Hebrew people *prior* to their "crossing of the Jordan River." Observe what follows: "What we do know about it is derived from the first five Biblical books, Genesis to Deuteronomy, and mainly from Genesis and Exodus." Why not the other books "mainly" as well as these two? Continuing: "Like *every* history of the beginnings of a race, it is told in the form of *stories,* which explain the origin of its institutions and describe its great leaders. Such *stories* are fascinating in their interest. They are the material out of which *wo make history,* but their greater value as Biblical material lies in their portrayal of strong, true types of character and in their emphasis upon God's share in human affairs.''

This evasive, *quasi* way of saying things is what we do not like in the class of writers to which our author belongs. Why do they not come out plainly and say they do not believe that the first five books of the Bible are historical, but are largely made up of traditions and folk-stories? Is this equivocal method adopted for an ulterior purpose? Look at the above. This history ''is told in the form of *stories.*'' But there are true and untrue stories. So here is a word used that has a double meaning. It looks as if he means that these stories are fictions. He says ''like *every* history of the beginnings of a race.'' This would seem to indicate that the Biblical ''stories'' are just like those of other nations. Then what is there to make the Bible a unique book, and a special revelation of God's character, works and redeeming grace? But out of such material as these ''stories'' ''we make history.'' That means that the stories are not history, but we must take them and disentangle from them the few threads of truth they contain. That is what it means, or it has no meaning. And that means again that we to-day, living over four thousand years after the events, must ''make history'' out of the tangle. What becomes of any special divine revelation from such a medley of fiction and truth? Yet this author proceeds to state that the greater value of this Biblical material lies ''in their emphasis upon God's share in human affairs.'' But if the majority of the events never occurred, how can you prove from them that God has had much share in ''human affairs?'' As we have said at other times, the difficulty with the rationalists is with their heads rather than with their hearts. Our perusal of many authors leads us to think that rationalists are the poorest reasoners in the world.

Note again on page 24 (he is speaking of the early chapters of Genesis) : "Nor do they, except in a *symbolic* way, throw light upon the exact method of man's creation or upon the origin of human occupations. God has given men the opportunity of discovering such facts for themselves. His message to the world through these *stories* was a *religious* message."

That word "symbolic" is *a la* the Cheyne-Driver-Kent school, but not according to their equals, if not superiors, Orr, Cave, Robertson, Urquhart, Green and Redpath. One of these references is to the Biblical account of the creation of man. If that narrative is "symbolical," in what way is it so? What are the points of comparison? The Genetical record is: "And Jehovah Elohim formed man of the dust of the ground, and breathed into his nostrils the breath of life; and man became a living soul." In what way is that a symbolical account? It is easy to give the interpretation of the parables of Uriah's ewe lamb and of the prodigal son; but we wish some liberal critic would give us the precise interpretation of this "symbolical" story of man's creation. A good symbol ought not to be difficult to explain. Nor can we see why the Biblical writer should have here used symbolical speech in describing the genesis of the human family. Of all places in the world, this would be about the most unsuitable one to use figures of rhetoric, instead of plain, literal prose. It is very poor symbolism, too, if that is what it is; for thus far it has led the vast majority of Jews and Christians to believe that it is literal history. Only a crude, not to say a dishonest, writer would write like that. Then what becomes of the "religious" value of such a bungling writer? However, if it is true history, and gives a true account of the beautiful, gracious, condescending way in which God brought man into being in His own image, then indeed is its *religious* value beyond computation; for then we perceive the basic reason for God's high evaluation of and wonderful love for man, and therefore why, when man fell into sin, He sacrificed His only begotten Son to redeem him.

Our author also contends that God has given men the ability to discover such facts as "the exact method of man's creation." We wonder when men have made that marvelous discovery. It must have been very recently. There are many guesses and hypotheses, but every true and modest scientist will tell you that no one to-day knows just the precise method of man's origin. Some of the radical critics ought to read the latest testimonies of science. Quite recently one of the greatest present-day scientists declared that, so far as science is concerned, the origin of man is wrapped in complete obscurity; science has no positive word to say on the subject. If man's origin is wrapped in obscurity, what do we know about the purpose of his being and about his destiny? But thanks be to God, the Bible tells us clearly and beautifully about his origin, his purpose and his destiny. This gives real meaning to life.

On page 25 Dr. Sanders gives his idea of the first chapter of Genesis. "This wonderful narrative," he says, "is really a stately *poem* about God." We are glad to note that our writer expresses here and there seemingly real heartfelt admiration for the Bible. In this respect he manifests a much better spirit than some of his fellow-writers who accept theoretically the same positions he occupies. However, here we note that what he formerly called a "story" he now calls a "poem." Of course, a poem may be a story too; yet it does seem that he is ready to call this part of the Bible almost anything but history. He continues: "It depicts an orderly, gradual process of creation under the guidance of God and in accordance with His will. But God and man, rather than the creative process, are the centers of real interest. The poem shows in dignified fashion how the whole universe finds its explanation in God."

Every evangelical believer will be glad for these tributes. Of course Dr. Sanders is a theist. No one would ever accuse him of being a materialist. Nevertheless, he picks and chooses among the statements of the Bible, as when he intimates above that we need not accept the Biblical statements about "the process of creation," but need accept only what is said about "God and man." So again it is human reason, not the Bible, that is the final judge. Afterwards he says that the "three great verses" of this first chapter of the Bible are the first, the 27th and the 31st, and some would add the 28th. But why make this distinction? Why not accept all the verses? Was not the getting of the earth into a habitable condition, so that man could dwell upon it and have communion with God,— was this not also of "religious" value? If our author should reply that "the process of creation" described here is not in harmony with science, we would ask, Whose science? That of Agassiz, Dana, Dawson and Quenstedt, or that of Haeckel, Vogt and Feuerbach?

Coming to the "story" of man's creation in Gen. 2:4-24, our writer remarks: "It answers, in the simple, pictorial form used by *primitive minds,* the question of the origin of human life." So it was only another of the "ideas" of the Hebrews. Again there is no revelation here; merely human ways of looking at things. The divinity of the book fades out almost to the vanishing point. See how he volatilizes everything into mere "symbolism"; a Christian Scientist could not do it much better: "But the garden of Eden was more a *symbol* than a geographical location" (p. 26). It means that God gave man every chance to exercise his powers and gratify his needs. The tree of the knowledge of good and evil signifies that man was not only to work and enjoy himself, but must also attain moral good, and so have a test. True manhood consists in free moral agency. Likewise, ''the beautiful *story* of the creation of woman *symbolizes* the true relationship of the sexes, the natural dependence of woman upon man, her fitness to share life with him, and the wonderful closeness of union in true marriage.''

This effort comes about as near interpreting the ''symbolism,'' if that is what it is, as any attempt we have yet seen. It is a revival of the old allegorical method of Origen, and has a touch of Swedenborgianism and Christian Science as well. By that method of hermeneutics you can find almost anything you want to in the historical narratives of the Bible. But we fear it will not answer for scientific theology and interpretation. It is reading very profound moral and spiritual truths into the story. But if this chapter is only ''the simple, pictorial form used by *primitive* minds,'' we wonder how such untutored minds could write ''poems'' and ''stories'' teaching such fine and exalted truths. We are sure that would not agree with the theory of evolution, which makes man with the ''primitive mind'' only a little grade higher than the ape. If you say it was divine inspiration that produced, through those ''primitive minds,'' these stories and poems, then we do not see why the divine Spirit did not lead the writers to narrate the process of human creation as it actually occurred. Why did the Spirit select a rhetorical form that has been mistaken for actual history by the vast majority of Jews and Christians through all the centuries? If man and woman were not brought into being as the Bible says, could not the inspiring Spirit of God just as well have told the truth as to make up this beautiful piece of fiction? On the other hand, if the narrative is not divinely inspired, then the thoughts symbolized are far too deep and high for the minds of primeval savages. However, if the narrative is accepted at its face value, and is the product of divine inspiration, both the form and the teaching are accounted for, and come down to us duly authorized.

The story of the fall of our first parents into sin is likewise vaporized into symbol or parable, but we cannot tarry here. In other writings we have endeavored to prove the historicity of this narrative (see "The Rational Test," Chapter V). Next we note that Dr. Sanders omits, without a word of explanation, the whole Biblical account from Adam to the flood. Was not this an evasion? Is that the way for a true and honest teacher of religion to treat the Bible? In spite of the great diversity of opinion on the subject, our author says the "story of the flood is of Babylonian origin." Is it right for him to keep his readers and students in ignorance of the fact that many great scholars think that the Genetical account of the flood is the original inspired history of that catastrophe, while the Babylonian story is a later version and perversion of it? And why should not that be the case? According to the Bible, Abraham, the Babylonians and all other people of the time were the descendants of Noah; and therefore, if Abraham was really chosen of God to be His representative, the father of His people, and the bearer of His redemptive plan, God could easily have kept the facts of the flood pure and uncorrupted in His servant's hands. This hypothesis will adequately account for the fact that the Biblical narrative, both in purpose and manner, is *toto coelo* above that of the Babylonians. (See Dr. George A. Barton's "Archeology and the Bible," 1916.)

It is a pleasure to admit here that Dr. Sanders, instead of finding fault with God for sending the flood, as Dr. Bade does, justifies God in thus punishing the wicked

world. While we are glad he does this, we think the force
of the moral lesson he derives is largely lost if the flood
was not a real historic occurrence. Fiction may have its
use for many more or less superficial people; but those
who think more deeply will be likely to say: "Oh! but
the incident never took place; it is only a bit of imagination." We cannot agree with the author when he grows
almost eloquent over the "pedagogical fitness" (p. 30)
of this symbolical method of conveying religious instruction. If the writer or writers, inspired or uninspired,
wanted to teach by parables, they should have given their
literary productions the parabolic cast and form. They
were not ethical, therefore, in using the historic form, and
thus deceiving the vast majority of Bible students.
Moreover, fiction is not the solid, deep and permanent form
of instruction, and for real pedagogical value is not to be
compared with facts. Besides, it is inconsistent to think
that God would give to the world a real religion, meant
for their highest temporal and eternal welfare, and yet
would separate it from the stream of human history, and
hang it up in the air in the form of imaginative stories.
While we believe that God cares for the more lightsome
moods of human life, yet we cannot help believing that,
when He is dealing in matters of revelation which involve
human redemption from sin and eternal death, He would
use the more serious and perduring pedagogical methods.

Our writer pursues the same course throughout his
book in dealing with the historical records of the Bible.
Nowhere will he accept the Bible at its face value. While
he differs from the more radical critics in defending the
teaching of the Bible—and for this we again commend
him—he otherwise accepts their premises and conclusions.
The patriarchs are rather nebulous characters in his
hands; the Bible representations are "idealized portraits"
(p. 31); sometimes they seem to have a little historic

reality; then they vapor off into tribal movements again. They shimmer and glance before you, but will not remain still and steady enough for you to get your camera focused upon them. Not so does the *Bible* represent them. But that boots little with the rationalists. With them, not the Bible, but their theories are decisive.

Dr. Sanders' treatment of Moses is no more satisfactory. This great character, so firmly and graphically drawn in the Bible, flits almost like a shadow across our author's pages. He seems to treat him as an actual historical character, and yet nowhere does he say so plainly, and thus we are left in doubt as to whether he is much more than an idealized hero of a fiction-producing age. For instance, he says (p. 67): "The casual references of these narratives to Moses are interesting." When you remember how boldly Moses stands out in the Biblical account, from the beginning of Exodus to the close of Deuteronomy, you wonder at the carelessness of such a remark. The author himself goes on to mention quite a number of very definite things that are ascribed to Moses, showing that the references to him were far from "casual." Then he actually stops to eulogize Moses, but whether he means a real Moses or a fictitious Moses, deponent sayeth not. At the close of this section (p. 68) he says: "It is not strange that Jewish *tradition* spoke of him in superlatives (Deut. 34:10-12), and loved to refer to him as 'Jehovah's servant' (Deut. 34:5) and as 'the man of God' (Ezra 3:2; Ps. 90:1)." So it is everywhere—"tradition," "story," "folk-lore," "symbolism," "idealization," "parable," "Hebrew ideas," "poetry," "popular tales," "primitive ideas"—yes, everything but what the evangelical believer wants and needs: history, fact, revelation, inspiration. And we are bound to say that you find almost everything in this professed "History of the Hebrews" but the *history!* If that is not rationalism, we beg to know what is!

With one breath the author tries to hold on to the Bible; with the next he spoils it all by trying to undermine its inspiration and authority.

Before we close, let us give a sample of his method of treating miracles, just to see what a past-master he is in "making" history instead of faithfully recording it. The miracles of crossing the Jordan and the fall of Jericho are handled in this free and easy way (pp. 78, 79):

"These two events were of first importance in the story of the Hebrew people." Note, "events" and "story." Can you get any determinate kind of teaching out of such use of language? "Hebrew poets and story tellers loved to recount the thrilling episodes which introduced the acquisition of their national home. God's share in the task was very clear to them." What a free use of his Biblical material! Where does he read that they were given to telling these marvelous tales? Perhaps they were, but where does the Bible say so? Then: "As in the case of the narrative of the Deliverance (section 114), the *story* of the crossing of the Jordan is a combination of more than one earlier account of the event. One of these, apparently the earliest, was relatively straightforward and simple. It represented Joshua as encouraging the people to expect aid of Jehovah in their emergency, and declared that, at a time when the crossing was unanticipated (3:15) by the Canaanites and unopposed, something happened far up the river, perhaps a distant landslide, which dammed the river temporarily, and left its bed exposed, so that the Israelites got across. The other narrative greatly magnified Joshua (3:7, 8; 4:9, 10, 14) and the part played by the priests and the sacred ark. It also *seemed* to state that the water of the Jordan stood just above the pathway of Israel like a wall (3:16a)."

Of course, we cannot now presume to make a refutation of this position. Our purpose is rather to show clearly this author's free and liberal way of handling the Biblical records instead of accepting them at their face value. However, if he had done the fair thing, he would have said that Lange and Keil do not accept the explanation here given, nor admit that the narrative is made up of several contradictory "earlier accounts." Besides, he should have known and explained that Prof. George Frederick Wright made first-hand investigations in the valley of the Jordan, and gives a lucid explanation of how the waters may have been parted, just as the Bible says, by God's miraculous use of secondary forces, just as He used the wind in the case of the parting of the Red Sea and the bringing of the quails in the wilderness. (See Wright's "Scientific Confirmations of the Old Testament History," 1906, pp. 130-144.) Here we merely pause to remark that, if our author uses so free a hand in getting rid of the supernatural in the Bible, is there no danger that its *religious* authority may be invalidated?

Just one more specimen (p. 79): "In the *story* of the capture of Jericho the *oldest* narrative stated that the little army marched around the city in silence for six days, then captured it with a *cheer* and a *sudden dash*. Such tactics agree with Joshua's generalship in other battles (8:10-21; 10:9). Whether the sudden collapse of the city walls is to be explained by a divinely ordered earthquake, or figuratively as an expression of the astonishing ease with which it was captured, no one can surely say."

We would advise one of this professor's students to ask him what the *Bible* says about this event, and that in the plainest and most vivid language. Note that our author *hints*—that is the worst of it, *hints*—that there were extant several contradictory accounts of Jericho's fall. That is what he means when he speaks about the "oldest" account. What becomes of the doctrine of the inspiration of the Old Testament in such hands? How can a book containing so many crude errors be a book of *religious* value, to say nothing of *religious authority?*

The limits of space forbid our pursuing the subject further; nor is it necessary. Our purpose in conducting this study and offering these strictures has not been primarily Biblical Criticism, but Apologetics. Wherever Biblical Criticism seeks to undermine the integrity and authority of the Biblical records and undertakes to pronounce upon the doctrine of inspiration, it invades the department of both Apologetics and Dogmatics, and therefore cannot be permitted to go unnoticed and uncensored. In the Evangelical Church especially, where we look upon the Word of God as the chief means of grace, it behooves us to defend the integrity and inspiration of the Sacred Scriptures.

We are constrained to add a paragraph at a later date, while revising our manuscript. In spite of all its defects, its lack of fairness and thoroughness, the publishers are still advertising Dr. Sanders' book and pushing its sale. A circular just at hand (July 22, 1919) has this to say of the book: ''The story of the Hebrew people in the light of the most recent scholarship is told in plain and simple words. *It is the best history of the Hebrew people in one volume.''* (The italicized sentence is underscored by the publishers for emphasis.) We rejoin that the work is *not* written ''in the light of the most recent scholarship,'' but only in accord with the partisan views of the liberalistic coterie, who read only one side of the controversy. It is *not* a ''history of the Hebrew people,'' but that history warped and twisted, shredded and frayed according to the author's subjective and one-sided opinions. The author has no historical perspective; he can see history only on a flat surface.

CHAPTER VII

THE WAYS OF THE CRITICS

A Sharp Contrast Between the Liberals and Conservatives *

A STUDY of a number of recent books on the so-called "liberal" side of the problem of Biblical criticism brings out some strikingly characteristic "ways of the critics." The thing that constantly surprises us is the *aplomb* of the liberalistic writers, their assumption of being in possession of the whole truth, with no recognition of the masterly works published on the evangelical side.

One of these recent books (1918) is Dr. W. E. Hopkins' "The History of Religion." The author seems to deal fairly and historically with the ethnic religions, but when he comes to the Hebrew religion, he loses his sagacity, and warps and twists the history in accordance with the theory of evolution, of which he is a proponent. No matter what the Bible says, he knows better than that revered Book. He merely echoes the views of the Graf-Kuenen-Wellhausen-Cheyne-Driver school, without so much as stopping to consider whether its teachings are well founded or not. Statement upon statement is made with a cock-sureness that would be amusing, if it were not so vital in its influence on

* This chapter repeats a few things that have been said in previous chapters. It first appeared as a separate and distinct article in *The Lutheran Quarterly* (January, 1920), and therefore had to be complete in itself. The author prefers to leave it, with some slight revision, in its original form, so that all the statements of the chapter may stand in their proper logical relations.

the destiny of immortal souls. Dr. Hopkins' treatment of Christianity is so inadequate and one-sided, so lacking in the spiritual and uplifting element, that, if it were a correct representation, our holy religion would not be worth holding and contending for. If Christianity is what he makes it out to be, we for one would be willing to renounce it as absurd. Apparently, however, the author is not acquainted with any historians save those of the latitudinarian order. Yet his work is intended for a text-book in our American colleges and universities.

Another book of the same sort is Professor Albert C. Knudson's "The Religious Teaching of the Old Testament." In this work the critical assumptions of the Cheyne-Driver school are all taken for granted. Says a competent critic of the book: "The long controversy about the Pentateuch has now reached a stage at which it is no longer possible for any writer who claims to be up to date simply to put before his public the exploded conclusions of the Astruc-Kuenen-Wellhausen school as the last word of scholarship." Yet that is precisely what Knudson has done. His work was published in 1918. Was he not aware of the publication of the International Standard Bible Encyclopedia, with its array of profound scholars on the conservative side? If he was, he gives no signs. If he was not, what is to be said of his "scholarship"?

Here comes another book copyrighted in 1919: "How the Bible Grew," by Frank Grant Lewis, issued by the University of Chicago Press. The very phrasing of the title gives a clew to the character of the book. The Bible "grew," was evolved; it was not God-breathed, divinely given and inspired! We quote with endorsement from a review of this book in "Bibliotheca Sacra": "This volume is devoted from beginning to end to popularizing the documentary theories of the Wellhausen school as applied to the Old Testament, and of the moderately radical critics of the

New Testament. It gives no indication of the writer's familiarity with the more recent discussions relating to the authorship of the Pentateuch, or of the most recent conclusions concerning the date of the writings of the New Testament books. There is scarcely a single reference to a conservative author. The lay reader will, therefore, find it a blind guide to the real truth.''

Another book, though printed in 1914, has just come into our hands. It is Dr. J. Paterson Smyth's ''The Bible in the Making, in the Light of Modern Research.'' There are many good things in this work. The author tries to uphold the doctrine of divine inspiration, and seems to think that he has succeeded. But a careful reading uncovers the fact that he trains in the Driver school of critics. With him the Bible is largely made up of tradition, folklore, legend and Hebraic ''ideas.'' How can he correlate this view with any doctrine of divine inspiration that is worth holding? Many fine recent writers have proved this position to be untenable. But note, there is no evidence in the book that the author is even aware of any of the many stalwart works in favor of the conservative position that have been issued in recent years. With the utmost cock-sureness the critical views are accepted and propagated as settled once for all. One is almost tempted to say that the ''advanced'' critics are becoming ultra-conservatives and extreme traditionalists.

Among the many recently issued liberalistic books, we call attention to Dr. Douglas Clyde MacIntosh's ''Theology as an Empirical Science'' (1919). * In dealing with this work, we shall make use of our own review of it in the January (1920) number of *The Lutheran Quarterly*.

Among its merits may be mentioned its intellectual qual-

---

* This book does not belong technically to the class of works dealing with Biblical Criticism; yet most of its theological positions are based on the assumptions of the more radical critics, and therefore it comes properly under the strictures of this chapter.

ity. It certainly is a labored attempt to reduce theology
to an empirical science, however short it may fall of the
goal at which it has aimed. The author is a Doctor of
Philosophy, and his work on every page indicates the depth
of his philosophical studies. Although he does not claim
the degree of Doctor of Theology on the title-page, we are
there informed that he is Dwight Professor of Theology in
Yale University. He is known as the author of several
previous works of a scholarly character. His researches in
philosophy have determined his style of presentation, and
have greatly colored his theological views. You must understand the abstruse terms of philosophy to understand
his writing.

We agree with the author that Christian theology is an
empirical science. Not only do we believe it to be so in
the restricted sense in which he uses the word "empirical,"
namely, "experimental" (p. 2), but also in the wider sense
of dealing with clearly observed and well-validated data
from which legitimate inductions may be drawn. However, the grave fault of the work is this: it whittles Christian experience down to the "irreducible minimum," and
that minimum is reached by a labored rationalizing process,
and not, after all, by a full, clear, simple, joyous Christian experience. And what is this much-shrunken "minimum" of Christian faith? It is that the God of the universe
is sufficiently dependable, and so His universe is dependable, and Christ is the one person in history who best taught
this doctrine and exemplified it in His life and experience.
God may not be omnipotent, but He is sufficiently powerful to hold the sovereignty of the cosmos in His hands,
and so we may rely on Him for help. Relevant to the last
point, just how, we beg to know, does the Christian soul
experience that God is powerful enough to be trustworthy
even though He may not be omnipotent? No; such an attenuated doctrine is not a matter of experience; it is a

rationalistic conclusion. But even at that it is not good, cogent reasoning; for if God were not all-powerful, and if, therefore, there were the least *strain* upon Him in upholding the universe, He would by and by, as the age-cycles pass, grow weary, and the universe would *drop*. If we are going to use reason instead of experience, let us make our rational processes more thorough-going.

As our author whittles down experience to the minimum, so he deals with the Bible, the Old and New Testaments alike. For example, he gets back to the only New Testament "sources" he is willing to acknowledge: they are Mark's gospel and St. Paul's letters. But even these he pares down to the "irreducible minimum." Mark gives the record of many miracles. Indeed, in proportion to the length of his gospel, Mark tells of more miracles than any other evangelist. But Dr. MacIntosh cannot admit these miracles, and therefore he criticizes and reduces even his original sources, and either cuts out the accounts of the miracles or tries to explain them on some kind of naturalistic ground. These supernatural occurrences do not fit into the mold of "the modern mind." Even the resurrection is denied, and the ascension of Christ to the right hand of God is laughed out of court as opposed to our modern views of astronomy, which are no longer geocentric.

We beg to ask whether this rationalistic denial of Biblical miracles can properly belong to "empirical" or "experimental" theology. Has any one ever learned by actual experience that the miracles did *not* occur? On the contrary, is it not a fact that many persons in the history of the Church who could not, in their natural state, believe in the supernatural element in the Bible, have been convinced of its reality by a genuine experience of regeneration? Usually the man who has had such an experience, no matter what his previous predilections may have been, has no difficulty in accepting the Bible miracles. Did the

apostles get their experience, for whose verity they were
willing to suffer and die, with or without miracles? Is it
not true that the great Christian souls of the centuries who
have had a great religious experience, one that made them
flaming evangelists and defenders of the faith, were brought
to believe in the Biblical miracles through the experience
of conversion? No; our author makes Christian experience too meager a thing to be of real value to the soul and
to fill it with missionary zeal.

As he can tolerate no miracles, so, of course, he cannot
endure the doctrine of the miraculous conception of Christ
by the Virgin Mary. Listen to him (p. 53): "In view,
then, of these various strands of damaging evidence, and
since, apart from this story, there is no basis for supposing
that human parthenogenesis is even possible, it seems not
unreasonable to suppose that the virgin-birth story is a
legend, comparable with the similar, although more crudely
expressed, birth-legends that grew up about Greek and
Roman heroes, and such religious personalities as Gautama
(the Buddha), Krishna and Shakara." We might quote
more to the same effect, but our sense of reverence is already sufficiently shocked by the above sentence. Our author devotes about a page and a third to the virgin-birth,
and then lightly dismisses it as unworthy of belief. What
are we to think of such scant treatment of a vital doctrine
in view of the great and searching works of Orr,* Sweet,†
Knowling ‡ and Thorburn § in vindication of our Lord's
virgin birth? No; the liberalist cannot get rid of the great
mass of facts and arguments that these scholars present,
simply by ignoring them. Moreover, does a rejection of

* "The Virgin Birth of Christ."
† "The Birth and Infancy of Jesus Christ" (a powerful argu-
ment).
‡ "Our Lord's Virgin Birth and the Criticism of To-day."
§ "A Critical Examination of the Evidences for the Doctrine of
the Virgin Birth." (See also Chapter VI of the author's book, "The
Rational Test.")

the miraculous conception of our Lord belong to the content of a Christian experience? We trow not. Then how can such categorical denial belong to a system of "empirical" theology? On the other hand, Christian history will be likely to afford indubitable proof that the most thorough-going Christian experience has always come with accept-ance of this doctrine. And why not? What is one of the outstanding elements of a complete and joyful Christian assurance? Surely that Christ was a supernatural being. Then he must have had a supernatural conception.

As for the doctrine of substitutional atonement, in which Christ really made expiation for sin by suffering the pen-alty of transgression in the stead of sinners, our author will have none of it. All the Biblical passages in both the Old and New Testaments that teach the doctrine of substitution are ruled out as speculations, illusions or later accretions. But that is rationalism, not empiricism. No one has ever experienced that Christ did *not* die to make propitiation for sin. Speculative theology may reject the doctrine of vicarious atonement, but experimental theology never can. On the contrary, we wonder whether many a Christian does not to-day experience the joy of pardon and salvation when he reads such passages as these: "He was wounded for our transgressions; He was bruised for our iniquities . . . and with His stripes we are healed;" "Herein is love, not that we loved God, but that He loved us, and gave His Son to be the propitiation for our sins;" "The Son of man came not to be ministered unto, but to minister, and to give His life a ransom for many." We venture to say that millions of Christian men, women and children have received their assurance of truth, pardon and salvation through the im-pingement and appeal of such passages as the above, ac-cepted in their literal sense and at their face value.

But we must not amplify further. We venture to say that a real, full, positive Christian experience, an experi-

ence "at its best," is not the be-littled and be-whittled
experience this author depicts. We also venture to assert
that our orthodox systems of theology are based more
soundly upon an empirical foundation than is the slender
structure of this Yale professor.

We had in mind to give a list of the liberalistic books
issued in the years 1918-1920—that is, since the war—but
we see no special need for advertising them here. One of
them (John W. Buckham's "Progressive Religious Thought
in America," 1919) is a veritable eulogium on the type of
theology held and taught by Bushnell, Munger, Gordon
(George A.), Tucker, Egbert and Newman Smyth, Gladden,
and others. And what has been the "progress" made by
these "advanced" thinkers? It is made up largely of nega-
tions: namely, that *systems* of theology are wrong and impossible, that the Bible is not infallible, that a piacular
atonement is absurd, and that orthodoxy is not progressive
and scientific. Of real constructive contributions to clear
theological thinking we find very few, if any. After reading the book through from beginning to end, we closed it
with the feeling that this kind of "progressive" theology
is vague and indeterminate, and seems to get nowhere; so
we fail to see the much-vaunted "progress" in it. Near
the close of his book the author admits that the New Theology has inadequate conceptions of sin and of its "flinty
factuality." But that is a *fatal* defect; for a defective idea
of sin spells a defective idea of redemption, and hence of
the Redeemer. Many of the good things that our author
claims as the discoveries of the "progressives" are to be
found in the conservative systems also, and some of them
were taught long ago. Take an instance, the ictus the
author places on personality; when has orthodox theology
not stressed the personality of God and of man? Take another case: the author seems to think that the doctrine of
the divine immanence is a recent discovery of the "progres-

sive" thinkers. Why, ever since the days of Christ and
Paul orthodox theology has inculcated the doctrine of God's
active omnipresence. There never has been a time when
evangelical thinkers held to the conception of a merely transcendent Deity. English Deism taught that doctrine—but
English Deism was an infidel propaganda, and was abun-
dantly refuted by the evangelical scholars of its day. Just
for a test we dip into Heinrich Schmid's "Doctrinal Theology of the Evangelical Lutheran Church," and we find
excellent discussions of the divine ubiquity by Gerhard
(1582-1637) and Hollaz (1648-1713).*

After this rather lengthy excursus, we must now proceed
with our main theme.

One of the strangest paradoxes in the advocacy of the
more moderate critics is their conception of divine inspiration. They insist that they have the true idea of divine inspiration and the correct evaluation of the Holy Bible,
and that to them it is a much more precious book because
of their critical conclusions; and yet, at the same time, they
speak of the Bible as being made up of legends, myths and
folklore, the conceptions of very primitive people, crude
and mistaken in many ways, with actual contradictions here
and there in the records. Is that an adequate and satisfactory conception of divine inspiration? Is it an inspiration
that is worth while and that makes the Bible a reliable book
in its religious teaching? Is it not too near the pantheistic
idea of divine inspiration—that is, that everything that
happens is inspired because everything is the evolution of
God in the universe? According to this conception, even
error and sin are to be attributed to the ultimate source of

* Even Irenaeus taught the doctrine of divine immanence. (*Vide*
Hitchcock's translation, Vol. II, p. 113). Indeed, we can go back
into church history even further than this father—to St. Ignatius,
who taught that Christ as God is ubiquitous. Note: "Nothing is
hidden from the Lord, but even our secrets are brought nigh unto
Him. Let us therefore do all things in the assurance that He
dwells within us, that we may be His shrines, and He Himself
dwell in us as God." (*Vide* Srawley's translation, p. 48.)

being. Moral distinctions fade out to the vanishing point. "Everything that is is right," according to the pantheistic world-view. Are not the modern exponents of evolution too much given to this conception? Hence they can get divine inspiration out of the errors and sins of primitive people. We are willing to believe that God can "bring good out of evil and make the wrath of man to praise Him"; but that is something totally different from a special divine inspiration on which men can rely for salvation both in time and in eternity.

A fatal difficulty with the radical criticism is that its logical outcome is rationalism pure and simple. If the Bible is partly inspired and partly uninspired, how are we to know which are the inspired portions and which are not? Each man must decide for himself. That makes human reason the final arbiter. What appeals to reason is called inspired; what is not according to reason is not inspired. If that is not rationalism, what is rationalism? Now, when we consider the achievements of unaided human reason historically, have we much encouragement to put confidence in its processes? The pagan nations of the earth have had reason to guide them all through their history in the absence of special revelation. What has been the result? Paganism in all its forms, from animism to pantheistic Hinduism and pessimistic and atheistic Buddhism. The ancient philosophers had reason to guide them, but even the best of them —Plato and Aristotle—thought that matter was eternal and that God was not the real Creator; while Democritus, Epicurus and Lucretius held to the materialistic world-view. How much agreement is there to-day among the apostles of pure reason? We have, among many other world-views, materialistic monism (Haeckel and Leuba), idealism, positivism, pantheism, theosophy, vitalism, "creative evolution" (whatever that means), and pluralism, not to mention a dozen more conflicting philosophies. Do all these fundamental divergencies beget much confidence in mere human reason as a trustworthy guide? Yet the dissecting critics would make reason rather than the Bible the final court of appeal. Even among them there is much difference of opinion as to which parts of the Bible are inspired and which are not inspired. On the ground of mere human judgment you never can arrive at a consensus among even a half dozen speculatists. No; the view of the critics respecting divine inspiration is illogical and inadequate. Let them spend half their time and effort in trying to reconcile *apparent* discrepancies in the Bible, instead of exploiting them, and they will readily find that its teaching from beginning to end is a wonderful unity.

Having pointed out "the ways of the critics" of the reducing school, namely, that they simply ignore the works of conservative scholars, or keep themselves uninformed regarding them, it is a pleasure to turn to a Biblical investigator of a different ilk. We refer to the Rev. J. S. Griffiths and his book, "The Problem of Deuteronomy," which we have read with much satisfaction. It was published in 1911, and won the Bishop of Jeune Memorial Prize for the best essay on "The Historical Truth and Divine Authority of the Book of Deuteronomy." The fact that it won the prize in a contest with other competitors is worthy of note, and gives the reader confidence to begin with. We have a special purpose in calling attention to the date of its publication—1911. That was before the radical books previously mentioned were issued—Smyth's in 1914, Hopkins' in 1918, Knudson's in 1918, Lewis's and MacIntosh's in 1919. Do these works make any reference to Griffiths' masterly treatment of Deuteronomy? They do not. They seem to be blissfully unconscious that so complete a refutation of their central position was ever given to the world. Now we maintain that such treatment of opponents is both unfair and unethical. No man who writes merely on one side of the

Biblical question has a right to speak of "the assured results of scholarship," when such a work as that of Mr. Grif-
fith's is accessible.

And what is "the way" of this scholar? The precise
opposite of the self-pluming critics. He takes nothing for
granted. His aim is to prove every position by the sound-
est rational process that he is capable of commanding. He
makes no assertions that he does not try to establish by
sound argument and by appeal to facts. Moreover, he does
not ignore his opponents, but mentions many of them by
name, quotes from their works, giving the titles and pages,
and then demolishes their conclusions. To our mind, he
does his work handsomely and thoroughly, not by dogmatic
asseveration, but by sound argument. We believe we can do
no better service than to indicate "the way" of this scholar
by making a number of quotations from his work, showing
how acutely he reasons.

Our author holds that Deuteronomy is "the pivot of the
Pentateuchal criticism" (p. 9), and quotes Graf, Dillman, Wellhausen, Kittel, Westphal and Addis in support
of the assertion. Note that, on the very first page of his
discussion proper, he mentions a list of opposing liberal
critics. How different his method from that of most of
the liberals! On pages 11-13 he argues for the Mosaic authorship of Deuteronomy. This he does against the critics,
who say that little or none of it is of Mosaic origin, and
fix the date of its composition at about 620 B. C. Dr. Driver
speaks of "an ancient traditional basis" and "an independent source, oral or written." "As if oral tradition and
tradition reduced to writing," exclaims our author, "were
not two things as far apart as heaven and earth!" Dr.
Driver suggests that the author of Deuteronomy may have
"derived his authority from more than one source; his
secondary authority being sometimes popular tradition,
sometimes, perhaps, his own imagination." On this point

our author reasons as follows: ''These scholars seem to forget that the 'value of tradition depends absolutely on the date at which it ceased to be oral by becoming fixed in writing. If recorded at first hand, or nearly so, it may have all the authority of contemporaneous history. But as generations come and go, and the events recede into the dim past, that which is handed down simply by word of mouth soon degenerates, and, parting with the reality of life, rapidly vanishes into the misty air of myth and fable. After the lapse of a few generations, oral tradition loses all pretense of simple truth' '' (quoted from Sir W. Muir's ''Authorship of Deuteronomy''). ''Meinhold (himself an 'advanced' critic) admits that if, on the grounds of literary criticism, Deuteronomy is to be dated at 620 B. C., no credibility can be attached to its historical statements. Besides, if the critical theory is right, the statements made in Deut. 1:1, 5, 29:1, 31:9, 24-27, must be false. And if the book is not to be believed when it distinctly affirms its Mosaic origin, on what grounds are we to accept its assertions on other points?'' The first passages cited above are (verse 1): ''These are the words which Moses spake unto all Israel beyond the Jordan, in the wilderness,'' etc.; (verse 5): ''Beyond the Jordan, in the land of Moab, began Moses to declare this law, saying,'' etc. If this is not reliable history, why should other parts of the book be regarded as reliable? That is Mr. Griffiths' argument. Then he continues:

''Again, if Deuteronomy is, as the 'advanced' critics claim, 'a protest of the prophetic party of the seventh century B. C. against the connection of unspiritual and heathen elements with the worship of Yahweh,' issued in the name of Moses by 'men who thought the time ripe for reform and had intelligently planned the way in which this was to be effected,' it is not easy to accept it as a divinely authorized code of laws. . . . But Deuteronomy speaks with an accent of *authority;* it lays down certain laws which were to be strictly observed by the Jewish people; and the authority which it claims is the authority of Moses as the 'man of God,' divinely commissioned to legislate for Israel. It was on this ground—that it was the genuine word of Moses—that its authority was recognized and its enactments obeyed by Josiah and his subjects. But if the book itself and most of the laws it contains were unknown to Moses, its claim falls to the ground. It is as certain as anything can be that, if King Josiah and his people had held the 'critical' view of the origin of Deuteronomy, they would never have accepted the book as divine.''

And yet the moderate critics make the claim that Deuteronomy was divinely inspired! What kind of divine inspiration would that be? It would be as futile for inspiration as the reasoning of the rationalists is for logic.

We must pass over a large part of Mr. Griffiths' book (though every page is worthy of careful perusal), and come to his analysis of the critical hypothesis that Deuteronomy was imposed upon the people of Israel as a reform document many centuries after Moses. We drop down on page 97 at Chapter V, ''The Critical Theory: Its Difficulties.'' Says our author: ''If Deuteronomy is not Mosaic, when and by whom was it composed? Modern critics cannot agree on an answer; and their lack of agreement on a point so vital undoubtedly tells heavily against the cause they represent. Two solutions are suggested.'' In a footnote a number of other theories are named, showing how much divergence of opinion there is among the ''scholarly'' critics. By the way, if the ''results'' of ''scholarship'' are ''assured,'' one would think that the ''scholars'' ought to agree. But they don't! Ewald, Bleek, W. R. Smith, Ryle, Driver, and others assign Deuteronomy to the reign of Manasseh; while Graf, Kuenen, Wellhausen, Cornill, Cheyne, and others assign it to the time of Josiah. In either case serious difficulties arise. The author deals more fully with the view that the book was imposed as a Mosaic document on the people of Israel in King Josiah's reign. He contends thus: "To say that Deuteronomy was written in the time of Josiah, and that Hilkiah and the priests were parties to its production," is "to cast a serious imputation on the moral character of these men. For the narrative expressly states that Hilkiah recognized the book as an ancient and authoritative law-book. He said, 'I have found *the* book of the law' (2 Kings 22:8), and in the Hebrew the definite article is emphatic. If Hilkiah was not deceived, he was himself guilty of gross deception; for, led by him, king and people accepted the book as an ancient code which had been disobeyed by their *fathers* (2 Kings 22:13). Here quite a number of awkward questions immediately rise up to confound the critics. Why should the law of a central sanctuary be invented at a time when almost all the rival sanctuaries had gone down in the ruin of the Northern kingdom? Why should the priests be so eager to foist upon the nation a code which certainly did not promote their interests, and in one particular—the law of Deut. 18:6f—was distinctly detrimental to them? And how did it come to pass that people, priests and prophets recognized as Mosaic, legislation which (according to criticism) was so opposed on many important points to all that up to that time had been regarded as such?

"But, indeed," our author continues, "that such a colossal fraud could have been carried out successfully is simply incredible. The *extent* of the alleged deception is truly marvelous. The whole nation with lamb-like innocence allowed themselves to be imposed upon. The priests of Jerusalem, to whom, as Kautzsch says, the book must have been intensely disagreeable; the priests of the high place whom it threw out of employment; the king whose ancestors it pilloried; and the people on whose cherished religious customs it poured the fiercest denunciations—all

were completely deceived. Even Jeremiah, who exposed
unhesitatingly the false prophecies of his own contemporaries (Jer. 29f), publicly defended Deuteronomy as the legislation of Moses (Jer. 11). This amazing fraud was successful—so we are to believe—in spite of the hostility which
must have been provoked by a work which assailed so many
interests, and in spite, too, of the searching inquiries to
which such hostility would give rise. According to criticism, the book contains many important modifications and
contradictions of the laws previously accepted as Mosaic—
discrepancies clearly evident to eminent scholars of the
nineteenth and twentieth centuries; yet these astonishing
Jews of the seventh century B. C., though they disliked it,
and after a brief period of alarm disregarded it, never
questioned its genuineness. Many persons must have been
concerned in its production, but no hint of the secret ever
leaked out. Even in the time of apostasy which followed
Josiah's reformation, neither kings, priests, nor people ever
tried to justify their relapse by impugning the Mosaic
authority of the book. Marvelous indeed was this deception,
so carefully carried out, so perfect in every detail. But far
more wonderful are those lynx-eyed critics who, after the
lapse of twenty-four centuries, are able to expose this ingenious fraud which the Jews of Josiah's age—though they
had every opportunity and incentive to do so—could not
pentrate!''

Then the author goes on to show that if the critics are
right, ''Deuteronomy is a deliberate falsehood. It is not
an adequate reply to say airily that, when the author assumed the Mosaic mask, he only 'made use of an acknowledged device,' and that men in those days 'perpetrated
such fictions without a qualm of conscience' (Kuenen).''

Here we would like to inject the question, On this hypothesis what becomes of the doctrine of divine inspiration?
Even if men in those palmy days would have perpetrated

"such fictions without a qualm of conscience," would the Holy Spirit have used the same dishonest methods? We have always thought that, according to the Holy Scriptures, the Holy Spirit was "the Spirit of truth." The critical conception of divine inspiration would surely be amusing if the results to the evangelical faith were not so calamitous.

But our alert author challenges Kuenen's assertion about such fictions being common in the days of Josiah (pp. 101, 102). "It is necessary," he declares, "that at least one undoubted instance should be quoted in evidence. But this the critics invariably omit to do. If fictions of this kind were common in the seventh century B. C., surely it would be possible to mention one instance. If none can be cited, how do the critics know that the practice was common? . . . But there is not a shred of evidence that such 'literary practices' were common or considered justifiable in the age of Josiah or at any earlier time. Galen, a very competent witness, assures us that it was not till the age of the Ptolemies, when kings were rivaling each other in collecting libraries, that the 'roguery' (so this unenlightened heathen regarded it) of forging writings and titles began. It is evident from this that the practice was not looked upon as lawful even among the heathen. How then can we reconcile such 'roguery' with the lofty religious and moral principles enunciated so fervently in the book of Deuteronomy? The so-called discrepancies between Deuteronomy and the other codes, which the critics parade with such pomp, fade into nothingness when compared with the astounding contradiction between the spiritual tone of the book and the fraud which gave it birth. 'Do men gather grapes of thorns or figs of thistles?' "

In the next few pages our author vividly portrays the remarkable sagacity of the author of Deuteronomy if he wrote the book in the times of Josiah. What a complete disguise the work was! He lived in the seventh century,

and yet transported himself so perfectly into the times
and circumstances of Moses eight centuries prior as to give
the whole record the air of historical verisimilitude, never
committing an anachronism. "When we reflect," says Mr.
Griffiths, "how difficult it is even to-day to reproduce with
exactness the scenery and circumstances of the past, we
must recognize in this nameless forger an antiquarian of
the first rank. Further, he not only adopts with conspicuous success the Mosaic garb; he embodies the Mosaic spirit.
He speaks in the tone and from the standpoint of the great
leader. He has caught and reproduced the emotions and
desires, the confident optimism and happy hopefulness of
Moses on the eve of the immigration. It is one of the greatest triumphs of the human imagination. So completely has
he transported himself into the Mosaic age that he is absolutely unconscious of his own environment. The intervening centuries, with all their doleful history of backsliding
and persecution, of disaster and defeat, are utterly ignored." There is more argument here to the same effect.
"He proclaims a war of extermination against the Canaanites, as though they had not been destroyed long before! . .
In a word, he never even for a moment drops the Mosaic
mask." He certainly was a past master of "camouflage."
That such a genius could have existed in the seventh century
B. C., and yet leave no trace of his identity, is beyond rational belief.

And think of it! This man of such commanding intellectual gifts and such "remarkable insight and lofty ethical
ideals," in order to bring about a reform "perpetrates a
fraud" upon his contemporaries—a fraud, too, "which he
himself denounces in the severest terms!" Then the author
cites Deut. 18:20: "But the prophet who shall speak a
word presumptuously in my name, which I have not commanded him to speak, or who shall speak in the name of
other gods, that same prophet shall die." If Hilkiah or

any one else in Josiah's day wrote that verse, and falsely attributed it to Moses, he was a hypocrite of the deepest dye. Is it any wonder that evangelical scholars contend that the critical position is destructive of the whole doctrine of divine inspiration and authority?

After thus dissecting the hypothesis of the dissecting Biblical critics, Mr. Griffiths concludes this part of his argument with these words, with which we are constrained to agree: "We may fairly claim that, whether we consider the literary influence of Deuteronomy, its relations to the other Pentateuchal books, the character of its contents, or the problem of its origin and authorship, on every point the critical theory breaks down completely. Our examination of its claims in the light of the available evidence has only served to demonstrate their falsity, and to show that no date and no authorship fit the book of Deuteronomy save those which it distinctly claims for itself."

There is much more fine argument in this book, but we need not continue our quotations. Three things are evident from the preceding presentation. The first is that the rationalists are the poorest reasoners in the world and the most consummate dogmatists and asseverators. The second is that their theories, if proven true, would undermine any view of divine inspiration that would be worthy of confidence. The third is that there is a marked contrast between the "ways" of the radical critics and those of the conservative scholars; the former mostly ignore the works of their opponents, and simply repeat over and over again their assumptions without argument and with constant arrogation to themselves of having attained "assured results"; while the latter—the conservatives—not only mention their opponents, cite their works, quote from them, giving title and page, but also enter into an elaborate argumentative process to prove their antagonists wrong and their own positions correct. Of the sharply contrasted ''ways of the critics,'' we greatly prefer those of the conservatives as being far the more rational, and, we are constrained to add, far more ethical.

CHAPTER VIII

THE BOOK OF JONAH

Is It Fact or Fiction, History or Parable?

A RECENT discussion of the book of Jonah in a minis-
terial association has set the subject vividly before our
mind. The aforesaid discussion has made it plain that
the methods and results of the Higher Criticism, both conservative and radical, have become widespread among ministers. The meeting referred to consisted of the ministers
of two inland towns of not more than 6000-7000 inhabitants each. Indeed, one of the ministers who advocated
strongly and intelligently the parabolic character of the
book, and quoted from Canon Driver and other Higher
Critics of that school, lived in the country, and was the
pastor of two or three rural congregations.

It is interesting to note how the association was divided
on the question at issue. The two Lutheran pastors present stood firmly for the historical character of the book;
in fact, were the most uncompromising advocates of that
view. The Presbyterian pastor seemed also to accept that
position, but contented himself with a cordial eulogy on
the Lutheran minister who had read the paper that started
the discussion. The two German Reformed ministers argued at considerable length that the book was an inspired
work of fiction designed to teach a moral lesson. The
Moravian and Disciple pastors accepted the traditional
view, declaring that the miracles recited in the book had

never disturbed their faith. One Methodist minister, not a pastor, stood without equivocation with the promoters of the fiction view. Another Methodist pastor seemed to be somewhat undecided, while a third averred that he did not see how any one could accept any view but the traditional one without compromising the distinct teaching of Christ. We detail these facts simply to show how the Higher Criticism has permeated the ranks of the ministry throughout the country, and is by no means confined to the great academic centers.

In entire fairness to those who differed from our view we should say that the more radical men were not irreverent. Rather, they contended that they were more reverent than the rest of us, because they did not make God do things that were grotesque and absurd. They also maintained that the book was inspired by the Holy Spirit, who moved upon the writer to compose the story for the purpose of teaching the Jewish people a much-needed lesson, just as He inspired the vision of Peter on the housetop in Joppa. When the meeting was adjourned, we said to one of the Reformed pastors that, if the book of Jonah was a parable, it was a very poorly constructed one, not worthy of a place in the mythical and allegorical literature of the world. What do you suppose was his reply? "That remark," he declared, "is a reflection on the work of the Holy Spirit, who inspired the allegory. It is an irreverent remark." We report this because we desire to be entirely fair and properly to represent the temper, as well as the position, of our opponents.

And yet, to be fully just, we must report something more. In the course of the promiscuous discussion we asked the more radical critics why they displayed so strong a disposition to prove the book an allegory or parable and were not willing to accept it as history. Their reply in substance was this: "The book contains such grotesque elements and such inconsistent miracles that we cannot credit its historicity.'' This remark, after all, disclosed the secret and motive of their advocacy—it was the spirit of rationalism; whether conscious or unconscious, it is not our province to say. However, the spirit displayed by the brethren of the more radical school convinces us that it would be wrong to impute unworthy motives to them, or accuse them of irreverence, while their arguments lead us to have respect for their intelligence. Therefore, the task we have assigned ourself in this chapter will be simplified thus far—that we may confine our observations simply and solely to the evidence and proof, and need employ no invectives in dealing with our opponents. Let us begin with giving them credit for sincerity and intelligence. The only question before us, therefore, is this: Is the book of Jonah history or fiction?

In the first place, what is the precise position of the supporters of the fiction theory? It is this: The book was intended by its author as a story with a moral lesson for the Jews. Christ himself made up stories for didactic purposes—the story of the Prodigal Son, the parable of the Rich Man and Lazarus. Stories of the kind are not unknown in the writings of some of the other prophets, such as Isaiah's song of the vineyard of his beloved (Isa. 5:1-7). Now, according to the critics, the Jewish people were narrow and sectional in their views, believing that God's mercy was confined to them as a nation, while all the heathen nations round about were under God's ban, designed only for destruction. They—the Jews—had no missionary and evangelistic spirit, no large vision of God's redemptive purpose. Even if God should want to show mercy to the Gentiles, the bigoted Jews would try to frustrate His plans. Therefore the Holy Spirit saw that they needed an allegory to show them their mistake, and to teach them that the mercy of God was of wider horizon than they conceived.

Now, in the reputed allegory Jonah represents the Jewish nation, which is commanded to preach the mercy of God to the surrounding nations. But just as Jonah tried to flee from the command of Jehovah, so the Jewish nation tried to evade its duty to the perishing Gentiles. As Jonah was overtaken by a violent storm, so the people of Israel suffered dire affliction from God's hand, especially through the persecutions of their enemies. Then, as Jonah was swallowed up by a great fish, so the Israelitish nation was swallowed up by the Babylonian captivity. The big fish disgorged Jonah; so Babylon returned the Jews from their exile. Still, Jonah was not pleased; neither were the Jews cured of their hatred of the Gentile nations, but rebelled against God's disposition to show mercy to them. Jonah's peevishness about the perishing of the gourd mirrors the smallness of the Jews in their conceptions of the plans and grace of God. The foregoing is the application of the so-called allegory of Jonah as set forth by George Adam Smith in "The Expositor's Bible," and Dr. Smith is one of the most reverent of the critics who lean toward the radical side, and also contends for the divine inspiration of the book.

The critics think that the key to the interpretation of the book is found in what Jeremiah says about the children of Israel in their exile in Babylon (Jer. 51:34, 44 and 45). "Nebuchadrezzar, the king of Babylon, hath devoured me, he hath crushed me, he hath made me an empty vessel, he hath, like a monster, swallowed me up, he hath filled his maw with my delicacies; he hath cast me out." Then Jehovah replies: "And I will execute judgment upon Bel in Babylon, and I will bring forth out of his mouth that which he hath swallowed up. . . . My people go ye out of the midst of her, and save yourselves

every man from the fierce anger of Jehovah.'' It is to
be noted here, in passing, that George Adam Smith does
not quote the intervening verses that lend no color to his
theory, but picks out from a large number of similes such
passages only as fit into the story of Jonah and the big
fish. We feel like adding that this passage, thus garbled,
does not strike us as a very good ''key'' to either a parable or a history.

In the next place, what are the critic's objections to the
historicity of the book of Jonah? One of the most serious
is the story of the Big Fish—which they write in capitals.
Such a miracle, they admit, is not impossible with God, if
miracles are granted at all, but it is so grotesque, so childish, that it has ever lent itself to ridicule. They cannot
conceive that God would perform a wonder like that. But
more serious still is the wholesale repentance of the Ninevites under the preaching of a stranger like Jonah. Where
is there any record elsewhere of a great city yielding so
quickly to the proclamation of the truth? In actual life
we know of no such event, for no matter how great the
revival in a city, there are always some who obstinately
refuse to repent. Moreover, the critics tell us that there
are no historical evidences of Nineveh's conversion, but
after this she was denounced by the prophets as a wicked
city, and at last met her doom through the punitive justice that overtook all the wicked ancient cities. Nor does
the story of Jonah's gourd, which sprang up in a night
and perished so quickly, impress the critics as a veritable
incident, but rather as a pretty fiction. Another objection urged by the critics is that the book is placed among
the minor prophets in the Old Testament, whereas, if it
is literal history, it does not belong there, but should be
placed among the historical books.

Before going further, it would seem to be advisable to
deal with these objections and see whether they are valid.

Take the first difficulty suggested—that the story of the Big Fish swallowing Jonah is grotesque and undignified. If that is so, would not the same objection hold against the composition as a *work of fiction?* How could an inspired writer—yea, rather, how could the Holy Spirit—hope to make an allegory effective by introducing an event that would strike the reader as absurd? Could He not foresee that many people would laugh at such a story, and find fault with it as a work of art? Surely, surely if the story is too unnatural to be believed as history, it is also too unnatural to be effective as allegory. Compare the naturalness, the simplicity, the wonderful art of the parables of our Lord with this strange parable of Jonah—if it is a parable. You can easily imagine the Jews casting ridicule at a story-writer who would suppose that so *bizarre* a tale, which they knew to be pure invention, would bring them to their senses.

That the people of Nineveh should be so readily won to repentance, and in so wholesale a style, strikes the critics as extremely improbable. But what do discerning readers think of a piece of fiction that seriously introduces the improbable element? They condemn it at once. Fancy a hard-headed Jew perusing this story, which he recognizes as a work of fiction directed at his own prejudices, and what would be his verdict? That the writer spoils the whole effect of his novel by overdoing it, by attributing a result to Jonah's preaching that everybody knows to be fantastic. A poor artist this story-writer. You and I know of Sunday-school stories that not only fail of their effect, but actually do harm by being overdrawn and ''goody-goody.''

Thus we feel like repeating our assertion that, if the book of Jonah is an allegory, it is a very lamely constructed one, lacking wholly in that winsome art and artlessness that characterize all the other parabolic portions of the Bible. Contrast it with the fine art and effective teaching of Christ's parables of the Good Samaritan and the Prodigal Son.

Let us now look at the positive and constructive argument for the historical character of the work. First, all the moral and spiritual lessons of the book are taught just as clearly, if the incidents recited are regarded as actual occurrences, as if they are looked upon as fictitious, and we cannot help thinking much more effectively. Jonah's attempt to run away from the Lord—how many other men have tried to do the same thing? If God employed so extraordinary a method of arresting Jonah and disposing him to carry the divine message to Nineveh, what a lesson for all men, whether Jews or Gentiles, that when God lays His hand upon a man, he cannot escape from His appointed work! Many a man, like Jonah, has declared that he would not preach the gospel, but God has brought him to his Nineveh by ways he little dreamed of. And Jonah's unwillingness to carry the gospel of mercy to a heathen city, because he thought its people were outside of the covenant of grace—what a picture of Jewish bigotry and selfishness—and of Greek, Teutonic, English and American narrowness as well! When the people of Nineveh repented and God relented and forgave them, the selfish Jews were taught two lessons that they greatly needed to learn; first, that heathen people were susceptible of repentance and salvation; second, that God's mercy was not confined to Jewish national life, but was as wide as the land and the sea. What a rebuke to sectionalism and bigotry wherever found! And how much more effective the lesson if the occurrence was real than if it was only a pretty piece of idealistic fiction! Even Jonah's littleness in feeling angry because his reputation as a prophet was injured holds the mirror up to some portions of human nature as it has always been known; not only to Jewish Pharisaism, but also to many a modern would-be prophet who thinks more of himself than of his message or the salvation of the people.

How powerfully all these lessons are impressed if the story is history! How much they are weakened if the story existed only in the fertile fancy of a romancer! Nor is that all. The lessons are so important, so much needed by the Jews and the whole human family, that it was worth while for God to perform the miracles recorded to impress those lessons upon the minds of the people of all times. And the more extraordinary the miracles performed, the more important the lessons God sought to convey. If God did nothing more than inspire a prophet to write a fictitious story, the lessons could not be so extremely vital. However, if God arrested and saved Jonah in the wonderful way described in the book, He must have regarded those lessons as of superlative value. When God places the stamp of the miraculous upon a doctrine, we know it must be heeded.

It will be granted by all that there must always be a sufficient ethical motive for the performance of a miracle. Can such a motive be found for the miracle of saving the prophet by means of a mammoth fish? We answer in the affirmative. The people of Nineveh were wicked, doomed to destruction, unless help came to them from some extraordinary source. If God saw that they would repent through the preaching of one of his prophets, surely no means for bringing about such a result would be too great or too extraordinary. God sent His only begotten Son into the world. Was the motive sufficient? Looking upon the lost condition of the world and remembering the value of a single immortal soul, it was. The explanation of the miracle of Jonah's rescue lies in God's estimate of the value of the souls in Nineveh.

This brings us face to face with the narrative of Jonah

and the Big Fish. It will not do to evade the issue by denouncing the doubter as a willful unbeliever and telling him that his salvation depends upon his accepting the story as history. That is not our way of dealing with the man who has intellectual difficulties, and it is not an effective way, either, but rather repels the skeptic. So let us deal with the miracle as thoroughly as we may.

Here the view of the allegorizing critics falls to pieces. As has been seen, they declare that the incident of the fish swallowing the prophet finds its analogy in the swallowing up of the people of Israel in the Babylonian captivity. However, God did not prepare the great fish to punish Jonah, but rather as the means of his deliverance from the sea, for the prophet was far from land; whereas the captivity of Israel in Babylonia was not intended for their deliverance but for their punishment and discipline. The comparison therefore is not well taken, and the allegory loses its force for lack of aptitude.

That the miracle of the great fish is the *gravamen* of the critics is evident from their manner of treating it. George Adams Smith places this rather scornful quotation at the head of his commentary on Jonah, and does not even give the name of its author: "And this is the tragedy of the book of Jonah, that a book which is made the means of one of the most sublime revelations of truth in the Old Testament should be known to most only for its connection with a whale." In the main part of his commentary he has this to say, after stating the allegorical interpretation of the event: "Such a solution of the problem has one great advantage. It relieves us of the grotesqueness which attaches to the literal conception of the story, and of the necessity of those painful efforts for accounting for a miracle which have distorted the common-sense and even the orthodoxy of so many commentators of the book. We are dealing, let us remember, with poetry—a poetry inspired by one of the most sublime truths of the Old Testament, but whose figures are drawn from the legends and myths of the people to whom it is addressed. To treat this as prose is not only to sin against the common-sense which God has given us, but against the simple and obvious intention of the author. It is blindness both to reason and to Scripture.'' Then he adds the following amusing foot-note: ''It is very interesting to notice how many commentators (e. g., Pusey, and the English edition of Lange), who take the story in its individual meaning, and therefore as miraculous, immediately try to minimize the miracle by quoting stories of great fishes which have swallowed men, and even men in armor, whole, and in one case at least, have vomited them up alive!''

Thus we see that it is, after all, the grievance against the fish swallowing Jonah that lies at the root of all skepticism and rationalism relative to this book. Is this such an unbelievable miracle as the skeptical world would have us think? We have often wondered why this miracle has been selected as the special object of ridicule and attack. Surely it is not so wonderful as many other miracles of the Bible. The saving of Noah in the great deluge was a much more stupendous miracle. The parting of the waters of the Jordan at the time of high water would require much more physical power. The halting of the sun and moon by Joshua is much more difficult to explain. The falling of the walls of Jericho at the blast of the trumpets is fully as mysterious. Christ's miracles of the loaves and fishes, walking on the water, stilling the tempest, raising the dead, and finally Himself rising from the grave—all of them have elements that are just as much beyond the range of common human experience as is this deliverance of the prophet by and from the great fish of the Mediterranean. And God's creation of the universe transcends all our conceptions of power and wisdom. If we can believe in miracles

at all, we can readily accept this one. The strange thing
about many of the critics is that they say they accept many
of the other miracles of the Bible, especially that of the
resurrection of Christ, and yet they pounce upon this
Jonah-fish miracle as if it were the one offender in the list
of wonders. That, to say the least, does not seem to be
consistent.

Now, we shall not proceed to "minimize" the miracle.
If the Scripture taught that the great fish was a whale, we
could still believe the story, for the God who made a whale
could manage temporarily to enlarge its throat so as to admit the body of a man; He could do that just as easily as
He could afterward keep the man alive amid the digestive
organs of the monster. But the Bible does not teach that
the great fish was a whale, in the technical sense, and if it
does not teach that, why should any one be called upon to
believe it or defend it? In King James's translation the
word *ketos* is translated "whale," but the Greek word simply means a *sea-monster,* and that name will apply to the
mammoth sharks of the Mediterranean Sea. And it is a
matter of sober record that these leviathans of the deep are
capable of swallowing a man whole. The great commenta-
tor, Dr. Keil, was as scholarly and sober as he was conservative, and he says in his work on Jonah (which, by the
way, is invaluable):

"The great fish (LXX. *ketos,* cf. Matt. XII. 40), which
is not more precisely defined, was not a whale, because this
is extremely rare in the Mediterranean, and has too small a
throat to swallow a man, but a large shark or sea-dog, *canis
carcharias,* or *squalus carcharias L.,* which is very common
in the Mediterranean, and has so large a throat that it can
swallow a living man whole. The miracle consisted, therefore, not so much in the fact that Jonah was swallowed
alive, as in the fact that he was kept alive three days in
the shark's belly and then vomited unhurt upon the land."

In a footnote he adds these observations: "The *squalus carcharias L.*, the true shark . . . reaches, according to Cuvier, the length of 25 feet, and, according to Oken, the length of four fathoms, and has about four hundred lance-shaped teeth in its jaw, arranged in six rows, which the animal can either elevate or depress, as they are simply fixed in cells in the skin. It is common in the Mediterranean, where it generally remains in deep water, and is very voracious, swallowing everything that comes in its way—plaice, seals, tunney-fish, with which it sometimes gets into the fishermen's net on the coast of Sardinia, and is caught. As many as a dozen undigested tunny-fish have been found in a shark weighing three or four hundredweight; in one a whole horse was found, and its weight was estimated at fifteen hundredweight. Rondolet (Oken, p. 58) says that he saw one on the western coast of France through whose throat a fat man could very easily have passed. Oken also mentions a fact . . . namely, that in the year 1758 a sailor fell overboard from a frigate, in very stormy weather, in the Mediterranean Sea, and was immediately taken into the jaws of a sea-dog (*carcharias*), and disappeared. The captain, however, ordered a gun, which was standing on the deck, to be discharged at the shark, and the cannon-ball struck it, so that it vomited up again the sailor that it had swallowed, who was then taken up alive, and very little hurt, into the boat that had been lowered for his rescue."

Our next quotation is from Dr. Geike: "Captain King, in his 'Survey of Australia,' says that he caught one (a shark) which could have swallowed a man with the greatest ease. Blumenbach even states that a whole horse has been found in this kind of a shark; and Basil Hall tells us that he discovered in one, besides other things, the whole skin of a buffalo, which had been thrown overboard a short time before. Brusch says that the whole body of a man in armor has been taken from the stomach of such a shark. It is not uncommon in the Mediterranean, and is met with also in the Arabian Gulf and the Indian Ocean.''

Well are we aware that such explanations sometimes bring a condescending smile to the lips of two classes of persons: First, orthodox believers who do not care to think and investigate, but prefer to swallow everything in a blind sort of way; second, the rationalizing critics who accuse us of holding to a miracle and then trying to reduce it to rational limits. Our reply is, the rationalists have proclaimed from the house-top that they cannot accept this miracle because it is so extraordinary and grotesque. We have shown by the facts cited that there exist in the Mediterranean Sea monsters which can easily swallow a man entire, and that therefore the miracle is not so fantastic as these men have thought. To orthodox believers who swallow every miracle as easily as the shark swallowed Jonah, and from their exalted Pisgah of credulity declare that they want no explanations, we have simply to say that they miss much pleasure in not trying to discover how beautifully God always in every miracle superimposed the supernatural upon the natural, connecting the two in the most vital way, thus showing that the natural is His handiwork as well as the supernatural, and that He will always honor the former as far as it will go in carrying out His heavenly plans. In feeding the multitude He used the loaves and fishes. In the miracle at Cana He made use of the water in the jars. In parting the waters of the Red Sea He used a strong east wind. In preserving Jonah He used a natural fish. This is a domain of thought worth investigating, and makes some of us respect the natural all the more, while it does not in the least diminish our faith in the supernatural. There is a sacred and heavenly economy in all miracles.

After the foregoing was written, we made an interesting

discovery, proving how the science of the day is coming to the fore to establish the historical verity of the Bible narratives. Frank Bullen is a modern writer of sea voyages and stories, and, so far as we know, his knowledge of marine life has never been called in question. In his "Cruise of the Cachalot" he says that he saw masses of cuttle-fish "as thick as a stout man's body, and with six or seven sucking discs, or acetabula, on it," all of which had been ejected from the stomach of a dying whale, and that, of course, through the throat. In one case he declares that "the ejected food was in masses of enormous size, larger than any we have yet seen on the voyage, some of them being estimated of the size of a hatch-house, namely, eight feet by six feet into six feet." That would be a good deal larger than the body of a prophet. It seems that the old scientific dicta as to the small size of the whale's throat applied only to the esophagus of the Greenland whale, whereas navigators and whalers have since discovered that there are other species of whales having enormous gullets. It would seem, therefore, that even the whale story need not be given up on the ground of its being scientifically absurd.

But the preservation of Jonah in the shark's stomach was the real miracle, and a miracle it must have been in deed and in truth. Still, it was not more marvelous than the preservation of Daniel in the lion's den, or the three Hebrew children in the fiery furnace. Then why should any believer in miracles stumble over it? The leading question is not, Was such a marvel possible? but, Was it justifiable, germain to the exigency, needful for the great object to be accomplished? We think it was. Jonah was out in the midst of a boiling, tempestuous sea, far from land. He was cast into the tumultuous waters. He was trying to flee from a work that God had determined to do and that was worthy of divine effort—the saving of a great city. God had given Jonah a degree of liberty, as

He does every man, prophet or layman, and in the exercise of his freedom Jonah had gone out upon the sea, meaning to escape to Tarshish. Now, if Jonah, flung out into the water, is to be saved to execute the great mission assigned him, a miracle must be performed. What kind of a miracle shall it be? God might have simply stilled the storm before so dire a calamity came. Then Jonah and his companions would have gone on their way to Tarshish, and God's purpose would have been balked. God might have given Jonah such superhuman strength as to enable him to swim through league upon league of briny water to the land; but that would have been as great a miracle as to allow a fish, which was a natural swimmer, to carry him. But some one says, "God might have sent along a ship that would have speedily picked up the prophet and borne him back to the coast of Phœnicia." Then Jonah would perhaps have failed to be impressed with God's earnest purpose and wondrous power, and would have made another attempt to run away from his divine call. It sometimes requires an extraordinary experience to bring men to their senses, especially if they are men of stubborn determination. Take the miracle as it is recited in the book, and it might as well have occurred as any other miracle, for all miracles are alike to a God of infinite power, and it taught the renegade prophet the lesson he needed, and taught it most effectively.

It was not only the most *natural* miracle, so to speak, that could have been enacted under the circumstances, but it was justified by the need of a preacher of punitive justice in sinful Nineveh, where God had determined either to destroy or to save the people. The critics are greatly troubled because Jonah's preaching was so exceptionally effective. Why, they say, no other case of a whole city's repenting after a few days' preaching is on record! Isn't that an indication of myth or fiction? No, indeed! It is rather a proof of the effectiveness of the miracle God had wrought. A prophet so wonderfully delivered would preach with an unction and power that could not be resisted. Yes, Jonah had attended a most proficient divinity school down there in the shark's stomach. He had been kept there long enough, too, to study theology and reflect on the doctrine of God's sovereignty. That is the reason the shark did not carry him at once to the shore. God wanted him to have time to think. Potentially God sometimes treats his prophets in the same way to-day.

Possibly we are ready now to consider the susceptibility of the Ninevites to the preaching of Jonah. The critics speak about the "conversion" of the whole city. Let it be understood that the Scriptures never speak about their "conversion," but simply about their repentance. By importing the word "conversion" into the event, and then arguing on that assumption, the critics suppose they make out their case against the historicity of the book, for they think there is no evidence that Nineveh had really turned to God; and the fact that it was afterward doomed to destruction on account of its wickedness seems to lend some color to their view. However, it is not to be assumed that, when the people of Nineveh repented under the preaching of Jonah, they were all thoroughly regenerated and became ideal worshipers of God. In many cases the repentance was formal, in others the result of sudden and violent fear of punishment. Perhaps the reformation was rather evanescent. If it was, it is not to be wondered at, for how often Israel turned to God under special punishment or kingly dominance, calling upon God for mercy, which he always displayed toward them; then soon went back to their idols and ungodliness. If with all God's care of them for centuries they were so wavering, can we wonder that the reformation of the heathen city of Nineveh was not permanent? The object of the book, as Dr. Keil has keenly pointed out, was to prove to Jonah and his fellow-Hebrews that God would be merciful to pagan penitents and that such people were capable of repentance and salvation; and when they repented, though their sorrow for sin may not have been deep or lasting, God for the time being stayed the hand of doom that was held over them. Thus we do not see that the temporary nature of the reformation in Nineveh is much of a stumbling-block to faith in the literal history of the book. The lesson of God's paternal love for all nations, and not merely the chosen people, would still be powerfully impressed upon the minds of the Jews.

From many sources come confirmations of the historical nature of the narrative portions of God's Word, including the book of Jonah. Here is something just at hand. The Rev. John A. Ainslee was for years stationed as a missionary at Mosul, near the site of the ancient city of Nineveh. In a letter written from Chatfield, Minn., to the editor of "The Bible Student and Teacher," * he says:

"There are several large Christian villages within twenty or twenty-five miles of old Nineveh. I worked more or less in many of these during the ten years that I was stationed at Mosul. One of these villages is Tel Kaif, having about 5,000 inhabitants. I found that in this village they keep a fast every year, a fast of three days, which is, according to their own story, a repetition of the fast ordered by the king of Nineveh in Jonah's time. It has been kept through all these generations, and is still kept in that village according to the 'custom' which means so much to an Oriental. The fast was ordered by a heathen king, and those who now keep it are nominally Christians. I do not know why they or their fathers should keep it, unless it may be that they are descended from those old Ninevites. Explorations may yet settle this fact. I can

* This magazine is now known as *The Bible Champion*, and is conducting a vigorous crusade in favor of the integrity of the Bible.

only report the fact, which can be tested by any one who cares to go to that village, that the old fast of the Ninevites is still observed.''

There is no need, we think, of attempting to explain or justify the miracle of the plant that grew up in a night and perished so soon, for if the greater wonders of the narrative can be accepted, this one will cause no difficulty.

Let us now note the position of this book in the sacred canon. It is placed among the minor prophets, on account of which the critics think it cannot be regarded as literal history, as it is the only work of the kind in that division of the Old Testament books. It contains no prophecy, but simple narrative. In that respect, we are frank to say, it is unlike the other books of its division. But how will it help the matter to call it an allegory? The other minor prophecies are not allegory; why should this one be placed among them? It is the only entire book of the Bible that is allegory, unless we except Job,* and therefore it ought either to be classed alone or be placed with the book of Job. Its position, therefore, among the minor prophets is no argument whatever for its allegorical character. More than that, we do not know that the most strenuous advocate of the plenary inspiration of the Bible would contend that the order and arrangement of the Biblical books is a matter of inspiration. However, if Jonah was a prophet—and he is so called in 2 Kings 14: 25—and if he wrote the book himself as an actual experience, that would be a good reason for classifying this work in the schedule of the prophets. The title of this special division is ''The Minor Prophets.'' Jonah was one of the minor prophets. Remember that the distinctive title is not ''The Minor Prophecies.'' Dr. Keil says: ''If then . . . the compilers of the canon have placed the book among the minor prophets, this can only have

---

* The author, however, does not accept the view that the book of Job is an allegory.

been done because they were firmly convinced that the prophet Jonah was the author.''

And more, every one at all versed in Biblical lore ought to know that a prophet is one who speaks for God, whether he predicts or not.* Did not Jonah speak for God when he preached to the Ninevites? God said to him (3:2): ''Arise, go unto Nineveh, that great city, and preach unto it the preaching that I bid thee.''

The critics maintain that the book must have had a late origin, exilic or post-exilic; that it was written by some unknown author long after the prophet's own time, which was the reign of Jeroboam II. The proof of this, they contend, is found in the language employed. In the compass of this chapter we cannot go into the linguistic and literary discussion, but will content ourselves with quoting the substance of the learned Dr. Keil's remarks on the subject: ''The Aramaisms''—here he mentions quite a long list of them—''belong either to the speech of Galilee or the language of ordinary discourse, and are very far from being proofs of a later age, since it cannot be proved with certainty that any one of these words was unknown in the early Hebrew usage. . . . The only non-Hebraic word, viz., *mayam*, which is used in the sense of command, and applied to the edict of the king of Assyria, was heard by Jonah in Nineveh, where it was used as a technical term, and was transferred by him. The reminiscences which occur in Jonah's prayer are all taken from the Psalms of David or his contemporaries, which were generally known in Israel long before the prophet's day.''

Christ's allusions to Jonah are of such a character as to be almost, perhaps wholly, convincing that He believed the prophet to be a historical personage and his experience in the shark's stomach and in Nineveh to be actual occur-

* The word ''prophesy'' does not mean to *foretell*, but to *speak for*.

rences. The most striking passage is Matt. 12:39-41. The
first two verses are as follows: "But He answered and said
unto them, An evil and adulterous generation seeketh after
a sign; and there shall be no sign given to it but the sign
of Jonah the prophet: for as Jonah was three days and
three nights in the belly of the sea-monster; so shall the
Son of man be three days and three nights in the heart
of the earth." It is just possible that Jesus *might* have
made use of a mythical story for the purpose of illustration, as men sometimes illustrate their sermons by reference to well-known fictitious incidents; but somehow there
is an air of verisimilitude about the language of our Lord
that makes one feel that he was alluding to something that
both he and his hearers believed to be an actual occurrence.
It is almost certain that the Jews to whom He spoke believed the story of the sea-monster to be a real event, and
if Jesus knew it was not, He was not dealing frankly with
them, but was rather lending countenance to their error.
Note the positive character of the language: "As Jonah
was in the sea-monster's belly, so *shall* the Son of man be
in the heart of the earth." If the Jonah incident was real,
the burial of Jesus would be real also. If the former was
mythical—well, to say the least, it would not have been a
very fortunate comparison, for some one in the audience
who was keener than the rest might have put the speaker
in a *cul-de-sac* by saying, "The Jonah-whale story is a
myth; so your statement about lying in the heart of the
earth must be myth too." Again, if Jesus did not know
that Jonah's adventure was merely legendary or parabol-
ical, what becomes of His divinity?

In the next verse—the 41st—He says: "The men of
Nineveh shall stand up in the judgment with this generation, and shall condemn it: for they repented at the preaching of Jonah, and, behold, a greater than Jonah is here."
The oftener you read that over, the more it sounds like the

clear statement of fact. "The men of Nineveh *shall* stand
. . . and *shall* condemn it." But suppose, on the judgment day, the men of Nineveh do not appear to condemn
those hardened Pharisees, because they—the Ninevites—
did not repent, after all, what then? Jesus was talking
about a serious matter in that discourse; would He have
been likely to make use of a myth to enforce the lesson?
Would He have solemnly told the Pharisees before Him
that they would be confronted and condemned by a host
of penitent Ninevites who, after all, had never repented?
In the great day to which we are all hastening, we wonder
whether those Pharisees will look around for those contrite
Ninevites, and will look in vain! However trenchant the
illustration may have seemed when it came from our
Saviour's lips, it will lose its force on the day of the great
assize—the very time, too, when He meant that it should
be verified and have its most telling effect. Mythical penitents surely will not put those impenitent Pharisees to
very great confusion on the judgment day!

Notice, too, that our Lord adds, "A greater than Jonah
is here." But if Jonah's preaching to the Ninevites was
only a bit of fiction, Jonah was not a very great preacher,
and the contrast loses its force. Would Christ in His infinite wisdom have called Himself greater than a mythical
personage? In the next few verses he refers to Solomon
and the queen of Sheba. Were they also mythical characters? If not, what right had He to make use of myths and
historical events in the same breath and to illustrate the
same truth without making any explanation or distinction?
To say the very least, that would scarcely have been disingenuous.

Our remaining arguments will be based upon the nature
and style of the book in connection with the general principles of evidence. It is not probable that a Jew would
have composed a parable like the book of Jonah, which

teaches doctrines entirely contrary to the conceptions of the Jewish people relative to the heathen. The Ninevites were among their enemies and oppressors, and the prophets were fortetelling that the time would come when Assyria would swallow them up in a terrible captivity. What Jew would care to compose and scatter abroad a book that would aim to teach the Jews that their arch foes were included in God's scheme of mercy? If the work is veritable history, God Himself became their teacher through an actual incident.

In reading the narrative one cannot fail to be impressed with the directness, simplicity and artlessness of its style and the air of verisimilitude that surrounds it. It does not read like fiction, like myth, like an Arabian Nights story. There is nothing in the manner of the telling to indicate that its author meant it as an allegory. Compare it with the historical portions of Isaiah or Jeremiah or even the strictly historical books of the Old Testament, and you will see that it reads just like them, bearing the marks of real history and not of fiction. If it is an allegory and was indited by the Holy Spirit, then the Spirit did His work in such a way as to lead the vast majority of readers in ancient and modern times to believe it to be veritable history, and that would be deception on a pretty large scale. An act that we are not willing to ascribe to the Spirit of God. If it is merely a story with a didactic purpose, we maintain that there should have been something to indicate that it was a piece of composition of that character. Look at all the parables of the Bible. In every instance there is something either in the context or the imagery that clearly indicates their figurative character. Not one of the parables of our Lord can be mistaken for literal history. On the other hand, no historical portion of the gospels can be mistaken for parable or simile.

But here is something still more serious. Jonah was a

real personage, a prophet living and prophesying in the time of Jeroboam II. Would a writer of his age or a later one have been so bold as to manufacture a piece of fiction like this book with a well-known prophet of Israel as its hero? And especially would he have dared to represent him to be of so narrow, squeamish and even peevish a disposition? Would not the Jews have resented such a story the moment it was circulated? Still more, would an allegorist have been so bold as to put the great and well-known city of Nineveh into his story and represent it as having repented so thoroughly at the preaching of a Hebrew prophet? Why, he would have brought down upon himself the ridicule of both Jews and Ninevites for composing so whimsical and improbable a story! And nothing so completely fails of its didactic purpose as a poorly constructed and unnatural piece of fiction, no matter how sincere the purpose of its author.

Taken all in all, therefore, we cannot help looking upon the noble and impressive book of Jonah as historical verity.

NOTE.—We recommend the following literature on the book of Jonah: C. F. Keil: "Commentary on the Minor Prophets"; J. W. McGarvey: "Jesus and Jonah" (contains a review of Driver on this book); R. A. Torrey: "Difficulties in the Bible" (pages 76-79); Von Orelli: "The Twelve Minor Prophets"; J. Kennedy: "The Book of Jonah"; J. R. Sampey: Article on Jonah in "The International Standard Bible Encyclopedia"; R. D. Wilson: "The Authenticity of Jonah" (*Princeton Theological Review,* April and July, 1918).

CHAPTER IX

CHRIST'S WITNESS TO THE OLD TESTAMENT

*Another Chapter on Biblical Criticism**

PERHAPS it will not be entirely superfluous to state briefly what is the teaching of the liberal critics relative to the Old Testament. We shall mention only the main points of their contention.

First, they hold to the documentary theory of the Pentateuch—that is, that at least four different documents are to be discovered in this portion of the Bible. These documents are labeled J, E, D and P, corresponding to the terms Jehovistic, Elohistic, Deuteronomic and Priestly. They were edited and welded together more or less crudely and blunderingly by various redactors, until they were finally cast into their present form. By a process of literary analysis and dissection the critics maintain that they are able to separate the Pentateuch—or, rather, the Hexateuch —into its various original component parts.

The original documents were not composed at an early age, as the Bible history would lead us to believe, nor even

---

* Several years after this chapter had appeared in a theological review, we learned of Dr. C. F. Noesgen's book, ''The New Testament and the Pentateuch,'' which was translated from the German by Mr. C. H. Irwin and was issued in English in 1905 by the Religious Tract Society, London. After reading this satisfying and masterly work, our wonder has grown to amazement that critics like Cheyne, Driver, Kent, Foster, Toy, Bade, Peritz, Sanders, *et al*, have had the conscience to go on and on repeating the stock tenets of their school without so much as naming this great conservative authority.

edited and compiled by Moses, but J had its origin about 800 B. C.; E about 750 B. C.; D about 620 B. C., and P about 444 B. C.; between the last date and 280 B. C. this last document was joined with JED by a final redactor; and thus we have the Hexateuch in its present form. Who the original writers were, and why they wrote, no one knows. By some of these critics not a word is said about the Holy Spirit having had any part in the composition of this portion of the Bible; all of it is attributed to a purely human origin and development. Others try to hold to a doctrine of inspiration, but it surely is very indeterminate and tenuous. There is, in fact, little or no intimation in the work of the critics that "holy men of old wrote as they were moved by the Holy Ghost."

In the second place, the narrative portions of the Old Testament are, according to the critics, not historical, but largely mythical, legendary or allegorical. To make good this statement, we insert here a quotation from a recent writer of this school who says: "Modern research has made plain that there are at least three stages of Old Testament history which vary in character and historic accuracy. We find in the first chapter of Genesis early traditions of creation, either from Babylonian or prehistoric Semitic tribes, adapted to the monotheistic belief of Israel. The ages described were marked by myth, allegory and primitive ideas as to the method of creation and the origin and distribution of tribes and languages. The second period—the patriarchal—was bathed in an atmosphere of legend. The core of the stories was historic, but the note of legend and romance gave an idyllic and patriotic halo to the early patriarchal life of Israel. Abraham, Isaac, Jacob and Joseph were actual personages, but their biographies move in a glow of heroic idealism." * Says Samuel

* Quoted from Edwin Heyl Delk's "The Need of a Restatement of Theology" (p. 31)—a work that is extremely radical in its liberalism, but lacks in logical coherence.

Davidson: "The narratives of the Pentateuch are usually trustworthy, though partly mythical and legendary. The miracles recorded are the exaggerations of a later age" ("Introduction to the Old Testament," p. 131). According to George Adam Smith, "the framework of the first eleven chapters of Genesis is woven from the raw material of myth and legend. He denies their historical character," and declares that he can find no proof in archeology for the personal existence of the patriarchs themselves. Later on, he admits the extreme possibility that the stories of the patriarchs may have historical elements at the heart of them. (See his "Modern Criticism and the Preaching of the Old Testament," pp. 90-106.)

In his Bampton Lectures for 1903, Prof. Sanday, who is regarded as quite conservative in comparison with Kuenen, Wellhausen and Cheyne, advances some very tenuous ideas relative to the "divine element" in the books of the Old Testament. Another says of Dr. Sanday's view of "the divine element": "What that really is he does not accurately declare. The language always vapors off into the vague and indefinite, when he speaks of it," that is, the divine element. "In what books it is he does not say." Here are a few quotations from Sanday: "It is present in different books and parts of books in different degrees"; "In some the divine element is at the maximum; in others at the minimum." He is not always sure where the divine element comes in. However, he is sure it is not in Esther, Ecclesiastes and Daniel. "If it is in the historical books," says a critic of Sanday, "it is there as conveying a religious lesson rather than as a guarantee of historic veracity; rather as interpreting than as narrating." Anent another crucial matter, Dr. Sanday says: "However much we may believe that there is a genuine Mosaic foundation in the Pentateuch, it is difficult to lay the finger upon it, and to say with confidence, here Moses himself is speaking." Again: "The strictly Mosaic element in the Pentateuch must be indeterminate." And yet the account itself says again and again, in Exodus, Numbers, Leviticus and Deuteronomy, "The Lord spake unto Moses," "Moses spoke to the people," "Moses wrote in the book of the covenant." For an offset to Sanday's grudging deference to Moses, let any one take a concordance and see how often Moses is mentioned in the four books named above.

The third point in the teaching of the critics relates to the manner in which the Old Testament literature was imposed upon the Jewish people. According to the simple narrative of the Bible itself (2 Kings 22 and 23; 2 Chron. 34 and 35) Hilkiah, the priest, in the days of King Josiah, discovered "the book of the law" in the temple, which was then undergoing repairs, and handed it to Shaphan, the scribe, who carried it to the king, and read it to him. On account of the revelations made by the book, Josiah became deeply penitent, and brought about a reformation among the people of Judah. The Chronicler (2 Chron. 34:14) says distinctly that the book was "the book of the law of Jehovah given by Moses." So far the Bible. It is all very simple and clear, has an air of reality, and reads like veritable history.

But the critics—what say they? To them it seems to matter little what the Bible itself really says; they must reconstruct the history to fit to their theories, which they do in this wise: Hilkiah and his fellow-priests, being moved by the laudable desire to reform the people of Judah, who had gone far astray from God, deliberately composed this book of the law themselves, pretended that they had found it in the temple, attributed it to Moses to give it an air of antiquity and authority, and thus foisted it upon King Josiah and his subjects. And king and people received it, too, apparently without question or examination. How they could be so easily deceived, if they really knew nothing or little about Moses and the book of the law, is, to our mind, one of the outstanding and astounding miracles of the disintegrating criticism. On the part of Hilkiah and his coadjutors this book of the law was a pure forgery, to call things by their right name; but the critics do not want so harsh a name given to the transaction. It should be called only a "pious fraud," and was quite justifiable in view of the righteous desire on the part of the priests to inaugurate a real reformation. Thus the Jesuitical motto, "The end justifies the means," finds advocates among the expert "modern" critics. And thus, too, the element of divine inspiration is carefully guarded and upheld by them! Perhaps the inspiration in this enterprise was the priestly desire to reform the people. Well, if the Holy Spirit moved the priests to try to bring about a much-needed reformation, why did He not inspire them as well to use honest and straightforward means? Another query that rises in our mind is this: If the people would believe the priests when they perpetrated a literary forgery, why would they not have believed them just as readily if they had come forward with a clear, ringing, honest proclamation of the law of righteousness and the need of repentance and reform? To our way of thinking, they employed the more difficult method, and the one that was the less likely to succeed.

However, this is not the end. The people of Judah soon relapsed into idolatry, and were carried away into captivity to Babylon. Under the leadership of Nehemiah and Ezra, many of them were led back from their exile, and then, in order to reform them again, Ezra and his priests had recourse to a method of forgery similar to the one that had succeeded so remarkably in the days of Josiah. Again the book of the law, falsely attributed to Moses, was brought out; and, as in the first instance, so now the people accepted the imposture, and followed the lead of their deceivers. Even the Samaritans, though repudiated by Nehemiah and plotting against the returned exiles, nevertheless, in some mysterious way, were induced to receive the Pentateuch from the hands of their enemies as the inspired writing of Moses! It is past belief what an influence that "mythical" Moses exercised over those Jews and Samaritans. In the hands of Hilkiah and Ezra his name seemed to be a name to charm by. What they as living, actual persons could not accomplish, that was comparatively easy for a mythical character to do!

Now, the foregoing, according to the critics, is the theory of the composition and history of the Old Testament; for the Psalms, Proverbs and Prophecies are treated in practically the same way by these dexterous analysts. Although we have hinted at some of the difficulties that these hypotheses encounter, our chief purpose in this chapter is to show that it is entirely out of accord with the testimony of the New Testament relative to the Old. We have no desire to use an *ad hominem* argument, nor to make an appeal to policy or fear; yet we do feel impelled to point out the gravity of the situation, if the views of the liberal critics should become prevalent. Every man should look before he leaps; that is only the dictate of common sense; and so the critics themselves should try to realize what will be the effect of their advocacy upon the faith of the people in Christ and His Gospel as set forth in the New Testament. However, if the pulverizing critics insist on looking at the Old Testament in a purely critical and dispassionate spirit, we will also try to consider, in the same temper, Christ's attitude toward those ancient Scriptures.

That Christ had before Him the same Old Testament canon that we have to-day no critic will undertake to deny. The Old Testament canon was established several centuries before the time of our Lord. We cannot take the time to prove this statement historically, but the facts are set forth in a number of recent works on Biblical criticism. We would especially refer to Dr. A. J. F. Behrends' valuable book, "The Old Testament Under Fire," pages 79-85. Even Prof. Sanday "cannot resist the historical evidence that a hundred years before Christ the Old Testament, as we now have it, was universally regarded as inspired Scripture"; so says Dr. Behrends. Let this fact be kept in mind, then, that Jesus referred always to the very same Old Testament which we have to-day.

Now, how did Christ look upon the Old Testament? It is evident that He regarded it as the veritable Word of God; else why would He say to Satan, "It is written," and then quote from Deuteronomy, as if that were the end of controversy? Why did He so often refer to incidents in the Old Testament as being paralleled by incidents in His own career? Why did He say, "To-day is this Scripture fulfilled in your ears"? Why did He say that not a jot nor tittle would pass from the law till all be fulfilled? Again and again He spoke about the prophecies of the Old Testament being fulfilled in Him. Since no one but God can foresee and predict the future, Jesus must have believed that the prophets were inspired, or they never could have uttered prophecies that were exactly fulfilled so many centuries after their proclamation.

Various subterfuges—at least, they seem so—are employed by the critics to account for Christ's attitude of reverence toward the Old Testament. Some of them maintain, for example, that He *accommodated* Himself to the views of the Jewish people with whom He associated. That means, put in plain language, that, though He knew better, He treated the Old Testament as if it were historical and the Pentateuch as if it had been written by Moses; and this He did simply because the Jews held that view, and He did not want to antagonize them. Was not that disingenuous in Christ? Was it not a case of trimming? Could He have properly called Himself "the truth," if He pretended that the Old Testament was historical and the law the work of Moses, when He knew they were not? Really what becomes of our Lord's integrity in such circumstances? More than that, if the critics are right, and He knew it, why did He not tell the truth about the Old Testament Scriptures? Why did He permit His followers for centuries to rest under error in so vital a matter? In a very few words He might have told them that much of the Old Testament was lacking in "the divine element," and that Moses wrote little or none of the Pentateuch. He was careful to tell the Pharisees that they had glossed and corrupted the Scriptures, and were teaching for the true Scriptural doctrine the traditions of men. He said bluntly to the Sadducees, "Ye do err, not knowing the Scriptures, nor the power of God." While He was so fearlessly pointing out their errors in this respect, why could He not just as plainly have told them the truth about the origin of the Scriptures? Instead of doing that, He actually defended the Scriptures against their false interpretations.

Perhaps it may be replied that it was not safe to disturb the faith of the Jews in the Old Testament. Then error is safer than truth, and yet Christ said, "Ye shall know the truth, and the truth shall make you free." And He promised His disciples that the Holy Spirit would "lead them into all truth." Besides, if it was not safe then for Christ to disturb the implicit faith of the Jews in their sacred writings, is it safe for the critics to disturb the faith of the people now?

However, the critics who are anxious to be considered evangelical have another explanation ready at hand, and that we must now deal with. They say that Christ, in the days of His humiliation, was not endued with all knowl-

edge; that there were many things He did not know, because He had assumed human nature and with it human
limitation. There was, they contend, an actual *kenosis* of
the divine. To uphold this view they quote Luke 2:52:
"And Jesus advanced in wisdom and stature, and in
favor with God and man." Also: "But of that day and
hour knoweth no man, not even the angels of heaven,
neither the Son, but the Father only" (Matt. 24:36).

But the arguments of the critics are not sound. In the
first place, Jesus was divine as well as human. While in
and of His humanity by itself He was not omniscient,
yet in His divinity He was, just as is declared in John
2:25: "He needed not that any should bear witness
concerning man; for He Himself knew what was in man."
Again and again He displayed wisdom and knowledge that
were far beyond mere human attainment; for instance,
when He said to the Scribes and Pharisees, "Why reason
ye in your hearts?" (Luke 5:22); when He knew the
woman had touched him in the throng (Mark 5:30);
when He predicted his own betrayal, death and resurrection, the destruction of Jerusalem, the day of Pentecost,
and the remarkable spread of His kingdom. Now if He
was endued with supernatural wisdom in so many ways,
why should He not have known that Moses did not write
the Pentateuch and that large portions of the Old Testament were mere myth and legend?

Again, even if we were to admit that, because of the
kenosis, Jesus did not know all things, especially such
things as the Father saw fit to hide from Him for the
time being, that is very different from attributing *erroneous*
teaching to Him. Nowhere did He admit that He taught
error; on the contrary, He always claimed to teach the
truth and only the truth. If He ever taught error, He
could not have been a perfect man, and therefore could
not have been a true example for the world. *Kenosis* or

no *kenosis*, He declared that He always did the will of His Father (John 5:30), and kept His commandments (John 15:10), and spoke as the Father taught him (John 8:28). Therefore He must have always taught the truth, having been, during the period of His humiliation, completely under the guidance of the Father, to whose will and direction He submitted in all things. But if He everywhere gave the impression that He thought the Bible was the fully inspired Word of God and that Moses gave the law, then He taught error by implication, and did it throughout His whole life, even after His resurrection. Surely that view would destroy the perfect manhood of our Savior, to say nothing of His Godhood. The doctrine of the *kenosis* of the Logos, therefore, even if it were admitted, cannot be employed to bolster up the disintegrating theories of the critics; for if Christ taught error, either directly or by implication, His Messiahship is made null and void; He broke the law of God, and so could not have fulfilled all righteousness. What that means respecting faith in Christ all must know without preachment on our part.

Nor is that all. If there was a *kenosis* of the Logos, it ceased with our Lord's resurrection, when His state of exaltation was in process. Read the beautiful story of Christ's meeting with the two disciples on their way to Emmaus, and you will see that He spoke most emphatic and unequivocal words respecting the Old Testament: "And He said unto them, O foolish men, and slow of heart to believe all that the prophets have spoken! . . . And beginning from Moses and from all the prophets, He interpreted to them in all the Scriptures the things concerning Himself" (Luke 24:25-27). And it would seem that the Holy Spirit sanctioned and emphasized His teaching respecting the Old Testament, for the two disciples afterward said one to the other: "Did not our hearts

burn within us, while He spake to us in the way, while
He opened to us the Scriptures?''

It may be said in reply that it was not important for
the disciples to know anything about the questions of criticism that are now agitating the public mind, and therefore He did not go out of His way to give them unneeded
information. If that is true, perhaps such information is
not important to-day. Why should it be needed now, if
not then? And if it is not necessary or important, why
all this painstaking and infinitesimal labor to establish
the critical theories? There are men in more than one
theological school who are spending all their time and
strength in searching land and sea to make good their
views and to exploit them before the world. And they are
compelling evangelical scholars to spend just as much
precious time and effort to investigate the facts and learn
whether the new theories are true or not. And all this over
questions that it was not worth while for our Lord even
to mention or hint at! What a big ado about a little!
Surely the work of the critics cannot be of much ''religious'' value.

Still another consideration is apropos at this place. We
have already said that Christ could never have taught un-
truth or error without nullifying His perfection as the
God-man. Still, we know that He reserved some truths to
be revealed by His Spirit after his ascension to the right
hand of God; for He said (John 16:12, 13): ''I have yet
many things to say unto you, but ye cannot bear them
now. Howbeit, when He, the Spirit of truth, is come, He
shall guide you into all truth; for He shall not speak
from Himself; but what things soever He shall hear, these
shall He speak: and He shall declare unto you the things
that are to come.''

The question now is, did the Holy Spirit ever impart
to the disciples any hint that the Old Testament was not

throughout the Word of God; that it was largely composed of myths, traditions, legends and allegories; that its historical narratives were bathed in an atmosphere of folklore; that only a very small portion of the Pentateuch was written by Moses; that the Hexateuch is composed of various documents loosely strung together by redactors; that most of the law and its historical setting was forged by Hilkiah and Ezra, and then foisted upon the people as an ancient composition to bring about a spiritual reformation? Were any of these "assured results" of the higher critics among the things that the disciples "could not bear" at the time, but that the Spirit afterward revealed to them? The answer is, No! On the contrary, the apostles everywhere treated the Old Testament just as their Master did— as if it were the veritable Word of God, and as if there were not the remotest doubt about it. At Pentecost, under the most powerful influence of the Holy Spirit, Peter arose and preached an epoch-making sermon that brought three thousand people to their knees. How did he treat the Old Testament? He quoted a long passage from the prophet Joel and two passages from the Psalms of David to prove that Jesus was the Messiah and that now He had poured out the Spirit upon His Church. He quoted from the Old Testament as final authority to those Jews who had crucified Christ, and never hinted that the Psalms were written in the days of the Maccabees, or that the prophecy of Joel was written long after the prophet lived! Under the Spirit's dominance that would have been the time to tell the truth and the whole truth. But how many people do you suppose would have been converted on Pentecost, if Peter had gone into the critical and dissecting process in his dealing with the Old Testament? The very fact that the Holy Spirit used the Word of God so effectively on that day, causing thousands to cry out, "What shall we do?" affords convincing proof to the evangelical scholar and believer that He—the Holy Spirit—placed His stamp of endorsement upon the Old Testament as God's inspired truth.

Subsequently when Stephen, at the time of his martyrdom and under the power of the Spirit, delivered his wonderful swan sermon, he recited a resume of the Old Testament history, beginning with the call of Abraham away back in Genesis. And he rehearsed it all as if it were actual history. Throughout, God is represented as inspiring and directing his servants, Abraham, Isaac, Jacob, Joseph, Moses, Aaron, David and Solomon. Nor is there a hint that any of these characters were mythical or legendary. If they were, the Spirit was not guiding Stephen into the truth.

In course of time Peter wrote three epistles. Did the Holy Spirit, whom Christ promised to the apostles, lead Peter to any of the higher critical conclusions respecting the Old Testament? Perhaps by this time, at all events, his faith would be strong enough to bear the truths that were too profound and mysterious for him before the Spirit came. But, no! instead of being led to treat the Old Testament as a human book, full of traditions, myths, legends and historical and other errors, he actually wrote the following sublime tribute to the Hebrew Scriptures (2 Pet. 1:19-21) : "And we have the word of the prophecy made sure; whereunto ye do well that ye take heed, as unto a lamp shining in a dark place, until the day dawn and the day-star arise in your hearts: knowing this first, that no prophecy of Scripture is of private interpretation;* for no prophecy ever came by the will of man, but holy men spake from God, being moved by the Holy Spirit." †

* Literal translation: "of its own unloosing"—that is, of mere human origin.

† Note how emphatic the precise order of the original Greek is: "But, being borne along by the Holy Spirit, spake the holy men of God."

This passage, this great passage, indeed, should be pondered well before men go over to the position of the radical criticism. Is it any wonder that many good men cannot see how any one can hold to that position and yet consistently law claim to being truly evangelical?

But perhaps Paul, who was a highly educated man and who also claimed to have the Spirit of Christ, received more light than his fellow-apostles as to the real status of the Old Testament. He was a bold and fearless thinker, never accepting anything except on the best evidence, and he was just as courageous in proclaiming what he believed to be the truth. Did he utter a word in all his writings that would give the least color to the "myth-legend-allegory" theory? Did he ever hint that anything in the Old Testament was not inspired, or that Moses was not a real character, or that he was not the author of the books commonly ascribed to him? Not a word! Had he known these things, he surely would have been honest enough to concede them. In his contest with the Judaizing teachers he might have made telling use of the higher critical theories, by saying that most of the Old Testament was legendary, that the "divine element" was very indeterminate, that the law was not Mosaic, that many of the prophecies were written after the predicted events had occurred, that most of the Old Testament was fiction invented by Hilkiah and Ezra, and that, therefore, they— the Jews—were entirely mistaken in supposing that they would need to keep the ceremonial law. What an advantage that would have given him in the argument! But, behold! he never used his opportunity. He treated the Old Testament as if it was the very Word of God, and mobilized his arguments along an entirely different line —that is, by showing that Christ was the fulfillment of all the divinely given types and symbols and prophecies of the Jewish covenant. Note his commendation of the Old

Testament in 2 Tim. 3:14-17: "But abide thou in the things which thou hast learned and hast been assured of, knowing of whom thou hast learned them; and that from a babe thou hast known the Sacred Writings, which are able to make thee wise unto salvation through faith which is in Christ Jesus. Every Scripture is God-breathed (*theopneustos*), and is profitable for teaching," etc. We give the translation which we believe to be the correct one. Does that sound like the declaration of a man who had vague, indeterminate ideas of the inspiration of the Sacred Writings which were "able to make wise unto salvation"? If the negative critics are right, the Holy Spirit must have led Paul into error rather than into truth.

And now having, as we think, established the position that Christ and His apostles looked upon the Old Testament as the veritable Word of inspiration, and that they never for a moment gave a hint that it was not historical when it professed to recite history, let us examine somewhat in detail Christ's treatment of its records. We will see that in every case it is diametrically opposed to the position of the analytical critics. True, as Dr. T. E. Schmauk says so well in his acute work, "The Negative Criticism and the Old Testament," we must not make Christ responsible for merely human teachings, speculations and interpretations; and therefore we appreciate that here we are treading on sacred ground, and must be as judicial as possible. However, knowing that in Christ's day the Old Testament canon was precisely what it is to-day and that the Jews regarded it as the Word of God, we may very readily infer Christ's attitude toward it from His manner of quoting it and referring to it. We will see that He treated all the books of the Pentateuch as Sacred Writing, and attributed at least large portions of them to Moses.

First, as to Genesis. In Matt. 19:3-12 there is the account of a contest between Christ and the Pharisees relative to divorce: "And there came unto Him Pharisees, trying Him, and saying: Is it lawful for a man to put away his wife for every cause?" Now observe His answer: "And He answered and said: Have ye not read that He who made them from the beginning made them male and female, and said, For this cause shall a man leave his father and mother, and shall cleave to his wife; and they two shall become one flesh? So that they are no more two, but one flesh. What therefore God hath joined together, let no man put asunder." Turn to Gen. 2:18-25, where you will find the writing or history to which Christ referred and from which He made a direct quotation. There is also a clear allusion to Gen. 1:27, where we read, "Male and female created He them." He refers to a book, for he says, "Have ye not read?" What book could it have been but the book of Genesis? Observe again that He says: "He who made them from the beginning." The antecedent of "He" is God. So Christ taught by the clearest possible inference that God created man and woman in the way described in the first and second chapters of Genesis, and on this divine and historical fact He bases one of the most vital practical laws of human life, namely, the true rule of marriage. But suppose the Genetical account is only "tradition," "myth," "allegory"! Would the divine Christ have founded an organic relation of human life on mere fiction? No, that would be frivolous, inane. What would you think of a reformer to-day who would try to base a fundamental law of life on the Greek or the Norse mythology? Therefore we have our Lord's own direct and unequivocal testimony to the historical veracity of the first and second chapters of Genesis. No doubt of this fact is possible because Christ adds: "What therefore God hath joined together let not man put asunder." What insincerity it would have indicated for Christ to say this, if He knew that the Genetical story was only mythical! That would have been using the *ad hominum* argument, and, worse still, would have been *ad captandum* trickery.

In the next place, Christ endorses the story of Abel as recited in the fourth chapter of Genesis. See Matt. 23:35 and Luke 11:51: "That upon you may come all the righteous blood shed on earth, from the blood of Abel, the righteous, unto the blood of Zachariah," etc. How could the hard-hearted Jews be guilty of the blood of Abel if he was only a legendary character? To give point to the reference, He calls him "Abel the righteous," showing that He accepted the Old Testament narrative at its face value and in all its details.

In Matt. 24:37-39 (also Luke 17:26f.) our Lord refers to Noah as a historical personage. The passage is familiar: "As were the days of Noah, so shall the coming of the Son of Man be," etc. If Noah was a mythical character, Christ surely would not have compared the event of the flood to His own second coming, which he meant to teach would be a real occurrence. Such an allusion would have indicated either misinformation or insincerity, and the illustration would have lost all point.

The patriarchal age is often said by the critics to have been "bathed in an atmosphere of legend," only "the core of the stories" being historic. Other critics go still further and deny the historic reality of the patriarchs *in toto*. Still others contend that they are only the names of tribes. What did Christ think, or, at least, what did He profess to think? "Jesus said unto them, If ye were Abraham's children, ye would do the works of Abraham. But now ye seek to kill me, a man that hath told the truth: this did not Abraham" (John 8:39-40). Later in the same chapter (8:56-58) he says, under the most solemn circumstances: "Your father Abraham rejoiced to see my day; and he saw it and was glad. . . . Before Abraham was born, I am." How could Abraham have been born and how could he have rejoiced, if he was only a mythical character? Or if only the "core" of the stories is true, how are we to know whether Christ had seized upon that core or not, seeing that He accepted the entire Old Testament as the Word of God? Again Jesus refers to the three patriarchs in one breath as follows (Matt. 8:11) : "And I say unto you that many shall come from the east and the west, and shall sit down with Abraham and Isaac and Jacob in the kingdom of heaven." That would be a most ridiculous way to refer to mythical characters, or even "actual person-ages" whose "biographies move in the glow of an heroic idealism." Perhaps, then, the kingdom of God is only mythical, or else only moves in a glow of idealism. We confess that we do not believe it right thus to destroy the reality and realism of the historical portions of the Bible.

Here is another of our Savior's marvelous statements: "But as touching the resurrection of the dead, have ye not read that which was spoken unto you by God, saying, I am the God of Abraham, and the God of Isaac, and the God of Jacob? God is not the God of the dead, but of the living" (Matt. 22:31-32). This remarkable passage de-serves special notice. First, it is a quotation from Ex. 3:6, showing that Christ regarded Exodus, as well as Genesis, as historical. Of course, in Genesis God is referred to more than once as the God of the three patriarchs, though perhaps they are not all mentioned there in a single sen-tence. Then, Christ says, "that which was spoken unto you by God." So it could not be a myth, according to the Lord. And again this passage proves that, in Christ's view, these patriarchs not only had a real existence on the earth, but had a real existence even in Christ's day, for "God is not the God of the dead, but of the living."

Note, too, how Christ refers to Abraham in his parable of the rich man and Lazarus, representing him as alive and fully conscious in heaven, called by the Jews Abraham's bosom.

Another Genetical reference is found in Matt. 10:15: "Verily I say unto you, it shall be more tolerable for the land of Sodom and Gomorrah in the day of judgment than for that city." Also Matt. 11:24; Luke 10:12. In this connection Luke 17:32 may be quoted: "Remember Lot's wife." Here we have Christ's own most solemn appeal to the people of his day to repent and accept His Gospel, upon the ground of the terrible fate that overtook the cities of the plains and the wife of Lot, as recorded in the nineteenth chapter of Genesis. If that story was a myth or fable—well, no more need be said. Thus we see that Jesus treats the outstanding events of the book of Genesis as historical. We have also noted that in one instance He appeals to an incident in the book of Exodus.

Let us now scrutinize Christ's allusions to Moses and his writings, and see whether He gives any color to the idea that Moses was mythical, or had only a small share in the production of the Pentateuch. Our first reference will be to Mark 12:26 (cf. Luke 20:37): "But as touching the dead that they are raised, have ye not read in the book of Moses, in the passage about the Bush, how God spake unto him, saying, I am the God," etc.? Here the reference is to Exodus 3:16. The negative critics say that Moses did not write the Pentateuch, including Exodus. But Jesus expressly calls Exodus the book of Moses. The issue seems to be squarely between the critics and Christ. Our Lord also treats the event as historical, while many of the critics regard it as merely legendary.

Our next reference is to Matt. 22:34-40, where Jesus told the questioning lawyer which were the greatest commandments—love to God and love to neighbor, adding: "On these two commandments the whole law hangeth, and the prophets." Now where in the Old Testament do we find

these passages? The second in Lev. 19:18; the first in
Deut. 6:5. That seems pretty strong endorsement of the
inspiration of those two books, especially in view of the
fact that He calls these two commandments the greatest
of all, and always insists on the keeping of them as essential to eternal life. Examine, next, John 3:14: "And as
Moses lifted up the serpent in the wilderness, so must the
Son of Man be lifted up; that whosoever believeth may
in Him have eternal life." Here is a reference to Numbers 21:8-9, giving Christ's sanction to this book of the
Pentateuch, and ascribing the lifting up of the brazen
serpent to Moses. Besides, here is Christ's positive admission of the miracle of healing that resulted from merely
looking at the suspended serpent. Unlike the rationalists,
Christ did not try to elide the miraculous element from the
Old Testament. The assertion of Samuel Davidson, "The
miracles recorded (in the Pentateuch) were the exaggerations of a later age," would hardly agree with the teaching of our Lord. We have now found Jesus making explicit reference to Genesis, Exodus, Leviticus and Numbers (as we shall also find in Deuteronomy, *ut infra*). At
the time of His temptation by Satan (Matt. 4:1-11) He
overcame the evil one by three quotations from the Old
Testament, all of them found in Deuteronomy, the last
book of the Pentateuch. (See Deut. 8:3; 6:16; 6:13.) In
each case He makes the solemn asseveration, "It is written," as if He were quoting from a divine authority that
even Satan would have to acknowledge. And it is a fact
that, according to the Gospel, these quotations from Deuteronomy did silence the devil, and cause him to relinquish
his enterprise of tempting the Son of God. Wonderful
that a myth or legend would have had such a crushing
effect upon the devil! One would have thought that he
would have gloated over Christ, and told Him that, in
the nineteenth and twentieth centuries, the critics would

prove the book of Deuteronomy to be only a ''pious fraud'' of Josiah's or Ezra's day! Note how decisive and sure Christ is about the inspiration of Deuteronomy: ''Get thee hence, Satan; for it is written, Thou shalt worship the Lord thy God, and Him only shalt thou serve.'' How does such language agree with the uncertainty of Sanday and some of the other critics, who say we cannot tell which parts of the Pentateuch are inspired and which are not?

Having seen that Christ puts His stamp of approval on all the books of the Pentateuch by quoting from them as authoritative, we must investigate His position relative to their Mosaic authorship. What does He teach? There is John 5:45-47: ''Think not that I will accuse you to the Father: there is one that accuseth you, even Moses, on whom ye have set your hope. For if ye believed Moses, ye would believe me; for he wrote of me. But if ye believe not his writings, how shall ye believe my words?'' He was rebuking the Jews, who misinterpreted Moses' writings and therefore did not see their inner prophetic character. What writings were regarded as the writings of Moses by the Jews—the very Scriptures on which they had set their hopes? They were none other than our present Pentateuch, which the Jews then, and for several centuries prior, believed was the composition of Moses. In this passage Christ takes it for granted that Moses wrote the Pentateuch, and even makes the remarkable statement that this writing would accuse the unbelieving Jews before God the Father. What absurdity this would be if the Pentateuch is made up of a number of unauthenticated documents, by whom written nobody knows, why written nobody knows, and when written nobody knows!

Another significant passage is Matt. 19:7-8: ''They say unto Him, Why then did Moses command to give a bill of divorcement, and to put her away? He saith unto them, Moses for your hardness of heart suffered you to put away

your wives; but from the beginning it hath not been so."
The reference is to Deut. 24: 1-4, which Christ attributes to
Moses. The same statement is registered in Mark 10:3.
Referring to Mark 12:18-27, we note that the Sadducees
said to Jesus: "Teacher, Moses wrote unto us, If a man's
brother die," etc. Jesus rebuked them in this way: "Is it
not for this cause that you err, because ye knew not the
Scriptures nor the power of God?" He admitted here
that Moses wrote Deuteronomy 25:5, and called it part of
"the Scriptures." We have already alluded to the 26th
verse of Mark 12: "Have ye not read in the Book of
Moses, in the passage about the bush," in which Jesus
calls Exodus the book of Moses. This is strengthened by
the parallel passage in Luke 20: 37, where Moses is again
mentioned in connection with the burning bush. It is most
significant that, in the parable of the rich man and Lazarus, Christ puts these words into the mouth of Abraham,
who was speaking to the rich man in torment: "They
have Moses and the prophets; let them hear them. . . . If
they hear not Moses and the prophets, neither will they
be persuaded, if one rise from the dead." As Jesus was
addressing this parable to the Jews, who regarded the
Pentateuch as the work of Moses, He must have meant
the same document, which He plainly teaches is of more
evidential and convincing value than the appearance of
one from the realm of the dead. No less striking was His
conversation with the two disciples on their way to Emmaus, after His resurrection (Luke 24:27): "And beginning from Moses and from all the prophets, He interpreted
to them in all the Scriptures the things concerning Himself." Afterwards they declared that their hearts burned
within them as He opened to them the Scriptures. Here
again the reference must be to the Pentateuch as the work
of Moses, which is sharply distinguished from the prophets.

Most significant is the passage in John 7:19: "Did not

Moses give you the law? And yet none of you doeth the law." Also verses 22, 23: "Moses hath given you circumcision (not that it is of Moses, but of the fathers); and on the Sabbath ye circumcise a man. If a man receive circumcision on the Sabbath that the law may not be broken, are ye wroth with me because I have made a man every whit whole on the Sabbath?" He asserts that Moses gave the law — Moses, remember, not some "great unknown." Moses also gave the Jews circumcision, referring to Lev. 12:3; and yet so accurate, so scrupulously true to the Old Testament history; He was, that He says parenthetically that circumcision was not really given by Moses, but that it came down to him from "the fathers." Now read Gen. 17:9-14, and you will see that Christ put His own divine seal upon the historicity of the covenant that God directly made with Abraham, when He commanded him to have every male circumcised. With our Lord there was no minimizing of "the divine element" in the Old Testament. Once when a leper was healed, Christ said to him: "See thou tell no man, but go, show thyself to the priest, and offer the gift that Moses commanded, for a testimony unto them." The Pentateuchal reference is to Lev. 13:49; 14:2ff. It would almost seem as if Jesus purposely meant to preclude the modern view that Moses had little or nothing to do with the production of the five books traditionally assigned to him.

And what was Christ's attitude toward the law as a whole, which He often called the law of Moses? Did He treat it as if it had come from God, and were an essential organism in the divine plan of redemption? Yes; He said (Matt. 5:17, 18): "Think not that I came to destroy the law or the prophets; I came not to destroy, but to fulfill. Verily I say unto you, Till heaven and earth pass away, one jot or one tittle shall in nowise pass from the law, till all be accomplished." In Luke 16:17 He puts it still more emphatically: "But it is easier for heaven and earth to pass away than for one tittle of the law to fail." Note Matt. 7:12: "All things therefore whatsoever ye would that men should do unto you, even so do ye also unto them; for this is the law and the prophets." When a certain lawyer came to Him and said, "Teacher, what shall I do to inherit eternal life?" Jesus answered, "What is written in the law? how readest thou?" Jesus had a remarkable habit of appealing to the law as the final authority. The lawyer than quoted two chief commandments from Deuteronomy and Leviticus, when Jesus made the following pregnant statement: "Thou hast answered right: this do and thou shalt live" (Luke 10:25-28). After His resurrection, in the solemn moments before His ascension to the right hand of God, as He was giving to the apostolic group His last commission, He said: "These are my words which I spake unto you, while I was yet with you, that all things must needs be fulfilled which are written in the law of Moses, and the prophets, and the Psalms concerning me" (Luke 24:44). Verse 45: "Then opened He their mind that they might understand the Scriptures." Can any one read such passages without realizing that our Savior accepted the Old Testament as the veritable Word of God? In one of His collisions with the angry Jews, He said (John 5:39): "Ye search the Scriptures, because ye think that in them ye have eternal life; and these are they which bear witness of me." Rebuking Peter in the garden of Gethsemane for using his sword, Jesus said (Matt. 26:53, 54): "Or thinkest thou that I cannot beseech my Father, and He shall even now send me more than twelve legions of angels? How then should the Scriptures be fulfilled that this must be?" In Mark 14:49 He said: "But this is done that the Scriptures might be fulfilled." On the cross He quoted from the twenty-seventh Psalm, when He cried: "My God, my God, why hast Thou forsaken Me?" Also in John 19:28: "After this Jesus, knowing that all things are now finished, that the Scriptures might be fulfilled, saith, I thirst." In this place the reference is evidently to Ps. 69:21. So intent was our dying Lord on fulfilling the Scriptures.

Let us examine Christ's testimony to other portions of the Old Testament which many of the critics have been dissecting and whose divine authority their views would practically invalidate. According to Luke, Jesus returned, after His baptism, to Nazareth, and went into the synagogue on the Sabbath. The prophecy of Isaiah was handed to Him, and He read from the fifty-first chapter. Then He said, "To-day hath this Scripture been fulfilled in your ears." Thus we have His witness to the book of Isaiah, which has been so much hacked to pieces by the more radical critics. In Matt. 13:14ff He quotes from Isa. 6:9, 10, where it is said, "By hearing, ye shall hear, and shall in nowise understand," etc. In Matt. 15:7ff. He quotes as authoritative Isa. 29:13: "This people honoreth me with their lips," etc. There is no hint in His reference of a *deutero* or conglomerate Isaiah. Jesus referred to both Elijah and Elisha in Luke 4:25-27 as historical personages, and also to Naaman, thus placing His endorsement on the historical character of First and Second Kings. He made allusion to Elijah in connection with John the Baptist. Also at the transfiguration scene He talked with both Moses and Elijah, and the subject of their conversation was His death at Jerusalem.

How numerous are His references to David! Again and again He accepted the title "Son of David" (Matt. 9:27; 15:22; 20:30; 21:9, 15; Mark 10:47; Luke 18:38). He justified David for eating the shew-bread (Matt. 12:3ff.; Mark 2:22ff.), an incident recorded in 1 Sam. 21:6, thus putting his stamp on another book of the Bible as properly historical. In the same passage He refers to Num. 28:9,

10, and quotes from Hosea 6:6, adding this book to the list which He treats as historical and authoritative. At Matt. 22:41-45 He not only admits that He is the son of David, but says: "How then doth David in the Spirit call Him Lord, saying, The Lord said unto my Lord," etc. What a crushing passage for the criticism of the pulverizing kind! The quotation is from Psalm 110:1, and Christ declares that David there wrote "in the Spirit." Yet many of the critics deny that any of the Psalms were written by David, but were composed during the exile and in the Maccabean time. They simply differ from Christ, that is all; but that is surely serious enough.

One of Christ's most telling references to the Old Testament is found at Matt. 21:42: "Jesus saith unto them, Did ye never read in the Scriptures, The stone which the builders rejected," etc.? The quotation is from Psalm 118:22. Another Psalm endorsed by our Lord as authoritative Scripture! Read Matt. 6:29 and Luke 12:27. Here Christ compares the lilies of the field to Solomon in all his glory, treating the great king as a real, not a mythical, character. At another place—Matt. 12:42; Luke 11:31—He refers to the visit of the queen of Sheba to Solomon, and then adds, "A greater than Solomon is here." Had Jesus known anything about the "assured results" of the critics of the present day, He would have trodden very lightly when He referred to Jonah, or, rather, would have avoided him altogether; but, surprising as it may seem, He referred to this runaway prophet with just as much assurance as He did to Moses, David, Solomon, Elijah, Elisha and Isaiah. His references are extremely significant (Matt. 12:39-41; 16:4; Luke 11:29, 30). In the first passage He even refers to the great *crux* of the critics, that is, the miracle of the sea-monster that swallowed Jonah, and He actually employs it as a precursor of His own resurrection. Then He bases another of his most vital teachings on the repentance of the Ninevites at the preaching of Jonah. Considering the importance, yea, the paramount nature, of the truths He desired to impress, it is inconsistent to think that He would have made such use of a merely fictitious or mythical character.

The book of Daniel has given the critics a vast deal of worriment, and they have handled it so ruthlessly that one conservative defender (Sir Robert Anderson), given a little too much to derision, has written a book entitled "Daniel in the Critics' Den." One of the critics—one, too, who desires to be regarded as evangelical—assigns the date of the book of Daniel to 164 B.C., and politely calls it "a romance." Such was not the view of Christ, who based one of His most solemn and urgent injunctions upon a prophecy contained in that book (Matt. 24:15-18): "When, therefore, ye see the abomination of desolation, which was spoken of through Daniel, the prophet, standing in the holy place," etc.

For a moment let us revert to Mark 7. After quoting from Isaiah, "This people honoreth me with their lips," etc., Jesus goes on to say: "Ye leave the commandment of God, and hold fast the tradition of men. And He said unto them, Full well do ye reject the commandment of God, that ye may keep your tradition; for Moses said, Honor thy father and thy mother," etc. Then He goes on to reprove them for saying "Corban," and adds this decisive statement, "making void the Word of God by your tradition." Now the references here are to Ex. 20:12; 21:17; Lev. 20:9, and Deut. 5:16, while the first sentence refers to Isa. 29:13. All of these Scriptures He calls "the commandment of God" and "the Word of God," and the Pentateuchal passages He attributes to Moses. At John 10:35 Jesus says in parenthesis, as if to make sure He would not be misunderstood: "And the Word of God cannot be broken."

So far as we are able at this time to pursue our study, we have examined our Lord's allusions to the Old Testament. Nowhere does He give any hint of a document theory, of a natural evolution of religious ideas, of an exilic and post-exilic origin of the Hexateuch, Psalms and prophecies, of literary forgery and pious imposture in the times of Josiah and Ezra; everywhere He treats the Old Testament Scriptures as the veritable Word of God and the ultimate authority. Strangely enough, Jesus *does not make a single reference to Josiah, Hilkiah, Nehemiah and Ezra*—the characters that bulk most largely in the estimation of the critics, and almost the only ones that they are willing to regard as really historical. We wish to make no appeal to fear, nor lay any embargo on scholarship and investigation; but we do desire to make plain this one thing—that the critics of the negative and meditating schools should be fully conscious of the seriousness of their undertaking when they seek to eliminate or minimize the divine element in the Old Testament and attribute it to human origins. On the seriousness of the situation we do not stand alone. We quote from Dr. Adolph Saphir, whose admirable and uplifting book, "The Divine Unity of Scripture," lies before us:

"It is most important that all Christians should be fully convinced in their own minds that the testimony which Jesus bears concerning Moses and the prophets is decisive. It leaves not a vestige of doubt in the mind of any one who acknowledges that Jesus is the Son of God. It gives us a perfect and incontrovertible conviction that the Scriptures of the Old Testament are the Word of God. Many doubts, many objections, have been brought against this view, and I can only remind you in a few words of the tactics of the rationalists who do not believe in the divinity of Christ, who attempt to show that our Savior accommodated Himself to the prejudices of His

contemporaries, and that, although He Himself did not
believe in the inspiration of the Old Testament, or in the
existence of Satan, or in those who were possessed of devils
as really possessed by them; still, adapting Himself to the
ignorance and weakness of the Jews, and wishing to lead
them, as it were, into a higher and nobler sphere of
thought, He argued with them from the things which they
admitted. Thus a course of action is suggested unworthy
of the character of an honest man, unworthy of the dignity
of a prophet, blasphemous as applied to Jesus, who is God
over all blessed forever. Jesus, who never for a moment
accommodated Himself to the prejudices of the Pharisees
and Scribes; who, with all the energy of His character,
protested against the traditions of the elders; who, not
merely in secret, but in the presence of all the people,
declared that every plant which His Heavenly Father
had not planted, however venerable and pious it might
seem, must be rooted up—how could He for a single
moment teach what He knew to be untrue?'' (pp. 52
and 53.)

Worth pondering is a quotation from the acute little
book of Dr. James G. Brookes, ''God Spake All These
Words,'' pp. 111, 112: ''If the manner in which the
writers of the New Testament speak of the Old is a proof
of its supernatural origin and inerrant inspiration, the
evidence is greatly strengthened by the reverence our
Lord Jesus Christ paid to the Book known as the Scriptures. He never gave a hint that they contain 'errors,'
'mistakes,' 'myths,' 'legends,' 'contradicitions,' or 'for-
geries,' and He never discovered that some of the books
were not written by the men whose names they bear. To
Him it is evident that 'God spake all these words.' ''
Referring to the use Christ made of the Scriptures in the
temptation after His baptism, Dr. Brookes adds: ''It is
a striking fact that the writings from which our Lord

quotes as His sufficient panoply are taken from the book of Deuteronomy, as if He would shield it from the infamous accusation of Higher Criticism, which pronounces it a forgery. 'Then the devil leaveth Him, and, behold, angels came and ministered unto Him.' He had honored the Word, and angels honored Him.''

Dr. John Smith, of Edinburgh, has written a scholarly and cogently reasoned book, entitled ''The Integrity of Scripture,'' in which he deals exclusively with the critical hypotheses. We have space for only a brief quotation from his work (pp. 107, 108): ''The point is: Did Jesus fundamentally misconceive the character of the Old Testament? Did He take for a creative revelation what was a slow and ordinary human growth? Did He take for prophetic insight of the patriarch Abraham words which some imaginative writer put into the mouth of a geographic myth, whom he first made a historical character? Did He take, for authoritative laws given by Moses, late codifications of Jewish common law wrought up with audacious fictions? Did the idea of a divine norm in the law which would yet receive an ideal fulfillment, and that other of the Scriptures governed in all its parts by a foreseeing mind, and pointing in all parts to Himself—did all that live as only a dream and illusion in His own mind? If these things were so; if all that is involved in these admissions were true; if we could for a moment believe them true—then what disparagement would fall on the judgment and insight of the Son of God! If He blundered regarding the preparatory dispensation—our pen trembles to write the words—may He not have misjudged regarding the platform on which He Himself stood?''

These are not the words of one who is seeking to frighten his protagonists, but of one who has calmly, critically and judicially gone over the whole question, has come to assured conclusions, and therefore feels a solemn

responsibility resting upon him to point out the seriousness of the positions taken by the critics.

When we started out in this study we meant to collate
the full testimony of the New Testament to the Old, but
our thesis has perhaps already grown to too great a length.
Some other time we may take up the subject again, and
point out the deference shown by the evangelists and
apostles to the Old Testament. Suffice it to say that, according to the investigations of Dr. James G. Brookes,
the New Testament quotes from the Old 320 times, besides
alluding to it almost as often. "Genesis is quoted 19 times,
and the quotations appear in nine New Testament books;
Exodus is quoted 24 times, and the quotations appear in
12 New Testament books; Leviticus is quoted 12 times,
and the quotations appear in nine New Testament books;
Numbers is quoted twice, besides many plain allusions to
its incidents as historically true, for example, 1 Cor. 10:
6-10, and these appear in nine New Testament books;
Deuteronomy is quoted 26 times, and these appear in 13
New Testament books; Isaiah is quoted 50 times in 11
New Testament books; Proverbs six times in six New
Testament books; Zachariah six times in four New Testament books; and other books of the Old Testament are
quoted as from God."

After the foregoing was written, we had the opportunity
of reading Dr. Franklin Johnson's scholarly book, entitled "The Quotations of the New Testament from the
Old," and we cannot refrain from calling special attention
to this work. For minute and thorough-going scholarship
it is equal to anything that has been published on this
subject, and is a complete refutation of the critics who
are so given over to finding occasions of stumbling in the
Bible. Here are noted the quotations that were taken from
the Hebrew Bible and the Septuagint, and in each case
the reason is given, and in each case, too, it is shown that

the New Testament writer or speaker was justified in his manner of quotation. Very many examples are given from classical and modern literature to show that other writers have made quotations and citations in precisely the same way as the New Testament writers did, showing that the Bible is constructed on the same literarry principles as are all the great literatures of the world. Dr. Johnson also upholds the inspiration and divine authority of the Scriptures. He answers most effectively the criticisms of Kuenen, Wellhausen and Toy.

This excellent orthodox work proves two things very clearly: 1. That the criticism of the pulverizers can be successfully answered; 2. That not all the scholarship of the day has gone over to the side of the liberalistic and pruning Biblical criticism.

CHAPTER X

VERY often to-day we hear the cry, "Back to Christ." When by this demand is meant that we should go back to the spirit and teaching of Christ and His inspired apostles in the entire New Testament, so that we may imbibe and practice them more and more, all of us will gladly assent. Every true reformation in the history of the Christian Church has been achieved by going back to the pure teachings of the New Testament.

However, the phrase, "Back to Christ," as it is currently used by a certain class of theologians, is not employed in the above sense. By some it means a disparagement, if not a positive rejection, of all the creeds of the Church, not excepting those that are called ecumenical. It is not our purpose in this article to deal with this specious use of the expression; therefore we shall stop merely to say that the theologian who ignores all the Christian thinking of the past, and especially that which has been crystalized in the great confessions of the Church at the most strategic epochs in the history of the Christian faith, surely does not prove himself a well-balanced and judicial thinker, but rather one who is surfeited with the sense of his own importance and ability; one who "thinks more highly of himself than he ought to think." As well might the botanist or geologist of to-day declare that he would go to the plants and rocks for himself, and would disregard all that previous thinkers and investigators had accomplished in those special sciences. While we cannot stop to dilate on this attitude of mind toward the past, yet we must add that, if you will follow the statements of the liberalist of the foregoing type, you will find, as a rule, that he has not deeply and thoroughly studied the theology of the creeds he belittles, nor compared them diligently with the teachings of Scripture.* Moreover, you will almost always discover ere long that he cherishes lax views of the inspiration of the Bible.

A second class of writers—and with these we shall deal in this chapter—whose slogan is, "Back to Christ," mean to set Christ's teachings as found in the gospels, especially the synoptics, in opposition to the teachings of His apostles in the Acts and the Epistles. That is, they mean, "Let us get back to Christ from Paul and the rest of the apostles." These men tell us that all of the New Testament that follows the gospels is the result of reflection and speculation after Christ's resurrection and ascension. Therefore much of it is merely human; it belongs to a theologizing period; it cannot therefore be placed on a par with the simple teaching of Jesus in the gospels, particularly the synoptics. Several members of the faculty of the Divinity School of the University of Chicago have been advocates of this view; so much so, indeed, that Dr. William Cleaver Wilkinson has come out in a pungent and incisive book against them—a book that, barring a little too much rhetoric, is to be commended as a most crushing argument against the specious position taken by the liberalists. The title of his book is, "Paul and the Revolt Against Him." We shall not follow Dr. Wilkinson in his

* For powerful defenses of the ecumenical creeds on the specified doctrines we would refer the reader to the following works: Canon GORE: "The Incarnation of the Son of the Son of God"; H. H. RELTON: "A Study in Christology"; L. G. MYLNE: "The Holy Trinity"; O. C. QUICK: "Modern Philosophy and the Incarnation." For a more general vindication of the orthodox credal doctrines, see Mr. QUICK's stimulating book, "Essays in Orthodoxy."

masterly arguments—though that would be well worth while—but shall look at the question as it appears to us.

Our main proposition is that Christ's teachings were not completed in the gospels; that He purposely left many things of vital importance to be revealed by Him through the Holy Spirit to His apostles, whom He inspired and equipped for this very purpose; and therefore the teachings in the Acts, the Epistles and the Revelation are just as much His own teachings and just as authoritative as are the teachings recorded in the gospels. Let us see whether this is not the clear doctrine taught in the New Testament.

First, what do the synoptics themselves teach, or, rather, what does Jesus teach in them? In Matt. 28:18-20 we read: "And Jesus came unto them and spake unto them, saying, All authority hath been given unto me in heaven and on earth. Go ye, *therefore,* and make disciples of all the nations, baptizing them in the name of the Father and of the Son and of the Holy Spirit; teaching them to observe all things whatsoever I commanded you: and, lo, I am with you alway, even unto the end of the world." What is the plain doctrine of this great commission? Note the logical force of the "therefore" which we have italicized. Because Christ had received all authority, *therefore* He commissioned His apostles go forth and teach His doctrines. And if they actually taught by His authority, as He bade them, would not their teaching be *His* teaching, and would it not be just as authoritative as that which fell from His lips during His humiliation? And what does He command them to teach? Their own speculations? No, indeed! but "all things whatsoever I have commanded you." Then He graciously promises that He will be with them alway. And why? Surely for the purpose of inspiring them and making them strong and inerrant in their proclamation. Now if the apostles obeyed His commission, they must have taught nothing contrary to His instructions to them during His earthly ministry. And where do we have the record of what they did and taught under this divine influence? Only in the Acts, the Epistles, and the Revelation.

Our next citation is Mark 16:15, 16: "And He said unto them, Go ye into all the world, and preach the gospel to the whole creation. He that believeth and is baptized shall be saved; he that disbelieveth shall be condemned." Here again Jesus indicates that the preaching of the apostles was to be authoritative, even on a par with His own preaching, for the salvation of those who heard the message was conditioned on their acceptance of it. Christ never made a stronger claim than that for His own personal teaching during His earthly ministry. This contention is further emphasized by the concluding verses of the same gospel: "So then the Lord Jesus, after He had spoken unto them, was received up into heaven, and sat down at the right hand of God. And they went forth and preached everywhere, *the Lord working with them,* and *confirming the word* by the signs that followed. Amen." Does not that statement make the preaching of the apostles the authorized preaching of the Lord Jesus Himself?

The following is Luke's statement of the last commission (24:44-48): "And He said unto them, These are my words which I spake unto you, while I was yet with you, that all things must needs be fulfilled, which are written in the law of Moses, and the prophets, and the Psalms concerning me. Then opened He their mind that they might understand the Scriptures. . . . Ye are witnesses of these things. And behold, I send forth the promise of my Father upon you: but tarry ye in the city until ye be clothed with power from on high." Here even the authority of the Father is added to that of Christ, enduing the apostles. This promise was made good on the day of Pentecost.

Next note the teaching of Christ in the gospel according to St. John; it will be seen to be quite as relevant. How significant are all Christ's promises of the Holy Spirit to His apostles! And He promised not only the Spirit, but also His own presence and that of the Father. John 14:15-18: "If ye love me, ye will keep my commandments. And I will pray the Father, and He shall give you another Comforter, that He may be with you forever, even the Spirit of truth; whom the world cannot receive, for it beholdeth Him not, neither knoweth Him; ye know Him, for He abideth with you and shall be in you. I will not leave you desolate; I will come to you." No less significant is John 14:25, 26: "These things have I spoken unto you while yet abiding with you; but the Comforter, even the Holy Spirit, whom the Father will send in my name, He shall teach you all things, and bring to your remembrance all that I said unto you." From this we may conclude that, if Christ afterward made good His promise, the Holy Spirit brought back to the memory of the apostles many of Christ's teachings that they would have otherwise forgotten. Would not this teaching, thus inerrantly recalled to their remembrance by the Holy Spirit, be in deed and in truth the real teaching of Christ Himself, the very doctrine that fell from His own lips? In John 15:26 the Holy Spirit is again called the "Spirit of truth," and the statement is added that He will proceed "from the Father," and "He shall bear witness of me." The only question is, Are we willing to accept the subsequent witness of the Holy Ghost as true? Observe how often Jesus calls the Holy Ghost "the Spirit of *truth*."

A decisive passage for the evangelical believer is John 16:12-15: "I have many things to say unto you, but ye cannot bear them now. Howbeit, when He, the Spirit of truth is come, He will guide you into all truth; for He shall not speak from Himself; but what things soever He shall hear, these shall He speak: and He shall declare unto you the things that are to come. He shall glorify me, for He shall take of mine and declare it unto you. All things whatsoever the Father hath are mine: therefore I said, He shall take of mine and declare it unto you." This sublime passage proves that Jesus purposely withheld certain truths from His apostles until they were endued and enlightened by the Holy Spirit so that they could bear them. Thus our Lord Himself teaches that He had no intention of completing His doctrines while He was here in His earthly state, but expressly left many things for subsequent revelation. Where do we have this supplemental teaching if not in the writings of the apostles? If we do not have them there, we do not have them at all; and that would empty Christ's promise of all content and leave it unfulfilled. Therefore to discredit the doctrines of the apostles is to discredit Christ's own teaching and promise. How can the liberalists avoid the fatal conclusion?

John 17 ought to be read in full. It records our Redeemer's intercessory prayer for His apostles. Again and again He prays for them. Verse 15: "I pray not that thou shouldest take them from the world, but that thou shouldest keep them from the evil one." How vital are verses 17-21: "Sanctify them in thy truth; thy word is truth. As thou didst send me into the world, even so sent I them into the world. And for their sakes I sanctify myself, that they themselves also may be sanctified in truth. Neither for these only do I pray, but for them also that believe on me through their word; that they may all be one; even as thou, Father, art in me and I in thee, that they also may be in us; that the world may believe that thou didst send me." If this does not mean a special enduement and inspiration of our Lord's apostles, the words are meaningless.

So much, then, for Christ's own teaching in the gospels. When and where did His gracious promises receive their fulfillment? We turn to the Acts of the Apostles, and find that, if we take the simple New Testament record just as it is, without prejudice or subjective theories, the whole teaching is beautifully consistent and self-interpreting. In Acts 1:1, 2 we read: "The former treatise I made, O Theophilus, concerning all that Jesus *began* both to *do* and to *teach,* until the day in which He was received up, after that He had given commandment through the Holy Spirit unto the apostles whom He had chosen." This agrees perfectly with John 16:12-15, where Jesus said, "I have many things to say unto you, but ye cannot bear them now"; therefore Luke says that Jesus, during His earthly life, simply "began" to do and to teach— that is, He did not complete His work or His doctrine, but laid down only the fundamental principles, the essential germs of truth, and then inspired His holy apostles to conserve and develop them. Then in the subsequent verses (4, 5, 8) He bids them tarry at Jerusalem, promises them the baptism of the Holy Spirit, the enduement of power, and adds: "Ye shall be my witnesses both in Jerusalem, and in all Judea and Samaria, and unto the uttermost part of the earth." Now the question is whether Jesus fulfilled His promise to be with them (Matt 28:20), and to guide them by His Spirit into all truth (John 16:13). The apostles returned to Jerusalem, and continued in prayer in the sacred "upper room." It being necessary to select an apostle to fill the place of Judas, the company prayed thus: "Thou, Lord, who knowest the hearts of all men, show of these two the one whom thou hast chosen," etc.; and in answer to their prayer, the lot fell upon Matthias. From this we see that Jesus began at once to redeem His promise of divine guidance.

Acts 2 recites the wonderful event of Pentecost, when the promise of Christ was literally fulfilled—the Holy Spirit was given and the apostles were baptized with power. Now how does Peter, who was the chief spokesman on that occasion, account for the outpouring of the Holy Spirit? We find it in Acts 2:32, 33: "This Jesus did God raise up, whereof we are witnesses. Being therefore by the right hand of God exalted, and having received of the Father the promise of the Holy Spirit, *He* hath poured forth *this* which ye *see* and *hear.*" The antecedent of "He" is Christ, and therefore it was Christ Himself who poured out the Holy Spirit on that day. Would not the work of the glorified and exalted Christ, performed through the Holy Spirit, be just as authoritative as what He did and said during His kenosis and humiliation?

A careful reading of the book of Acts will convince any one that the apostles and their chosen helpers always spoke and acted as if they were in the presence of Christ and were guided by the Holy Spirit. For instance, Peter disclaimed having healed the lame man by his own power, but declared that the miracle had taken place through faith in the name of Jesus. When Stephen had concluded his wonderful address, he saw heaven opened and the Son of Man *standing* on the right hand of God—not sitting, for He was then in the attitude of one who had risen to help and welcome His faithful witness. Paul, as well as the rest of the apostles, claims the same enduement directly from the exalted Jesus.

In the opening verses of both of his epistles Peter calls himself "an apostle of Jesus Christ," and throughout he speaks in a tone of authority that betokens the consciousness of divine direction. In 2 Pet. 3:1, 2 he says: "This is now, beloved, the second epistle that I write unto you;

and in both of them I stir up your sincere mind by putting you in remembrance; that ye should remember the words which were spoken before by the holy prophets, and the commandment of the Lord and Savior through your apostles"; a passage that invests the apostles with an authority equal to that of the prophets. The apostle John indicates that he writes by divine authority, or at least by positive and certain knowledge (see 1 John 1:1-5). In the Apocalypse he claims to have direct communion with the exalted Redeemer and to receive dictation from Him as to what he shall write to the seven churches.

It might be said that the apostle Paul is almost *persona non grata* to the liberalizing theologians. They censure him for having "theologized" about Christ, for having developed a system of theology by means of his speculations. Thus they think he has interjected confusion into the simplicity of Christ's teachings. He has added to it a well-wrought-out theology of the person of Christ, of the vicarious atonement, of justification by faith alone, salvation by grace, the resurrection of the body, and a good many other doctrines. Such a determinate doctrinal system the liberalists do not like. A good many of these doctrines their rationalistic temper cannot abide. So they look back to the gospels, and do not find these doctrines so fully developed there; from which they leap to the conclusion that Paul was a speculative theologian, a dogmatician, who unfolded a system that finds no warrant in Christ's teaching. Little wonder that these men do not relish the Pauline theology. They have almost as little regard for him as they have for the definite theology of the Nicene and Athanasian Creeds. A theology of tenuity is much more to their liking.

But before we consent to have Paul discredited and cast overboard, we would better look into the status of his case. Of course, if we choose to throw away the evan-

gelical records, or manipulate them according to preconceived notions, neither Paul nor Christ can say an authoritative word for us. However, it is not our purpose to go
into the question of the criticism of the gospels and epistles, but simply to show what they teach regarding Paul's
relation to Christ. There will be an advantage in this
method, for if we can make our contention good, it will
show that the quarrel of the liberalists is with the evangelical records, not with orthodox theologians.

The New Testament witness is clear that Paul received
his commission as an apostle directly from the exalted
Christ. Luke tells the story of Paul's conversion in Acts
9:1-19; Paul tells it himself in Acts 22:3-21, and again
in Acts 26:9-23. He lays claim to the apostleship—Rom.
1:4, 5: "Even Jesus Christ, through whom we received
grace and apostleship"; 1 Cor. 9:2: "If to others I am not
an apostle, yet at least I am to you; for the seal of mine
apostleship are ye in the Lord"; Gal. 2:8: "For He that
wrought for Peter unto the apostleship of the circumcision wrought for me also unto the Gentiles." In almost,
if not quite, all of his epistles he calls himself an apostle,
e. g., Rom. 1:1, 1 Cor. 1:1, Gal. 1:1, and so on with the
rest. He contends earnestly for his apostleship against all
gainsayers. 1 Cor. 9:1: "Am I not free? am I not an
apostle? have I not seen Jesus our Lord? are not ye my
work in the Lord?" 2 Cor. 12:11, 12: "For in nothing
was I behind the very chiefest apostles, though I am nothing. Truly the signs of an apostle were wrought among
you in all patience, by signs and wonders and mighty
works." Rom. 11:13: "Inasmuch then as I am an apostle
of Gentiles, I glorify my ministry." He contends that he
received his call from God (Gal. 1:15-17). It was God
who had "separated him," even from his mother's womb,
to "reveal His Son in" him, that he might "preach Him
among the Gentiles." Thus called, he says: "Straightway

I conferred not with flesh and blood, neither went I up to Jerusalem to them that were apostles before me.'' He tells plainly his authority for the gospel (Gal. 1:11, 12): "For I make known to you, brethren, as touching the gospel which was preached by me, that it is not after man. For neither did I receive it from man, nor was I taught it, but it came to me through revelation of Jesus Christ.'' He bears similar testimony in 1 Cor. 11:23: "For I received of the Lord that which also I delivered unto you," etc. He asserts that he was "called to be an apostle of Jesus Christ through the will of God.'' He claims to have the Spirit of God (1 Cor. 7:40). Even if an angel from heaven should come to preach another gospel, Paul pronounces him anathema (Gal. 1:8). Another of his claims was that Christ lived in him (Gal. 2:20); also that the love of Christ constrained him (2 Cor. 5:14).

Now the argument stands thus: Was Paul either an imposter or a fanatic? There is no internal nor external proof that he was either—none whatever; on the contrary, every circumstance proves that he was both sincere and well-balanced; that he spoke forth "the words of truth and soberness" (Acts 26:25). Then he must have spoken the sober truth when he contended that he had received his call and commission directly from the glorified Christ, who met him on the way to Damascus, and ever afterward was present with him. Now, if he received the vocation to the apostleship from the glorified Christ, we beg to know why such a call would not be just as authoritative as it would have been had he received it from the Master in the days of His humiliation? And if Christ's promise that the Holy Spirit would lead His apostles into all needed truth was fulfilled by our Lord (and this promise surely would pertain to the greatest of all His apostles), we fail to see why the doctrines of Paul would not be the veritable doctrines of our divine Lord and Saviour. Does

Christ have less authority in His glorified state than He had during the *kenosis?* In the days of His humiliation He did not set up the claim of having all authority in heaven and on earth; it was only after His resurrection and just before His ascension that He made this claim. Moreover, it is a strange mode of interpretation which attributes more authority to Christ's words while He was here on earth than to the inspiration of His Spirit after He had ascended to the right hand of Omnipotence. While Christ was here in the earthly state He did not confer great power on His apostles; indeed, they were a weak company of men; one of them denied Him; all of them forsook Him and fled; they could scarcely be convinced of His resurrection from the dead; they were full of doubts and fears. Only after they had seen Him alive a number of times, and had witnessed His ascension into the heavens, were their doubts allayed; only when the exalted Christ had poured His Spirit upon them, did the last vestige of doubt and timidity disappear; only then were they clothed with a superhuman power that made them steadfast in all danger and trial. Thus endued, they were able to do even greater works than their Lord had done in the days of His self-limitation (John 14:12).

And, by the way, it will be worth while to pause a moment to examine the passage last cited, as it will support our present view. Here Jesus said: "Verily, verily, I say unto you, he that believeth in me, the works that I do shall he do also; and greater works than these shall he do." And why? "Because I go to the Father; and whatsoever ye shall ask in my name, that will I do, that the Father may be glorified in the Son." Note that the very reason assigned for the greater ability of believers is that Christ will ascend to the Father to be clothed with divine power, and thus enabled to do all that His disciples may ask in His name. Why then was not Paul's vocation as valid and authoritative as that of the rest of the apostles? Why, too, were not the post-ascension commissions and enduements of the whole apostolic college completely authoritative?

If it should be said that Paul never met Christ personally while He was here on earth, and never heard any of His instructions from His own lips, our reply is, If his own story of his conversion on the Damascus road is true, he met the *ascended* and *glorified* Christ, and received his apostolic authority from *Him.* This would more than compensate for his failing to know Christ "according to the flesh."

It should be remembered that some of Paul's letters were written before the gospels were composed. It is not likely that he had any of our present gospels before him when he wrote these letters. His sources of information relative to Christ must, therefore, have been just as reliable as those of Mark and Luke. It is strange, therefore, that some of the liberalists, who regard the gospels of Mark and Luke as authoritative for Christ's teaching, should in the same breath discredit Paul's teaching. What were Paul's sources? First, the Old Testament prophecies, to which he had the same access as the evangelists; second, the reports of the immediate disciples of Christ; third, direct revelations from the exalted Messiah. All of these combined would make Paul an authority for Christ, and just as much of an authority, indeed, as the writers of the gospels, whether apostles or only disciples.

It may be asked how it occurs that Paul carries the doctrines of salvation so much further than do the gospels; that he presents a fuller doctrine of grace, faith, justification, atonement, and of the divine-human person of our Lord Jesus Christ. In reply we would say, we have studied the writings of Paul for many years, and are convinced from the internal evidences that they are more than merely human compositions; that such depth and elevation of thought are beyond unaided human acumen; that, therefore, the only adequate explanation is that which Paul himself assigns, namely, that he received his vocation from God in Christ, and wrote under the inspiration of the Holy Spirit. Indeed, if we did not have the teachings of the apostles and the inspired history of their works after the ascension of Christ, we should have a very meager and indeterminate body of doctrines, and the way of salvation itself would be obscure. However, with the completed revelation, the way of life is made plain even for wayfaring men, and we also have a sufficiently full and definite body of doctrine to satisfy those who are interested in scientific theology.

Truly enough, all the precious doctrines of our religion are found in seminal form in the gospels; but how nobly Jesus led His apostles by His inspiring Spirit to develop those doctrines! Take the doctrine of Christ's atoning sacrifice; if we did not have the inspired development by Paul and Peter and John (Rom. 3:25,26, 1 Pet. 3:18, 1 John 2:1, 2), we should have a meager and unsatisfying idea of the meaning of Christ's passion and death. With the teaching of the whole Bible before us, however, we are able to formulate a doctrine of atonement that satisfies the heart, wins the affections, and fulfills all the ethical demands of the enlightened intellect and conscience. The same is true of Christology: the synoptics set Christ forth as the Son of Man; John's gospel exhibits Him as the eternal Logos and the Son of God; while Paul, Peter and John, besides portraying Him in His humiliation, also depict Him in His exaltation at the right hand of power and glory, where He is filled with all the fullness of God. How meager would be our doctrine of Pneumatology if the Acts and the Epistles had never been written! Without Paul our conceptions of grace and faith would be so defective that we doubt whether the doctrine of salvation would have endured throughout the centuries. Christ taught a very meager Ecclesiology; only twice in the gospels does He mention the Church (Matt. 16:18 and 18:17). Can any one believe that this is all He ever meant to teach respecting that divinely instituted organization of which He Himself declares that "the gates of hell shall not prevail against it?" And where do we find the doctrine and mission of the Church developed and clearly set forth? In the Acts, the Epistles and the Revelation. As to the last things—Eschatology—we need all the invigorating teaching of Paul, Peter and John in their epistles and the Revelation, to make the future life sufficiently attractive to be a real incentive for following Christ in times of great tribulation.

While we desire to be generous, yet the truth compels us to say that, whenever you find a theologian who repudiates the development of the doctrine by Paul, Peter and John and the history of the Church recited by Luke in the Acts, all you need to do is to push him to define his doctrinal system, and you will find that it is very misty and indeterminate; that he does not accept the orthodox and confessional doctrines of the Trinity, the person of Christ, the substitutional atonement, justification by faith alone and salvation *sola gratia;* while on the doctrine of Biblical inspiration he is likely to be far off to one side. Many of the liberalistic theologians do not accept even the synoptic gospels in their entirety, but slice away such portions as do not comport with their critical theories and doctrinal preconceptions.

Another matter is worthy of comment. Some investigators make a mistake, we think, in their efforts to work out a complete system of Christian doctrine and ethics from the gospels alone. If Jesus had meant to complete His system of redemptive truth during His earthly life, such efforts might succeed; but we know from His own express statements that He simply aimed to lay the foundation in teaching, example and atonement, and then, after His ascension and glorification, endue His apostles with the Holy Spirit, who should direct them in erecting the superstructure of truth and salvation. This is evident from His last commissions, from His promise of the Spirit who would lead His apostles into all truth and endue them with power, from the actual history of the Church after our Lord's ascension, and from the many truths added to the gospels by the apostles themselves under the inspiration of the Holy Spirit. Therefore, it is narrow and one-sided to try to work out a complete theology and ethic from the gospels alone. It is not fair to Christ Himself who told His apostles expressly that the Holy Spirit would lead them into further truth. An excellent writer (evangelical, too, as far as we can judge) has, we think, made this mistake in a recent book dealing with the ethics and social teaching of Christ. By a somewhat labored effort he seems to make out his case— that is, he proves that the teachings of Christ in the gospels are the real solvent of all ethical and social problems. However, how much easier would have been his task, and how much clearer a light he might have thrown upon life's problems, if he had used the whole New Testament! Let us illustrate our viewpoint. If you were to consider Christ's teaching in the gospels alone as to the treatment of the poor, there would be danger of pauperizing many people, and encouraging in them a spirit of dependence; but co-ordinate it with Paul's teaching (which is also Christ's teaching, for Paul was inspired), and you will see how every danger is avoided: "If any man will not work, neither shall he eat" (2 Thess. 3:10); "For each man shall bear his own burden" (Gal. 6:5). Again, observe how Paul completes and balances the teachings of the gospels regarding the relations of masters and servants, husbands and wives, parents and children. Yes, we need the whole New Testament—the whole Bible, indeed—to give us a complete and satisfying conception of doctrine, ethics and practical Christian living.

In the interests of evangelical truth, it is time to call a halt to the liberalistic effort to "rob Paul to pay Christ," as some one has tersely put it; for Paul, having received his commission from the exalted Christ and being endued with His Spirit, was in every way fully as competent to represent His Lord as were Mark and Luke and even Matthew and John. If we are to know the whole teaching of Jesus, we must study the whole New Testament; yes, and the Old Testament as well; for Christ was the inspiring personality even in the preparatory dispensation; such is the declaration of an inspired apostle (1 Pet. 1:10, 11): "Concerning which salvation the prophets sought and searched diligently, who prophesied of the grace which should come unto you; searching what time or what manner of time *the Spirit of Christ which was in them* did point unto, when it testified beforehand the sufferings of Christ, and the glories which should follow them." Thus the whole Bible is an organism, a divine unity; all inspired by the same Spirit of our Lord and Redeemer; and in order to formulate a complete and satisfying theology, a complete and satisfying system of ethics, a complete and satisfying scheme of redeeming grace through Christ, we must accept the hallowed teaching of the whole sacred Volume.

CHAPTER XI

THE BIBLE A BOOK OF RELIGION—AND MORE

At a recent convention we listened to a rather striking
address by a professor in a theological seminary. He said
many good things, some of them in an original way. However, he said some things that raised question-marks in our
mind. Were they as careful, exact and discriminating as
they should have been? Did he say all he meant to imply,
or was there at least some "camouflage" in his remarks?
There seemed to us to be a disposition to *hint* at things
rather than to speak them right out with entire frankness.
He evidently did not want to go too far, so that, if you
should interrogate him, he could easily beat a retreat and
exclaim, deprecatingly: "Oh! I did not mean to imply
the conclusions you have drawn from my remarks. You
must not be too ready to make inferences. Pray do not
be a heresy hunter!"

You see how it is, reader. The obscurantist always
knows just about how far to go to keep from committing
himself. If you try to corner him, and ask him to say
precisely what he means, he will warn you not to appoint
yourself a guardian over other people's theology. But he
will always do one of two things—either stir up more dust
to cloud the issue, or else quickly declare that he is "perfectly evangelical," and that you mistook his meaning.
But we think it better, braver and honester not to make
any dark hints, and thus make room for inferences, mistaken or otherwise, but to say frankly just what you be-

lieve and what you do not believe. Oh, this thing of having "something up your sleeve" which you cannot bring out into the open—how we dislike it!

But to come to the point. Our speaker declared over and over and over again that "the Bible is a book of religion, not of physical science." More than once he made a statement something like this: "If I want to know something about religion, I go to the Bible. If I want to know something about science, I go to a text-book on astronomy, geology, biology or physics." Then he used an illustration: "Here is my watch," holding out a fine gold timekeeper; "if I want to know the time, I look at *it;* but if I want to know what the temperature is, I do not look at my watch; I consult a thermometer." Over and over he rang the changes on his illustration, which he evidently took to be very apt. At one point he said that, when the young student begins to study astronomy, he questions the miracle of the sun and moon standing still for Joshua; and then the speaker dropped the matter without any attempt at an explanation. Why did he suggest the difficulty at all? * Our orator also made the assertion that "the Bible was not intended to teach history, but religion only."

Now-a-days it behooves defenders of the faith to examine and analyze every statement. So many assertions are made that do not say precisely what is meant, but that carry a dangerous implication. So let us look judicially at this statement that "the Bible was not intended to teach science." First, who has ever held that such was its main purpose? Where is the statement made in any of our evangelical books and periodicals that the Bible was written primarily to teach science? We cannot remember that,

* By the way, not to do as the speaker did, we refer the reader to Dr. Robert Dick Wilson's fine article on this subject—that is, the above-named miracle—in the January, 1918, number of *The Princeton Theological Review.*

in all the multitude of writings we have examined, we
have ever seen the asseveration made that the Bible was
written to teach science. So why do some men to-day
want to lay such a tremendous emphasis on the statement.
Why emphasize a platitude? Why put such an *ictus* on a
truth that no one has ever denied? There is nothing new
or original about the statement. It does not even have
the merit of being a smart epigram, and it throws no light
on the problems of the Bible.

Therefore we must know what is the ulterior motive in
reiterating such a commonplace statement. Is there some
"camouflage" about it, or is there not? Is not this what
is meant by the repeaters of the saying, "The Bible was
not intended to teach science"? They mean a *therefore,*
and this is what it is: "Since the Bible was not intended
to teach science, *therefore,* when it touches on any of the
data of science, it may be greatly in error, but that will
not affect its religious teaching." But what does that sig-
nify? That God gave to mankind an inerrant religious
revelation, and then put it into a book full of scientific
errors and crudities! Not only so, but its history is also
unreliable. What then? Well, by means of your reason you must go through the Bible and disengage and
disentangle its religious teaching from its multitude of
historical and scientific blunders. Biblical astronomy and
cosmogony are away "off," say the critics—but its spiritual teaching, that is reliable.

How marvelous is the reasoning of these rationalists!
It amounts simply to this, that God gave to mankind a religious revelation, and embroidered and inlaid it with
multitudinous errors; also that he separated religion from
the stream of history, from the facts of the physical cosmos, and kept it far up in the air somewhere until these
recent times of science and Biblical criticism, when He
has at last consented to let it come down to the earth and

find "a local habitation and a name." Can you and I believe that our holy and practical religion is a quixotic windmill like that? For our part, we continue to maintain that the religion which God gave us in the Bible is a historical religion, and that the Bible itself gives us its true history, and indicates unequivocally just what is its relation to the general history of the world.

"The Bible was not intended to teach physical science." No, not primarily. But it does touch and invade the realm of physical science in many places. In its first chapter it gives a cosmogony. If God simply meant to teach religion in that chapter, why did He add so detailed a description of the method of creation? In order not to get His revelation mixed up with false science He should have stopped with the first sentence, "In the beginning God created the heavens and the earth." But he did not stop there; He went on to tell us just how the primordial material was molded into shape and the earth prepared step by step for man's residence. In the first chapter, therefore, He gave us some distinct teaching in regard to astronomy and cosmology. In telling about the beginning of light, He dealt with the science of optics. With the origin of life He ventured into biology. When He told how vegetables came, He turned to botany. In describing the incoming of the animal kingdom He—or the writer He inspired—moved into the science of zoology, including entomology and ornithology. When He described the atmosphere—called the "expanse"—He was dealing with the science of meteorology. And when, in the latter part of the first chapter and the early part of the second, He recited the beautiful story of man's creation, He handled the material of the great and worthy science of anthropology.

Now we leave it to any one who will use his reason logically whether the first chapters of our Bible separate the *religious* teaching from the sciences with which it is connected. Does this part of the Bible set off religion by itself as if it were something isolated and alone? Is not this rather the real teaching, the full-orbed and all-comprehensive teaching, of the Bible—that its primary purpose is religion, but religion set vitally and organically in a scientific and historical environment? The world was to be gotten ready for a religious inhabitant, and so God tells us, so far as was necessary for His wise purpose, just how He got the world ready for him. And why did God use that method? For the very purpose of showing us that man's religion was not to be something mystical, tenuous, and up in the air, but something right down here on the ground, vitally connected with the practical affairs of this mundane sphere; not a religion divorced from and lifted far above the natural sciences, but one that lives amicably with them and breathes with them the same atmosphere. Yes; the same God who gave us our religion also gave us our scientific world-view in its fundamental conceptions, so that our science might be religious and our religion scientific. Biblical religion is not narrow, exclusive nor seclusive, but inclusive—inclusive of all truth. It is not a religion for anchorites and mystics, but for men who live in the world and do the real work of the world. "Godliness is profitable unto all things, having the promise of the life that now is, and of that which is to come." It is for this world as well as for the next.

"The Bible was not intended to teach history"; so shout the liberalists. That is only part of the truth; it is not true as a blanket statement. It has just enough truth to be specious and dangerous and to lead the superficial mind astray. We should put our statements more discriminatingly, more accurately: The Bible was not intended to teach *all* or *universal* history, for we know it does not do that; but it was intended to teach enough history to prove how our holy religion came down to us from the beginning of time to the fullness of time—to the complete revelation of God's redemptive plan in Jesus Christ. Wherever it does teach history, it teaches it truly and accurately. More and more is the science of archeology confirming before our very eyes the historicity of the Bible.

"The Bible is a book of religion!" dins the liberalist over and over again into our ears. "A book of religion only!"

How do you know that, friend? Where does the Bible say so? Can you point to a single passage of Scripture which tells you that the Bible was meant to teach only one thing? The best way to determine the purpose of the Bible is to read it, to master its contents. When we do that, what do we find right on the surface? That, while it is pre-eminently a book of religion, it teaches a great many other things in connection with its religious teaching and not separate and distinct from it. It teaches how the cosmos and man were created, and probably from two-thirds to three-fourths of the contents of the Old Testament are made up of historical narratives, as is also a large part of the New Testament. Pray tell us why God inspired men to write so much history if "the Bible was not intended to teach history." Surely every one ought to be able to see that where the Bible recites history, it was meant to teach history. Of course, it is history connected with religion, but religious history is just as historical as is any other kind. A more rational statement would be, The Bible was *intended* to teach whatever it *does* teach. All through it teaches religion—but in the first chapter it also teaches cosmogony; in innumerable places it teaches anthropology; and almost everywhere it teaches history, for almost every spiritual doctrine has a historical setting, and moves along in the historical current.

It is almost too trite to take space to say that there is a vast amount of science that the Bible says nothing about. We would not go to the Bible to learn the details of any modern science, such as physics, chemistry and biology. This is not a matter of speculation or conjecture, for, when we look into the Bible itself, we do not find it teaching the minutiae of any physical science. But this is what we maintain—when the Bible, in giving a revelation and history of our holy religion, touches on the domain of any physical science, there it speaks truly; it does not trip, falter and fall, and commit egregious blunders, as do the cosmogonies and religions of the heathen world. Read the crude and absurd account of the creation according to the Babylonian monuments, and compare it with the Genetical account in the Bible, and you will see the difference between the guesses of the human intellect and the inspiration of God. There is just enough of truth in the Babylonian account to prove that it is a human perversion of the true record.

When a man makes the assertion that the Bible is a "book of religion only," we must ask him what he includes in the term "religion." This is a very pertinent and important question. He seems to imply that there are some things in the Bible that do not belong to the realm of religion. If so, we should like to know what they are. Let us have something definite. Pray come out of the fogland of obscurantism. Is there anything in the Bible that does not have a religious significance and bearing? If there is, we should be greatly obliged if the critic would separate the religious teaching of the Bible from its other teaching. The fact is, until the critical oracles make some definite statements along this line, the whole discussion is in vain; it comes to no head.

Suppose we take the first and second chapters of Genesis, and see whether the whole teaching, every verse of it, does not have a religious implication; whether religion is not in it all either explicitly or implicitly. The liberals will probably admit that the first verse teaches religion, because it tells us that the God with whom we have communion was the Creator of the universe. Then they will be likely to stop there, and aver that the *method* of creation (see men like Driver and Dods) is not vital, and must be left to the discoveries of science. But how arbitrary and illogical that is! If the divine creation itself belongs to "religion," will any one tell us why the *method* of divine creation is not also religious? Is not the method of creation also attributed to God as well as the creation itself? And does not everything that God does belong to the sphere of religion, whether it is creation *ex nihilo* or the molding and developing of the material that has been created? Why did the Spirit of Elohim brood over the face of the abyss and bring order out of chaos? Why did God make light, separate the land and the water, form an "expanse" between the waters beneath and those above, and cause the waters and the land to bring forth vegetables and animals? Did He not do all that to make the world ready for man's residence? He surely did, according to the Bible. Well, then, that whole narrative belongs to the realm of religion, for it betokens God's wise and gracious plan for man's well-being, and proves His interest in him. If that is not religion, then what is religion? Yes, the cosmogony of the Bible and its religion go hand in hand and stand or fall together. The creation of man in the divine image is pre-eminently religious, for that is where man received his spiritual nature. As to the method of man's creation as detailed in the second chapter of Genesis, that is distinctly religious, too, because it describes God's immediate action, showing that God formed man's body from material substance and then breathed into it the spiritual entity which gives to him the divine stamp and image. Here religion and anthropology meet and blend most beautifully, and you cannot put asunder what God has joined together. If the Bible is God's revelation— as even the liberal critics admit—would He have surrounded man's creation with a lot of crude and erroneous details as to the method? If the Bible was meant merely to teach the great religious fact that man is God's noblest handiwork, it surely was superfluous to say anything about the method by which He brought man into existence; not only superfluous, but most injudicious and confusing. However, our chief point is that God's whole method of dealing with man as recorded in the Bible belongs to the domain of religion. Wherever God comes in contact with man, or does anything for him, there you have religion. You cannot divorce the religion of the Bible from its science and history.

The critics find much fault with the Biblical narrative of the flood. However, that narrative is surcharged with religion. The reason the flood came upon the world was on account of the wickedness of the people which God could no longer brook. He saved Noah and his family because He had found them righteous in His sight. God gave Noah specific directions as to the building of the ark, because it is not to be supposed that any one at that time knew enough about the art of ship-building to construct such a vessel for such an ordeal. Was not that religious, and intensely so? God instructed Noah as to the animals, both clean and unclean, which he should take with him into the ark. Was not such guidance from God religious? And God saved Noah and his family and the animals, and thus made wise and ample provision for the re-peopling and re-stocking of the world; and after the flood had subsided, Noah built an altar and offered sacrifices to God. Religion! Thus you note that you cannot separate and tear apart the various fibres of the Bible's cloth of gold. If you do, you will destroy the whole fabric.

Here we will give an apt quotation from Dr. Henry A. Redpath's "Modern Criticism and the Book of Genesis." Speaking of "the vast majority of Christians," who, he declares, have "spiritual insight," he says (p. 43) : "It will be a long time before they will accept the dangerous doctrine which is presented to them to-day, that, in an admittedly inspired book, you may have set before you religious truth and scientific and historical error. The science and history of this book are not the science and history of the twentieth century. At the same time we feel quite sure —and the opinion is a growing one—they are not opposed to it. The book is not in its primary intent and in its content a scientific or a historical manual; its purpose is a much higher one; and that purpose it will be found more and more to fulfill, without in the least traversing any *absolute* truth which science or history may finally arrive at. A divinely inspired book could, we feel sure, never deny truth."

Some of the illogical rationalists make the claim that the history in the Bible is only a parable to prove how God always watches over and cares for His people. It is not to be accepted at its face value, but only for its religious value. But if such is the case, how do we know, after all, that God *actually* exercises a special providence over his people and cares for them? Mere legends and fictions never can establish a fact. They may be only the imaginings of men. No one would go to Walter Scott's novels for a real historical fact, if that fact had not been previously established by actual history. The truth is, no scholarly person thinks of going to the historical fiction of any time for his facts; he goes to them for their literary value, their value as efforts of the human imagination, their skill in weaving a little history, gathered from genuine historical sources, into the fabric of an imaginative piece of writing. In all historical fiction the history is only a modicum; the fictitious element is the predominant element. So we say that if we have no better basis on which to ground our faith in God's providence and interest than a collection of legends and folk stories, we have a very poor basis, one that will not bear the stress and shock of times of trial. On the other hand, suppose that the Bible gives us literal history, that God did really care for Enoch, Noah, Abraham, Moses and the people of Israel as the Bible narrates, then who can doubt the doctrine of His general and special providence? No; if we are to have a solid and bracing religion, it must have a substantial foundation in history. A foundation of mere fiction and parable would be a foundation of straw. A man who can retain faith in a religion with a fictitious basis has not a true intelligent faith, but one that is, *ipso facto*, mere credulity.

The speaker with whose address we started out in this chapter used, as we have said, an illustration of a watch and a thermometer. In trying to prove that the Bible is exclusively "a book of religion and not a book of science," he held out his watch somewhat dramatically, and declared: "When I want to know the time, I look at my watch; but when I want to know the temperature, I do not consult my watch; I consult a thermometer. So when I want to know something about religion, I go to the Bible; when I want to know something about science, I go to the text-books of science."

Many people are led astray by an illustration. They make up their illustration in such a way as to fit the case, and then apply it, and, presto! they think it an argument and jump to the conclusion. But an illustration never *proves* a proposition; it simply illustrates it after it has been proved. When you know that your proposition is true, you can make it plain and impressive by means of imagery; but you cannot use the illustration as a proof. Why? Because you have fixed up your illustration to fit the case, and so you must first prove whether the illustration is apt, relevant, to the point. Now, we hold that the illustration about the watch and thermometer is not a true parallel; it does not fit the case. And why? Because you first have to prove that "the Bible is purely a book of religion," and that it does not teach, with the religion, a good many other things. What are the facts in the case? When we come to look into the contents of the Bible, we find that it does teach a very distinct cosmogony; not, it is true, in much detail, but in broad, vital and general lines that are, we hold, strictly in accordance with the established facts of physical and anthropological science. It tells us how the universe was created and prepared for man, and then it tells us how man was brought into existence. True enough, all this is intensely religious, but it also invades the domain of certain physical sciences, and recites—or professes to recite—actual history. Besides, when we read the Bible, we discover at once that, after the narrative of the expulsion of man from the garden of Eden, it continues to give a historical narrative of the experiences of the human family.

Therefore we see that the Bible, though primarily intended to teach religion, teaches a good many other things besides, giving the religion a scientific and historical basis and environment. So the watch-thermometer illustration is not apropos. As a method of proof it is a fallacy, a *proteron hysteron*. To make it fit the real exegencies of the case you would better use an instrument which measures both the time and the temperature, with its chief purpose that of a time-keeper. Moreover, can any watch be made, and made a reliable time-meter, without reference to the temperature? Must not the material be so made and the mechanism so constructed as to remain almost, if not quite, immune from the changes of temperature and humidity? Make a watch of wood, and see how trustworthy it will be in ticking off the seconds. No; we do not believe in making the religion of the Bible an isolated thing, divorced from the science and history into whose warp and woof it is woven, just as we do not believe in separating the practice of religion from the history, science, thought and every-day life of our times. True religion ramifies the whole realm of life and experience. It is Ritschlianism, always narrow and one-sided, which tries to make a kind of mystical anchoritism of religion. With the liberal mystics, religion is nothing but a kind of watch, intended to register the emotional moods and tenses. But with orthodox Christians it is something practical and all-inclusive.

To conclude and get right down to the facts, what is the precise relation of the Bible to science? The way to decide this question is not to formulate a theory, and then make the Bible fit into it, but to study the Bible itself. When we do this, we straightway learn that it is not a book that teaches a great deal of science; it does not go into many of the details of astronomy and cosmology; it teaches very little geology, biology, botany and ornithology; scarcely any, if any, chemistry is taught on its pages. It does not even set out in a formal way a sytem of theology. But when that is said, the facts compel us to say more. At certain points, and those very vital ones, it connects its religious teaching with some of the sciences, as, for example, in the first and second chapters of Genesis. Our position is that, whenever and wherever it does this, it sounds the note of truth, absolute truth; it does not err and blunder, as do other humanly made systems of religion and the mere speculations of men, but its teaching is in strict accord with the ascertained results of the science of our times and of all times. * So far as regards those large areas of science on which the Bible, empirically tested, does not touch, we are only too happy to consult the reliable works of technical science; and we believe that the Bible student who studies the marvels of scientific investigation will become all the better a theologian on that account. He will be heartily glad to accept the truth wherever he finds it.

* In this chapter it has not been our purpose to show how beautifully the Bible and science agree wherever they come together. This has been amply done by the authors cited in our ''Selected Bibliography,'' under the heading, ''Science and Philosophy.'' Special attention is called to the works of Dawson, Wright and Azbill.

CHAPTER XII

SOME THOUGHTS ON THE INCARNATION

It is not our purpose in this chapter to treat all the points
pertaining to the doctrine of the incarnation of the Son
of God, but simply to present some of the results of our
recent thinking and study on this great topic of theology. *
The doctrine of the person of Christ, or what is known as
Christology, is a subject of perennial interest. This is
evident from the large number of books that have been
written on the subject, many of them within the last few
years.

To try to prove that the divine incarnation is a Biblical
doctrine would be superfluous, as our readers are familiar
with all the classical passages. We will pause here to make
only one citation. In John 1:1 we read: "In the beginning was the Logos, and the Logos was with God, and the
Logos was God." Then in the 14th verse this is said:
"And the Logos became (*egeneto*) flesh, and tabernacled
among us, and we beheld His glory, the glory of the only-
begotten of the Father, full of grace and truth." If this passage does not mean a divine incarnation, it is devoid of any
signification that can be made clear to the mind. As we
proceed with our discussion, we shall cite other revelant
proof-passages.

The incarnation of the divine Son of God connotes sev-

* The *rationale* of the incarnation is presented, in a somewhat
expanded form in the author's work, "The Rational Test," Chapter
VII, with many arguments not here given.

eral doctrines that are vital to it. One of these doctrines is—

The Miraculous Conception

Those theologians who deny the miraculous conception, or the virgin birth, of our Lord are compelled to reject those parts of the evangelical records, namely, Matt. 1:18-25 and Luke 1:26-56, which give a clear account of such a conception, and carry the air of historical verisimilitude. Into the critical question respecting these records we have no desire to go, nor is it necessary. For able and convincing discussions of the problem we refer the reader to Dr. James Orr's great work, "The Virgin Birth of Jesus Christ" and Prof. Louis Matthews Sweet's searching book, "The Birth and Infancy of Jesus Christ." Another excellent book, not so large as the two just mentioned, but very able, is Dr. R. J. Knowling's "Our Lord's Virgin Birth and the Criticism of To-day." No less heartily do we commend Dr. T. J. Thorburn's "The Virgin Birth: A Critical Examination of the Evidences of." The last two works are published by the Society for Promoting Christian Knowledge, London, as is also Dr. H. M. Relton's "A Study in Christology," referred to later in this chapter. The above-named society publishes many safe and conservative works marked by saneness, scholarship and evangelical earnestness. The difficulty with the critics who reject these birth narratives is that they manipulate them to conform to their subjective views, and hence their treatment cannot truly be called *historical* criticism. With them it is a foregone conclusion, to begin with, that such a miracle as a pure conception by the Holy Ghost is impossible and absurd.

Now our purpose shall be to try to show that the miraculous conception is not absurd, but reasonable and necessary, and that, therefore, the narratives of Matthew and Luke may stand in all their beauty, simplicity and historical integrity. With us it matters little about the "sources," about which the critics to-day make so much ado and over which they spend so much time in airing their speculations and conjectures. The fact is, Matthew was an apostle of Jesus Christ, associated with Him for some three years, and so Christ Himself would be his best source. Luke was closely associated with Paul, and no doubt wrote his gospel under the direction of that apostle, and Paul met the immediate disciples of Christ again and again, and surely must have known the chief facts of Christ's life. Moreover, Christ promised His apostles the inspiration of the Holy Spirit, who, if He guided them in their oral teaching, would surely have also directed them when they came to make the records that were to carry the message of salvation in trustworthy form down through the ages. The difficulty with many of the liberal critics is that they never mention Christ and the Holy Spirit among the "sources" of the gospel writings. That would be too simple a process; would get too near the supernatural and miraculous, and especially would not give them an opportunity to display their labored and technical "scholarship."

What would it mean to say that Christ was not "conceived by the Holy Ghost, born of the Virgin Mary?" It would mean that there was no divine incarnation, no God-man, and therefore no Redeemer of the world. If He, the Christ, was not the Redeemer, the world has never had a Redeemer; we are still groping in darkness, and none of the problems of sin, salvation and eternal destiny have been solved. For, if Christ was conceived by natural generation, He was a sinful being like the rest of us, and therefore could not have redeemed even Himself, to say nothing of redeeming the world.

Here some one replies: "But, though naturally procreated, He was immaculately conceived." We answer, that is simply substituting one miracle for another, and we can see no good reason for the substitution. Besides, there is not one iota of Scriptural or historical evidence for an immaculate conception of Christ, in which God merely prevented the transmission of congenital sinfulness. There is no more proof for the immaculate conception of Christ than there is for the immaculate conception of the Virgin Mary, which is a tenet of Roman Catholic theology. Moreover, the redemption of the world from sin requires something more than merely an immaculate man. At the very most an immaculate man could have made atonement for only *one* sinner; yes, and perhaps not even for *one*.

But other absurdities would follow if Christ was engendered in the natural way. Then a human person, an ego, would have been brought into being. If the Logos, who was also a person, had united Himself with the human person thus born, Christ would have been two persons; or the two persons would have been consubstantiated into a *tertium quid;* or the one would have been absorbed by or transubstantiated into the other. All these suppositions are untenable because they are absurd. Take the idea that Christ was a being with two egos—who can tolerate such a thought? To our mind, it is more than preposterous; it is monstrous. More than that, it would destroy the unity of Christ's self-consciousness, on which even the liberal theologians and critics of the day are insisting most strenuously. Where did Christ ever give the faintest intimation of a dual consciousness? He always spoke of Himself in the first person singular. Never once did He speak of Himself as "we." In His first recorded utterance He used the pronoun "I": "Wist ye not that *I* must be about *my* Father's business?" None of the evangelists and none of the apostles ever applied to Him a plural pronoun or cognomen, but always the singular. If He had a dual personality, He either did not have a clear self-consciousness, or else He gave a false revelation of Himself; and either alternative would prove that He could not have been even a reliable teacher and a true example, to say nothing of being the divine Redeemer of the world.

Or suppose His human ego was absorbed by the divine ego of the Logos; then He was not truly human, not "very man of very man," and so you run off into docetism. Besides, would it not be absurd beyond comprehension for God to permit a human ego to be brought into existence, and then transubstantiate or absorb it into the divine ego? That would be like the pantheism of the Hindu religion. And we might well ask, what was the purpose of bringing a human ego into being only to destroy its human quality by divine absorption? To suppose that the divine ego was absorbed by the human ego would be too absurd to be cherished for a moment, and, besides, would border on irreverence. The same might be said of the conception that the two egos were merged into a *tertium quid*, which would be neither divine nor human. A being thus constituted would be too anomalous to be the world's Saviour.

It may be thought that there is still another alternative: namely, that Christ was naturally generated, and that God simply united Himself with Him in an ethical or mystical way. This is the view, with various shades of differences, of such theologians as Ritschl, Rothe, Beyschlag, Lipsius, and many others. However, such a view is untenable for a number of reasons. First, it would have been no divine incarnation, but only a mystical union of the divine and human, such as all regenerated persons have and experience; it would have been no hypostatic union, only an ethical union. According to this view, Christ was not a unique being, a theanthropic person, but was like all believers, differing from them only in degree, but not in kind; therefore not the God-man, not the Saviour and Redeemer. Of Him it could not be said that He was "Immanuel, God with us," or "the Word become flesh," or "God manifest in the flesh.'' Such a being, that is, merely a ''God-filled man'' (Schleiermacher, Martineau, *et al*), could not have made ''propitiation for our sins, and not for ours only, but for the whole world,'' nor could He have ''tasted death for every man,'' nor could ''the iniquity of us all'' have been laid upon Him. Not only is such a doctrine un-Biblical, but it is unreasonable; because, if Christ was a divinely filled man, and thus was without sin, He still would be a great miracle. If men can accept such a miracle, why should they stumble over the miracle required by the evangelical doctrine of the Church—that of the conception by the Holy Ghost? It should be remembered, too, that a God-filled man would be adequate to only a part of the task required of the world's Redeemer—that is, He could be nothing more than our teacher, leader and example; whereas a true God-man could be these, and could, in addition, perform the greater and more necessary task of making propitiation for the sins of the whole world, satisfying the principle of eternal justice, and upholding the moral economy of the universe. Why should not theologians be scientific by assigning an *adequate* cause for every effect in the religious and ethical realm as well as in the physical?

The view of Rothe, that Christ was only a man, but through divine influence gradually developed into Deity, is also untenable, because, as Dr. James Orr* points out so effectively, that process would virtually add another person to the Godhead. Besides, the very idea of a human being unfolding into a divine being is metaphysically absurd, and is more like Hindu pantheism than like Christian theology.

Therefore we conclude that the conception by the Holy Ghost of the Virgin Mary is the only scientific and adequate

* *Cf.* his ''The Christian View of God and the World,'' *in loco* (consult index).

doctrine; and if we can believe in the supernatural at all, it is very reasonable that God, the Holy Spirit, could enter the procreative depths of the Virgin, take from her seminal substance the essence of human nature, and unite it hypostatically with the person of the divine Logos. It may be said that such a conception has never been known to have taken place anywhere else, and therefore it cannot be accepted here. Certainly it has never taken place anywhere else! If it had, Christ would not be unique. What is it that makes our Lord different, *unus et unicus?* The very fact that He was chosen to be the Redeemer of the world. Therefore, if His vocation was so utterly unique, His conception must also have been unique.* This brings us to another vital question:

How a Divine Incarnation Was Possible

If, instead of thinking along mere human lines, which are always more or less narrow and one-sided, we will study and accept the whole completely rounded Biblical teaching, we shall see how "sweetly reasonable" it was for the divine Son of God to become man. Go back to the Biblical narrative of the creation, and all will be plain. There it is said that God made man in His own image. With God there can be no after-thoughts. If there were, if He did not and could not foresee all things, and thus provide for every possible contingency, His universe would some time be hurled into ruin. So when God determined to create the cosmos, He foreknew that man would sin; therefore He created the cosmos and His highest creature, man, in view of the fact that He would redeem them through the incarnation of His only begotten Son. Thus He made man in the divine image so that there would be so close a kin-

* For additional reasons for the miraculous conception of Christ, see the author's "The Rational Test," Chapter VI.

dredship between the divine and the human natures that
the divine could become incarnate in the human. God's
whole plan is a solidarity; it is one—one plan in creation,
preservation and redemption. Thus man was originally
created with these two fundamental possibilities: first,
that the divine Logos could be hypostatically united with
human nature; second, that we, through the power and
grace of that union, might be mystically reunited with
divinity. Could anything be more structural, more organic,
more credible?

The Anhypostasia of the Human Nature

What was it that the divine Logos assumed in the incarnation—a human person or human nature? This is a question that has been much controverted. A liberal theological
writer, Edwin Heyl Delk, in his booklet, "The Need of a
Restatement of Theology," scoffs at the doctrine of the
Anhypostasia; but, as usual, he offers no argument against
it, or in favor of his own view, if he has a clear one. He
also seems to put Seeburg and Loofs on his side.

Lutheran theologians, however, generally accept the doctrine of the Anhypostasia,* though most, if not all, of them
prefer the term Enhypostasia. Among these we mention
Hollazius, Quenstedt, Gerhard (cited in Schmid's "Doctrinal Theology"), Jacobs, Weidner, Graebner and Blomgren. Of course many theologians of other communions
might be cited. John of Damascus and Peter Lombard
stoutly upheld this doctrine, and Dr. James Orr argued
for it most convincingly. However, instead of merely citing authorities, let us consider the problem on its own
merits.

In the first place, if Christ's human nature had a human

---

* This term means that the human nature of Christ was without
(an) personality, and that, therefore, the divine Logos supplied the
Ego in the incarnation.

person, the virgin birth was unnecessary, for the normal way of bringing a human person into being would have been by natural procreation. In such a case the law of parsimony would have been violated in the very incarnation itself. In the next place, is not the very thought of the Holy Ghost constituting a human person in the womb of the virgin, and then uniting it with another person, that of the Logos, an absurdity? Let us go further. If a human ego was constituted, Christ must have been two persons, must have had two egos; which is an absurdity, and would destroy the unity of Christ's consciousness. Or else the human ego was destroyed, which is a monstrous supposition. If it was destroyed, why was it constituted at all? Or else it was absorbed in the divine ego—transubstantiation—or the divine ego was absorbed by it, or the two were merged together. None of these suppositions is rational, nor is there any Scriptural basis for them.

The only tenable view is that egoity was supplied from the divine side—that the person of the Logos posited Himself in human nature, put himself under truly human conditions, and lived here on earth a truly human life. We leave it to any man who can think lucidly whether this is not the only way in which there could have been a real divine incarnation, the only way in which the Logos could have become (*egeneto*) man and tabernacled among us (John 1:14). On any other theory you have either an anomaly or only a mystical union, but not a divine incarnation. The choice lies between the doctrine of the Anhypostasia of the human nature, or the rejection of the Divine-human Redeemer, the theanthropic person of Christ, and the hypostatic union.

In reply to the objection, raised, no doubt, by sincere thinkers, that, if our Lord's human nature was without personality, Christ would not have been truly human, because personality is an essential element of human nature, we have to reply that the objectors fail in deep and fundamental thinking. Personality—which means self-consciousness, the ability to say "I"—is not something that is peculiar to man; it is something that he has in common with God and the angels. All of them say "I," and they mean by it one and the same thing—the quality or power of self-cognition. But what is it that is *sui generis* in man? It is his human *nature*. That is the very reason it is called *human,* thereby distinguishing it from the divine and angelic natures. We can think of at least four particulars in which human nature is unique: First, it is dual, being constituted of mind and matter, body and soul; second, it is capable of being procreated from one generation to the next; third, after the original creation of the man and the woman, it develops from an embryo and is born in the infantile condition; fourth, it must reach many of its thought conclusions by discursive processes. In all these particulars it is differentiated from both the divine and the angelic natures.

Now note: When the ego of the divine Logos posited, enfolded and ensphered Himself in human nature in both parts, somatic and psychical, did He not become truly human? Did He not assume human nature in all its distinctive elements? Did not the divine ego function in a truly human way? Yes; here you have a real divine incarnation, not a makeshift, not an evasion. And you can say truly, "The Logos *became* man, and dwelt among us." You can also subscribe *ex animo* to the noble old ecumenical creed, which says that Christ was "very man of very man," as well as "very God of very God."

This matter will become still clearer when we consider our next *locus*:

The Kenosis

That there was a *kenosis* of some kind the Scriptures teach both explicitly and implicitly (Phil. 2:7, and many other passages). Of what, then, was there a kenosis? Most of our Lutheran theologians correctly teach that there was no *kenosis* of the divine *nature* or *substance*. Among the most recent writers who hold this view we may mention Jacobs, Weidner, Valentine, Voigt, Graebner and Blomgren. Others who held the same view were Dr. James Orr and Dr. Francis J. Hall.

And why can we not admit the doctrine of the *kenosis* of the divine nature or substance? Because the Son shares the divine nature or substance with the Father and the Spirit. That is what the three persons of the Godhead have in common—*homoousios*. Therefore if the divine nature would have been renounced, there would have been a *kenosis* of the whole Godhead. Then who, during the period of the humiliation of the Son of God, would have upheld and directed the universe? It is plain that God would not have dared to abdicate His throne, not even for a moment.

Of what, then, was there a *kenosis?* Most certainly of the human nature. To that all evangelical theologians will agree, for the empirical fact is that the human nature was not at once glorified, but passed through all the stages of humble life. Only at times was there a partial *majestaticum* of the human nature, as, for example, at the transfiguration, in the miracles, and especially during the interim of the forty days after the resurrection.

However, may we not, in the light of the whole Biblical teaching, go a step further in regard to the *kenosis?* We give the following thoughts only tentatively, and ask for them fair and judicial scrutiny. Nothing is asserted dogmatically here, but we simply ask for a serious consideration of the following arguments on the part of evangelical theologians. While there could not have been a self-emptying of the divine *nature,* might there not have been such an emptying of the divine *person* or *ego* of the Son? We mean this: Might not the ego of the Logos voluntarily, lovingly and for our sakes have posited and enfolded Himself in human nature and put Himself under human limitations for the time being, and thus have lived a truly human life on earth? If the blessed Son did this, would not such an act have been a real divine incarnation, and would not the person of the Logos have become "very man of very man?" Would not this view explain all the human conditions under which Jesus lived and to which He was subject? It would not mean that He renounced His deity, but that for the time being and for our sakes He placed His self-consciousness under human limitation.

It may be said that we cannot separate the divine person of the Son from the divine nature. That is true, but our view does not propose to *separate* them. However, we do *distinguish* between the divine substance and the threefold divine personality. We say God is one in essence and three in persons. Hence we distinguish the three persons from the one divine essence, and we say the three persons have the essence in common, but each has His own ego or person. The Scriptures themselves make this differentiation, or orthodox theology would not dare to make it. "In the beginning was the Word, and the Word was with God, and the Word was God." Jesus always addressed the Father as a distinct person, and also spoke of the Holy Spirit in the same way. All the New Testament writers make the same immanent distinction in the Godhead, taking it for granted.

What is the true doctrine of the Trinity? That in the one Godhead there are not three individuals, but three centers or *foci* of self-consciousness, whereby He is, and has been from eternity, the loving Father, Son and Holy Spirit, the ground and source of all threefoldness and diversity in the universe which He created. He is an immanent Trinity, not merely a modal or economic Trinity. Now, if each member of the Holy Trinity has His own self-conscious ego distinct from the other two, while yet all have the same essence, how rational and how kind it was for the Father to "send" the Son, and for the Son to "come" of His own good will, and enshrine His self-consciousness in our human nature, and live our human life here on earth; while at the same time the egos of the Father and the Spirit, through the divine nature, which the three have in common, streamed forth to Him, enlightened Him, upheld Him and directed Him during His period of *kenosis,* never trenching on His assumed human freedom, and yet never deserting Him. By this view the three persons of the Godhead were kept in their integrity and in vital contact, and at the same time their sovereignty over the universe was not renounced, because there was no *kenosis* of the divine nature or substance, nor of the egos of the Father and the Spirit.

Let us note how many things in the Holy Scriptures this doctrine will explain. It will explain how there could be a real conception of Christ by the Holy Ghost; how He could be an unconscious babe in His mother's arms; how He could really and truly, and not merely docetically, "grow in wisdom and stature, and in favor with God and man." It will throw light on His saying, "The word which ye hear is not mine, but the Father's who sent me" (Jn. 14: 24; also verse 10). Note too: "The Son can do nothing of Himself, but what He seeth the Father doing" (Jn. 5: 19); "I can of myself do nothing; as I hear I judge; and my judgment is righteous, because I seek not mine own will, but the will of Him that sent me" (Jn. 5: 30); "I do nothing of myself, but as the Father taught me I speak these things. And He that sent me is with me; He hath not left me alone; for I do always the things that are pleasing to Him.'' Our view will also explain another marvelous saying of Christ: ''And now, Father, glorify thou me with thine own glory, with the glory which I had with thee before the world was'' (Jn. 17:5). If the last passage does not connote a divine renunciation of some kind, it is difficult to say what plain language means, for it is evident that the preëxistent glory of the Son could not to be applied to the human nature. The view here proposed will also explicate Christ's admission that He did not know the day nor the hour of the last judgment (Matt. 24:36; Mark 13:32). It also explains His prayer in Gethsemane for the cup to pass, ''if it be possible,'' and yet His leaving it to the Father's will; and, best of all, it will explain his plaintive cry on the cross, ''My God, my God, why hast thou forsaken me?'' It also affords the most satisfactory explanation of the classical text, Phil. 2:1-11. The whole luminous passage should be read with the foregoing observations in mind. Note also how our view irradiates Heb. 5:7, 8, 9: ''Who in the days of His flesh, having offered up prayers and supplications with strong crying and tears unto Him who was able to save Him from death, and having been heard for His godly fear, though He was a Son, *yet learned obedience* by the things which He suffered; and *having been made perfect,* He became unto all them that obey Him the author of eternal salvation.''

Thus we see that the holy and self-sacrificing Son of God, in infinite love, voluntarily renounced the exercise of His divine self-consciousness (but not His divine nature), in order that He might function in and through a truly human life here on earth. Yet, though thus self-limited, He never sinned and never erred; His life was sinless and His teaching inerrant, because, as He says, He always kept

Himself in contact with His Father. Had He broken that connection for a moment, as Satan tempted Him to do with an "if thou be the Son of God," all would have been lost. But, thanks be to God! He won in every contest with evil, and hence became the "Captain of our salvation."

Let us illustrate. We human beings have at least adumbrations of this unique power of putting a limitation on our self-consciousness. By acts of the will we may elide many things from our minds. We make the effort to forget, and in some measure we succeed. Sometimes we can even forget ourselves for a while. But let us take two examples. When Father Damien went to the leper community to live and die, did he not put a kind of *kenosis* upon his consciousness? Did he not voluntarily renounce much of the knowledge of the stirring outside world? David Livingstone immured himself for years in darkest Africa, living among the poor negroes. Was not that a voluntary *kenosis* of the knowledge of the world and its activities that he might otherwise have enjoyed? And do you not suppose he drove many things from his memory which, had he not done so, would have made his seclusion unbearable? But he found his compensating joy in the help he was able to bring to his poor, benighted Africans.

These are perhaps feeble illustrations, but do they not give us something of a clew to the possibilities of self-renunciation in the infinite divine love and power? Thus, without trying to explain away its force, we may accept the inspired declaration that Christ truly emptied Himself, truly humbled Himself, and became obedient unto death, even the death of the cross. We are also prepared to accept what follows: "Wherefore God hath highly exalted Him," etc. Yes, the divine Son has been restored to complete divine self-consciousness and glory, and has borne to the same exalted state the human nature in which He once imprisoned Himself for our sakes. For this reason we shall some time partake of His excellent glory: "Though He was rich, yet for our sakes He became poor, that we through His poverty might be made rich" (2 Cor. 3:9).

After the foregoing had been written and sent to the printer (it was first printed in *The Lutheran Church Review* in April, 1918, but written some months earlier), a new book (1917) came into our hands. It is Dr. H. M. Relton's "A Study in Christology: The Problem of the Two Natures in the Person of Christ." It is a most illuminating work, and reviews the whole history of the Christological problem. To our mind, it is a better work than Sanday's "Christologies, Ancient and Modern," because the author has thought his way through to clear views and a firm conviction. He advocates the doctrine of the Anhypostasia of the human nature of Christ, but calls it Enhypostasia, which, while it virtually means the same thing, may be the preferable word; it means that the human nature of Christ was never without personality, because, in its very formation or conception, it was made personal in and by the person of the Logos. The main point is established by this profound author, we think, namely, that the egoity of Christ is that of the Logos, not that of the human nature. In one respect, however, we do not think that Dr. Relton clears up the problem as much as he might. He admits of no *kenosis* of the ego of the Son, but assumes that Christ from the beginning of his earthly life had full divine self-consciousness and was also limited by His assumed human nature. To our mind, this view still attributes to our Lord a double instead of a single consciousness. Dualism in our Lord's *consciousness* cannot be permitted, while dualism of His *natures* must be upheld, if we accept the *whole* teaching of the Holy Scriptures.

The Hypostatic Union

This is the term in theology by which is meant the union of the divine and human natures in the person of Christ. Of course it has depths which the human mind cannot fathom; and yet we believe that the orthodox view can at least be shown to be reasonable. However, our purpose now is to answer a few objections to the orthodox doctrine which were made several years ago by a liberal theologian (Dr. Edwin Heyl Delk), who felt sure at that time that "a re-statement of theology" was necessary for the world's well-being. We shall let him speak for himself:

"The metaphysical and docetic atmosphere in which most of the earlier treatises were projected has been superseded by the historical, human approach in the study of our Lord's personality. Not that the supernatural factors, as declared in the New Testament, are ignored or denied, but that the earthly, human side of Jesus' nature and career has become the starting-point for the study of His person. Albert Schweitzer, in 'The Quest for the Historical Jesus,' has given us the classic study of this phase of the person of Christ."

The reflection on "most of the earlier treatises" as "metaphysical and docetic" is untrue and unjust. That there were docetists—those who denied the reality of Christ's human nature—in those days is true enough, but they were always condemned as heretics by the orthodox party. Dr. Delk's sweeping assertion would seem to include even the framers of the Nicene Creed, which asserted the true manhood of Christ; and so did the Athanasian Creed; so the Augsburg Confession; and we do not know of a single evangelical theologian who has not rejected docetism, and taught that Christ is "very man of very man." But our author holds that "the human side of Christ has now

become the starting-point in the study of His person."
That is just the danger of this radical "modernism"; it
puts so much emphasis on the human side that, if it does
not deny, it at least neglects, the divine side. It even tries
to account for the person of Christ by evolution. We have
read Albert Schweitzer's book, "The Mystery of the Kingdom of God," which is a later work than the one that Dr.
Delk praises so highly, and we are bound to say that he
makes Christ so decidedly human, with His mistaken and
even fanatical notions of eschatology and apocalypse, that
we cannot see where His divine nature could have a place.
To attribute human frailty and error to Christ is certainly
to destroy His value as the divine-human Saviour of the
world; the One in whom we can repose unfaltering trust
for our eternal salvation.

At all events, to make Christ's human nature the starting-
point is not the Biblical way, which emphasizes both the
divine and the human elements in His person proportion-
ately and correlates them properly, and thus forms the
basis for our evangelical creeds and systems of theology.
Suppose we scrutinize the Biblical method for a little while.
In Matt. 1: 18-23 we have the narrative of the interview of
the angel of the anunciation with Joseph, in which Joseph
was told that Mary, his betrothed wife, was with child by
the Holy Ghost. Then the angel said: "And she shall
bring forth a son; and thou shalt call His name Jesus; for
it is He that shall save His people from their sins." And
the name Jesus, when traced back through the Hebrew,
means Jehovah-Savior. Here both the divine and human
elements are indicated. A little later the angel said, "And
His name shall be called Immanuel, which is, being interpreted, God with us." Here the Deity of Christ is clearly
indicated. The gospel, according to St. John, does not
start with the human nature of Christ, but the very opposite. Note the first two verses: "In the beginning was

the Logos, and the Logos was with God, and the Logos was
God. The same was in the beginning with God." Then
observe that in the fourteenth verse we read: "And the
Logos became flesh, and tabernacled among us, and we beheld His glory, the glory of the only begotten of the
Father." This is the precise opposite of Schweitzer and
all the Schweitzerized liberalists of England and America.
The Bible does not make the human nature "the starting-
point." We confess to a decided preference for the Biblical
way of putting things. It does not put them one-sidedly.
In St. Luke's account of the angel Gabriel's visit to the
Virgin Mary, we find the same beautiful coördination of
the divine and human elements in Christ's person. And
all through the thrilling narratives of the evangelists both
natures proceed together in the unity of the person. Now
this nature, now that, comes most to the fore; but Christ
is always the one person, the one "I," the one "He." For
the most part, Jesus lived a natural human life, but here
and there His divinity flashed out in a wonderful way, just
as should have been the case if He was the incarnate Son
of God. From the full Biblical representation our evangelical theologians have drawn and formulated their Christological doctrine.

Again we quote from our author: "But the abiding
fact of the indwelling of the divine nature in Jesus does
receive a different interpretation from that presented in
the Chalcedonian Creed, or that of the speculative *communicatio idiomatum.*"

It certainly is poor theology to speak of "the indwelling
of the divine nature in Jesus"; at least, it is an ambiguous
mode of expression. It sounds as if the author believed
that Jesus was merely a human being in whom the divine
nature dwelt. If that is what the author meant, he is
wrong theologically, and his teaching is absurd and puerile.
For if Jesus was merely a human person in whom the

divine nature dwelt, then Jesus was one person and the divine nature another, and that would make Him a being composed of two persons; which would be an absurdity. No; the divine nature was a constituent element of Christ; indeed, it constituted the *ego* of Him. The divine Logos assumed human nature, not a human person. If the divine Logos, who was a person from eternity, had taken a human person into His Godhead, the result would have been a being with two *egos;* which, as we have said, would have been an absurdity, not to say a monstrosity. It would have made the unity of Christ's self-consciousness impossible. Then He would have had to say "We," and could not have said "I." On the other hand, if the divine nature merely dwelt in Jesus as a human person, then there was only a *mystical* union between Him and the Logos; there was no hypostatic union, no divine incarnation. The proper Deity of Christ would thus be nullified. If He would differ from the Christian believer, who is also mystically united with God, it would be only in degree. He would not be unique; He would not be the God-man; He would not be the Redeemer of the world and the Lord of creation.

Observe that our brother cannot away with the Christology of the Chalcedonian Creed. This we regret exceedingly. The great creed in question makes one of the clearest, fullest, profoundest and most discriminating statements of the person of Christ that was ever formulated. It sets forth precisely the doctrine found in the Nicene Creed, the Athanasian Creed and the Augsburg Confession. We quote from the creed of Chalcedon:

"We, then, following the holy Fathers, all with one consent, teach men to confess one and the same Son, our Lord Jesus Christ, the same perfect in Godhead and also perfect in Manhood; truly God and truly Man, of a reasonable soul and body; consubstantial with the Father, according to the Godhead, and consubstantial with us, according to the Manhood; in all things, except sin, like unto us; begotten before all ages of the Father, according to the Godhead, and in these latter days, for us and for our salvation, born of the Virgin Mary, the Mother of God, according to the Manhood; one and the same Christ, Son, Lord, Only-begotten, to be acknowledged in two natures, 'inconfusedly, unchangeably, indivisibly, inseparably'; the distinction of natures being by no means taken away by the union, but rather the property of each nature being preserved and concurring in One Person and One Subsistence, not parted or divided into two persons, but one and the same Son, and only begotten God the Word, the Lord Jesus Christ; as the prophets from the beginning have declared concerning Him, and the Lord Jesus Christ Himself has taught, and the Creed of the Fathers has handed down to us.''

Marvelous! sublime! discriminating! Biblical! true! There we have the whole doctrine of the adorable person of our heavenly Lord and Savior. We can accept it *con amore.* Note the unity of the person, hence oneness of self-consciousness; veritable Godhood (''consubstantial with the Father''); true Manhood (''in all things, except sin, like unto us''); the two natures in holy and most intimate union and communion, and yet without consubstantiation (''unconfused''); without transubstantiation (''unchanged''); without separation in respect to place (''indivisible''); without separation in respect to duration (''inseparable''). All the *loci* are beautifully correlated, and all apparent contradictions harmonized. Do we really need a restatement of the doctrine to put it in accord with the so-called ''modern thought''? If we do, let us have greater clearness, not greater confusion and ambiguity. We challenge the whole modernist school to make a restatement of Christology that will excel, or even equal, the statement of the old Chalcedonian Symbol. In comparison, Dr. Delk's "restatement," made either by himself or by the authors he quotes, is hazy, nebulous; above all, partial and one-sided. And why? Because he and his school have not gone to the "pure fountains of Israel," the inspired Word of God, but to their own rationalistic thinking.

Our author also criticizes the Lutheran doctrine of the *communicatio idiomatum,* or the communication of properties in the person of Christ. He calls it "speculative." But it is drawn from the Holy Scriptures, was taught by Luther, even if he did not use the term, and is advocated and defended in the Formula of Concord and by all our orthodox Lutheran theologians from Chemnitz and Gerhard to Krauth, Jacobs, Valentine, Graebner and Blomgren. This doctrine has been developed in the Lutheran Church in opposition to the Nestorian heresy, which so separated the divine and human natures as practically to divide the person of Christ. The dogma is a marvelous correlation of the whole Scriptural teaching on the person and natures of our Redeemer. Let us see if it is not so. There are three *genera* of the *communicatio idiomatum.* When Christ said, "The Son of Man hath power on earth to forgive sins," He used one form of the *Genus Idiomaticum;* that is, He predicated a divine attribute of the human concrete (the person viewed from the human side). When He said, "Father, glorify thou me with thine own glory, with the glory which I had with thee before the world was," He employed the *Genus Majestaticum;* which means that the divine properties were communicated to the human nature. For other conspicuous examples of the same *Genus* see Matt. 28:18; 28:20; Col. 2:9. When Paul declared that "Christ died for our sins according to the Scriptures" (1 Cor. 15:3), he made use of the *Genus Apotelesmaticum,* meaning that both the divine and human natures shared in the death of Christ; the human nature dying, and the divine nature sympathizing with it in its suffering, supporting it through the ordeal, and giving infinite value and efficacy to the sacrifice. Call it "speculation," if you will, it is all taught clearly in God's Word.

Some of our liberal friends do not believe in these "fine-spun distinctions," as they call them. That is the trouble with the school; they seem to want to blur all distinctions. Is it because they do not have the mental acumen to see distinctions where there are differences, or have they in heart gone over to monistic pantheism, and yet have not the courage to say so? We should like to know what their philosophy is—dualism or monism. Let us remember the good old adage: *Bene docet qui bene distinguit.*

Next our polemist dissents from the orthodox doctrine of the "two natures" in Christ, which, he asserts, "in its traditional form, imparts into the life of Christ an incredible and thorough-going dualism. In place of that perfect unity which is felt in every impression of Him, the whole is bisected by the fissure of distinction. No longer one, He is divided against himself."

Here he is wrong again. The distinction of natures taught by evangelical theology creates no schism in the person of Christ. "God was in Christ reconciling the world unto Himself." It was the very purpose of the incarnation to bring the two natures into the most intimate and harmonious conjunction and relation, so that, when our humanity is united by regeneration and faith with Christ, it is truly, lovingly united with divinity again. The moral and spiritual gulf between God and man that was caused by sin has been bridged by the incarnation of the divine Son of God. Originally God and man were in loving spiritual communion; then sin came and broke that fellowship; but the Logos came and restored it in and through His incarnation and soteriological work. It certainly is a beautiful, rational and organic method. There is nothing artificial and mechanical about it.

Nor is it true that this conception introduces "into the life of Christ an incredible and thorough-going dualism." There is no "bisecting," no "fissure." Just as before sin came into the world there was no schism between man's body and soul, so there is no antagonism between the divine and human natures in the person of Christ. True dualism there is, just as there is dualism in man, who is composed of body and mind, but no opposition, no antinomy. It is a curious thing that some would-be modern thinkers cannot see that two different entities can be joined in a most beautiful harmony is a universe that God has made. If He could make two different substances, mind and matter, He certainly could so constitute them that they would blend into a perfect harmony, and that, too, without consubstantiation. So God could blend into a perfect union divinity and humanity in the one person of Christ without a consubstantiation of them. He who cannot believe that would better announce himself frankly as a pantheist.

Again Dr. Delk: "The self-consciousness of Jesus, as depicted by the evangelists, we may call divine or human as we please; to express the whole truth, we must call it both at once. But it is single consciousness after all; it moves always as a spiritual unity, and separatist or divisive theories do a grave disservice, not merely to clear thinking, but to religious truth and power. It hypostatizes falsely two *aspects* of a single concrete life," and so on through a sentence that vapors off into obscurity.

We deny point-blank that the last sentence quoted above states the truth. The evangelical doctrine of the two natures in Christ does *not* "hypostatize" them. If this writer uses the term "hypostatize" accurately, he means that the traditional view *personalizes* each nature in Christ, thus making Him two persons. In the name of reason, why should any one so distort history? Orthodox theology, from the days of the council of Nice to the present time, has always opposed the Nestorian doctrine of separating the two natures of Christ into two persons. On the contrary, it has always insisted on the unity of the person in the two natures. Read all the ecumenical creeds and all the evangelical symbols, and see what the facts are. This is a marvelous thing—that a would-be modern thinker, who feels it his duty to restate Christian doctrine to bring it up to date, should accuse traditional theology of teaching the very heresy that it has always rejected with heart and soul.

Our author also introduces confusion and error into his thesis when he represents the two natures in Christ as only "two *aspects* of a single concrete life." That means that the two natures are merged into one nature, which is consubstantiation; and surely, surely he cannot believe that there was a consubstantiation of the divine and human natures in the person of Christ. Why, that was the old Eutychian and Monophysite heresy of the first three centuries of the Christian era, which was condemned by all the orthodox councils of those times.

Next, we must enter the field of ontology, for our essayist leads us into these difficult and metaphysical spheres. On page 39 he quarrels with the idea of two natures "inseparably joined together" in a person. "To put it frankly," he says, "when we abstract personality . . . what we vaguely call 'human nature' is not human nature in the least. There is no such thing as an impersonal human nature. In earlier theology human nature *is* taken as real apart from personality—the manhood is anhypostatic." This doctrine our protagonist rejects, and calls on Seeburg and Loofs to abet his views.

We see no way but to think this matter through, difficult as it is. First, we think it a vague and indeterminate kind of philosophizing. If a "restatement" of doctrine means to substitute vagueness for the definite and comparatively simple statements of orthodox theology, we do not see that anything is to be gained. But, next, let us enter in *medias res*. Take the proposition: Apart from personality there is no such thing as human nature. That is to confuse quality with substance, *phenomenon* with *noumenon*. Personality is a quality, not an entity, not a substance. Is it not clear that without substance, you could not have quality; without the *noumena* you could not have the *phenomena?* True, we do not know what substance is, but we do know intuitively that, if the world is not a mere phantasm and delusion, there must be something there, the thing in itself, the *ontos*, or there never could be the attributes of weight, force, light, life, consciousness, egoism or personality. If there were no mental substance, there would be nothing to carry on thought processes. An absolute blank could not think; a piece of nothing could not feel or will. Figure it as you will, there must be "the thing in itself." One of the best definitions of mind that we have ever seen was made by a recent scholar and philosopher: "Mind is self-conscious substance."

Now, following the same kind of reasoning, we contend that there must be the *substance* of human nature, or there never could be human egoity. And God must have created the substance which He endowed with personality and all its other qualities. Therefore in the seminal depth of every human being there must lie the substance of human beings yet unborn, and therefore still impersonal, only awaiting the conditions of fertilization and procreation to be evolved into personal beings. There can be no "I" until conception (perhaps not until birth) has taken place. Only when the proper conjunction of the man and the woman occurs, is a new human *ego* born, but it is born from the latent, seminal, and as yet impersonal substance of human nature carried down through the generations from the first human pair. There must be such a perduring human substance, or the race could not be perpetuated.

Apply this reasoning to the person of our Lord. The divine Logos, a person from eternity, entered the seminal depth of the Virgin Mary, and took from her the substance of human nature, both psychical and somatic, purified it from all sin and corruption, and assumed it into His Godhood in that mysterious act which we reverently call the incarnation. The Logos was a person, and therefore had no need to add another person to Himself. He did not first produce a human person in the Virgin, and then unite Himself with it; but in the very act of assumption He took only human nature into His Deity. Yes, the human nature was "anhypostatic" before the incarnation, but in the *unitio* it became "enhypostatic," receiving its personality from the divine Son of God. Why, it *must* have been so. Suppose for a moment that the Holy Ghost would have brought forth a human person, and then would have united it with the personal Logos, there would have been produced a being who was two persons; which would be a preposterous conception. It is not theologically correct, therefore, to say that the divine Logos assumed *a* human body and *a* human soul, for then He would have taken a human person into His Godhead. We should say, He assumed human nature in both parts, psychical and somatic.

Therefore, when the personal Logos assumed human nature, or, to put it more accurately, ensphered Himself in human nature, He became truly human, and hence could enter to the uttermost into the fellowship of all our joys and sorrows. It is the fact that the divine Son of God took our human nature into His very Deity that makes His companionship and sympathy so real and precious to us. The Bible way is always the right way, the profound way, the organic way.

.   .   .   .

While revising the proofs of this book, an additional thought relative to the *kenosis* of the Logos comes to our mind. Why was the Son conceived by the *Holy Ghost?* Why did the *Holy Spirit* perform the act of the miraculous conception in the womb of the Virgin Mary? Why did not the *Son Himself* perform that sacred function? There is always a divine rationality in the ways of God. It was the *Son,* not the Father or the Holy Spirit, who was to be passive in the act of incarnation, who was to make the great surrender; in other words, who was to empty Himself, which is the meaning of the *kenosis.* Therefore the Son submitted willingly and sacrificially to the dominion of the Holy Spirit, who enwrapped and enshrined Him (the person of the Son) in human nature that He function in and through it for the purpose of human redemption. Thus the Son surrendered Himself gladly and completely to the will of the Father and to the brooding care and guidance of the Holy Spirit. "Great is the mystery of godliness: He was manifest in the flesh"—HE, THE ADORABLE AND ETERNAL SON OF GOD.

CHAPTER XIII

GOD AND IMMORTALITY

With Special Reference to Leuba's Arguments and Findings

RECENT investigations seem to indicate that mere human and worldly learning does not lead to belief in spiritual realities. Fundamentally the explanation may be that given by the apostle Paul: "Now the natural man receiveth not the things of the Spirit of God: for they are foolishness unto him; and he cannot know them because they are spiritually judged" (1 Cor. 2:14). Perhaps it will be said that it is prejudging the case to make this excerpt from Paul; and, besides, some people may even think it ungenerous to charge academic men with lack of spiritual discernment; yet this must be said: we have never known a person who has accepted Christ by faith, and has thus received the witness of the Holy Spirit in his heart, to question the existence of God and the immortality of the soul. The assurance of the divine existence is based on the saying of Christ: "I am the way, and the truth, and the life; no man cometh unto the Father but by me" (John 14:6). The assurance of immortality results from an experience of this inspired statement: "These things have I written unto you that ye may *know* that ye have eternal life, even unto you that believe on the name of the Son of God" (1 John 5:13). Thus a simple Christian experience will solve the problems over which worldly wise men are vainly racking their minds.

However, when you are dealing with men to whom the spiritual and experiential appeal cannot be made, you must go to them where they are; you must meet them on their own arena, that of reason, science and philosophy. That is what we shall endeavor to do in this essay.

Dr. James H. Leuba's recent book, "The Belief in God and Immortality," has created a good deal of stir, especially in intellectual circles. It is little short of sensational; not, however, because the subjects are so well reasoned, but because the author's method is somewhat unique. He sent out questionnaires to some six hundred college people and others, asking them whether they believed in God and immortality, and in this volume their replies have been published (in part), tabulated, compared, and displayed in a somewhat spectacular way. The strange thing, indeed, the surprising thing, about this experiment is that, taken all in all, the majority of the respondents expressed non-belief in God and immortality. Moreover, this non-belief seems to grow more pronounced and definite the further advanced the respondents are in erudition. To make the matter clear, there were fewer college juniors and seniors who expressed belief in God and immortality than there were freshmen and sophomores. Among the more renowned historians, scientists and psychologists there was less belief than there was among those who were less well known. To sum up the findings of Prof. Leuba, we may put it thus: the more learning the less theistic belief.

No doubt this display will be distressing to those who have never been truly converted. There are people who are greatly affected by exhibitions of human learning, and are apt to go with the crowd of scholastics, thinking them able to say the last word on almost all subjects. Upon this class the book will no doubt have a harmful effect, because they will want to decide these questions on the basis of human knowledge, instead of going to the true source of assurance on spiritual matters, namely, Christ and His Word. And, indeed, in one respect the situation is alarming to the Christian. Are our colleges and universities not only leading men and women to reject Christianity, but causing them to plunge into downright atheism? If so, are these academic institutions more harmful than beneficial? And does human learning profit the race? These are questions that well may "give us pause." * It certainly is time that the theistic proofs be restated, defended and confirmed in such a way as to convince the minds of our educated and semi-educated men and women both in and out of college. A stalwart course in scientific Theism should be placed in the curriculum of every college in the land, and taught by an instructor who has both the spiritual mind and the requisite mental equipment; one who knows the field, appreciates the danger, and holds to the higher ideals of life and destiny.

We cannot help pausing here to inject an observation. Many good and sincere people have attributed the sad downfall of Germany in the late war to her prevalent rationalism, materialism, and other departures from the evangelical faith. That country, it is said, forsook God, and so God either punished it, or left it to its own devices. But if Leuba's representations are true, what about America? If atheism and agnosticism have affected our academic centers so seriously, how long will it be be-

---

* In accepting this essay for publication in *The Lutheran Church Review* (October, 1917), the Editor, Professor T. E. Schmauk, D. D., LL.D., expressed much concern regarding the gravity of the situation in our country resulting from the attitude of many of our colleges and universities and scientific teachers toward religion. He declared that it was indeed time for the Church to be awake to the crisis at hand. In a vigorous book entitled "The Menace of Modernism," the Rev. William B. Riley, D. D., of Minneapolis, Minn., has called attention to the liberalism that prevails in many of our academic institutions; and still more recently Rev. Dr. G. W. McPherson has sounded the alarm in an eye-opening book, "The Crisis in Church and College."

fore we are inundated by a wave of popular apostasy? Will God then give America up to her vain devices, and raise up some foreign nation to defeat and enslave us and our children and children's children? Surely these reflections, in the light of Professor Leuba's findings, ought to cause us serious thought. It is also a matter for grave reflection that few scientists of the country, so far as we know, have made public protest against Leuba's representations.

In this chapter it is our purpose to analyze somewhat critically the mental status and logical acumen of the so-called "representative American scholars" who express unbelief respecting God and immortality, to discover whether they show themselves competent to lead the world of thought on these vital and exalted themes. Are their scholarship and rationality so thorough-going, are their views so well digested, are their investigations so profound and comprehensive, as necessarily to command a large following among thinkers?

The Learned Specialists and Their Views

Passing, for the present, the replies of the college students who had part in this quiz, we will subject the replies of the representative American scholars to examination. They include historians, scientists (physical and biological), sociologists and psychologists. The table of comparative percentages will help us to evaluate the opinions of these scholars.

We note, first, that, of all these classes except the psychologists, more believe in God than in immortality. Among the historians 51.6 per cent. believe in immortality, while only 48.3 per cent. believe in God, a difference of 3.3 per cent.; among the physical scientists the relative per cents. are 50.7 and 43.7; among the biologists, 37.7 and 30.5;

among the sociologists, 55.3 and 46.3. Note that among the scientists of both kinds the difference is 7 per cent.—that is, 7 per cent. more believe in immortality than believe in God. With the historians the disparity is 3 per cent., while with the sociologists it runs up to 9 per cent. We would respectfully ask what degree of rational acumen is exhibited by seven out of every hundred scientists and nine out of every hundred sociologists who reject the doctrine of the divine existence and yet cling to belief in personal immortality (for Dr. Leuba's questionnaire was respecting *personal* immortality)? What order of mentality must such men have? If there is no God, how can there be personal immortality for man? For if there is no God, the universe must be composed of only material substance; there can be no such thing as spiritual entity. But if there is nothing but material substance in the universe, there can be no personal immortality. We are puzzling over the conception of these 3 to 9 scholarly gentlemen concerning the human soul that they think it can be immortal in a purely material monistic cosmos. Is a person who can commit such a hiatus in reasoning as to be an atheist, and yet believe in personal immortality, entitled to confidence when he gets out of his special field and pronounces judgment on matters that belong to the higher spiritual sphere?

The psychologists differ from their fellow-savants in several respects. Of them only 24.2 per cent. believe in God, and only 19.8 per cent. believe in immortality, the disparity being 4.4 per cent. We cannot help wondering what kind of rational processes these 4.4 per cent. must carry on. What sort of a God would He be who would bring into existence rational and aspiring beings, and then, after they have spent a few years of earthly toil and struggle over many perplexing problems, blot them out of conscious existence for ever and ever? A God who could or would find pleasure in doing such things would surely not be worth believing in. Atheism would be better than such deistic belief.

Next, we would remark that these statistics do not reflect much credit on the psychologists of the country. Observe that they rank the lowest in theistic belief and in belief in immortality. Nor is the above the worst showing they make; for the table shows that the more eminent psychologists tip the scale at only 13.2 per cent. for belief in God and only 8.8 per cent. for belief in immortality. Those of less note mark respectively 32.1 and 29.9 per cent. The average is 24.2 and 19.8 per cent. These figures afford food for serious reflection. Think of it for a moment. Among the more eminent psychologists only 13.2 out of every hundred express belief in God's existence, making 86.8 of them out of every hundred atheists or agnostics; and, worse yet, 91.2 out of every hundred reject the doctrine of personal immortality!

Pray what is the matter with the psychologists of the country? Have they been spending more time in dissecting human brains than in studying the noble faculties of the human mind? Have they become physiologists instead of psychologists? Have they come to think in terms of materialism rather than in terms of mentality? Is it not marvelous that a class of scholars who deal with the royal powers of the human mind, its intellect, its sensibilities, its will, its conscience faculty, its theistic faculty, its ability to conceive of the infinite and eternal, its natural longing for God and immortality—is it not marvelous that this class of men, of all men in the world, should go over to atheism and materialism, and should deny an immortal destiny to the human soul? Have they actually accepted the crass theory of materialism, that thought is only a secretion of the brain as bile is a secretion of the liver? If this statistical table is a true index of the trend to-day, it is time we were getting back to the noble science of psychology pure

and simple. We wish to register our admiration for and
confidence in the 24.2 per cent. who hold to belief in God
and the 19.8 per cent. who have not abandoned belief in
immortality to serve the mammon of materialistic physi-
ology. Cannot psychologists see that mental and material
phenomena belong to entirely different categories? A
thought, which is a mental product, is not a material substance like bile, which is the product of the action of the
liver. Material substance has no consciousness; mental
substance has. Material substance cannot initiate motion;
mental substance can. The former cannot think and plan
and purpose; the latter can. The former cannot will and
choose; the latter can. The former has no moral sense, no
spiritual aspiration and experience; the latter has. While
the mind and the brain are vitally connected and related,
they are different quiddities, because their functions and
phenomena are fundamentally different. You cannot trans-
late consciousness, emotion, volition and conscience into
terms of material substance and mechanical force. What
the majority of the above psychologists need is to learn to
think in terms of mentality and spirituality instead of in
terms of materiality; that is, they need to get rid of their
crassness.

Another interesting point is the disparity of the opinions
collated in this list of "representative American scholars."
Take, first, the divergence between the physical and biological scientists: of the former 43.9 per cent. believe in God;
of the latter only 30.5 per cent.; a difference of 13.4 per
cent. That is rather a large disparity. At all events, it is
far from a consensus. Why this difference? The physical
scientists, for the most part, deal with physics, chemistry
and mathematics—that is, with dead things; while the biologists deal with living organisms. Of course, along the
frontiers these sciences must overlap considerably. Yet we
cannot help wondering what there is about the data of these

two scientific fields to cause 13.4 more out of every hundred of the one class than of the other to believe in God. Are the wonders of living organisms less impressive than the wonders of chemical affinity? Can it be that some scientists fail to see God in a living cell, while others see him in the electrons, atoms and molecules that compose the cell? Surely these differences and incongruities greatly minimize the value of the conclusions of these scientists. If their investigations give them any actual worth, there ought to be greater unanimity among them. You take a thousand Christians who have had a real experience of salvation through Jesus Christ, and you will find them a unit on the existence of God, and a personal, loving and holy God at that. Talk about diversities of opinion among Christian people! Why, they are a happy and united family compared with the scientists.

In regard to immortality precisely 13 per cent. more physicists than biologists believe in it. What is there about physics, chemistry and mathematics to cause people to believe in the immortality of the soul, while biology leads a good many more to the opposite conclusion? To our mind, there is no rational explanation of this divergence of opinion, except the subjective and undigested speculations of the scientists themselves; for if their conclusions were based on real scientific data, there surely would be greater unanimity of view among them.

Let us make another comparison, this time between the historians and the psychologists. Of the historians 48.3 per cent. are theists, while the psychologists fall below 24.2 per cent., a difference of 24.1 per cent. The former deal with the workings of the human mind in history, in the movements and progress of the race; the latter deal with the human mind through direct observation of its functions and experiences. Yet there are twice as many theists among the historians as among the psychologists. Why the difference? Is there anything about the data with which the historian deals that would tend to make him more theistic in his convictions than the psychologist who deals with a somewhat different class of data? This large disparity between the two classes proves that their conclusions are not based on rational inductions from observed facts, but only on subjective and *a priori* conjectures.

On the subject of immortality the historians and psychologists differ still more widely—31.7 per cent. Think of that diversity—31.7 more historians than psychologists out of every one hundred believe in the immortality of the soul. If "representative American scholars," working their minds vigorously, cannot come nearer an agreement on immortality, we do not feel that their wisdom is acute enough to command our confidence. Take as many Christian men and women, such as have had a genuine experience of God's reality and grace through Jesus Christ, and they would be an absolute unit on both the existence of God and the immortality of the soul. Talk about the differences among Christian people!

Another comparison is interesting. Of the sociologists 46.3 per cent. believe in God and 55.3 per cent. believe in immortality. The historians are ahead of the sociologists 2 per cent. on belief in God, while the latter exceed the former 3.5 per cent. on belief in immortality. Thus these scholars go see-sawing back and forth, their opinions determined by no apparent guiding principle.

A still greater dissonance appears among these scholars when we take into consideration the percentage of atheists and agnostics. Begin with the historians. Of the "lesser" ones 63 per cent. believe in God, leaving 37 per cent. who are atheistic or agnostic. A very small per cent. are agnostics, perhaps 2 per cent. Of the "greater" ones 32.9 per cent. believe in God, leaving one-half, or 50 per cent., atheistic, and the rest agnostical or doubtful. So there you have it—out of 100 of these great scholars and thinkers, selected expressly on account of their eminency in the world of research, 32.9 believe in a personal God, 50 do not, and 17.1 do not know what they believe. Here is plenty of the spice of variety; the showing certainly indicates anything but unanimity of opinion. Suppose Christian people differed so widely in their views about God, what would the world say? Would the people of the world have any confidence whatever in Christianity? Why, then, should they have faith in the *ipse dixits* of these scientific gentry? Yet you may go the world over among truly converted Christians, and you will find them of one accord to the last man respecting the existence of a personal God. Talk about divisions among Christians!

Among the other scholars who had a part in this questionnaire there was practically the same amount of divergence of opinion. It is sad to contemplate that the minority of all classes of scholars believe in God; or, to put it positively, the majority were either atheists or agnostics. This is not a very encouraging showing for secular scholarship —that it should go so far astray on the most noble and exalted subject of human thought; for we take it that no other conception is so vital, so paramount, as the doctrine of the divine existence. For if there is a God who created and controls the universe, He must be good, wise and all-powerful; then all will be well with those who believe in Him and do His will, and some time all their problems, no matter how perplexing, will be solved. But if there is no God, the world is indeed a riddle; and the worst of it is, we shall soon die and perish with the brutes and the weeds, and our riddle will never, never, never have a solution. What a small outlook has the man who rejects God and eternal destiny!

With regard to the believers in these lists, it is fair to say that, most likely, all of them have either had a definite

Christian experience, or, if not, are men of high ethical ideals, which demand a personal God as the ultimate ground of right. They are perhaps believers, not because they are scientists and scholars, but because they are Christians and thorough-going ethicists. If this is a fact—and its factual probability is very great—it will still further reduce the value of merely human science and speculation regarding spiritual matters; for James Martineau well said: "Man does not believe in immortality because he has proved it; but he is ever trying to prove it, because he cannot help believing it." The same epigram will apply to man's attempts to prove the existence of God.

The Questionnaire to College Students

The author submitted four questions to all the non-technical students of "nine colleges of high rank" (author's language), and one normal school. We observe (p. 186) that 927 answers were received from the four classes (Freshmen, Sophomores, Juniors and Seniors) of those "nine colleges of high rank." If you divide 927 by 9, you will have 103, showing that those "nine colleges of high rank" had an average of only that many non-technical students, and each class averaged about 21 members. It does not strike us that those "colleges of high rank" were very large institutions; or perhaps we do not understand! The author says (top of page 186): "These data have special value, because *every student* of the class, when the questionnaire was distributed, answered." Moreover, it turns out (same page) that 289 of the answers from these young college people were from men and 638 from women, while 78 were from students of a normal school.

We must examine the questions which our professor inflicted upon those innocent and undeveloped young people. The first question, "Do you think of God as a personal or an impersonal being?" perhaps cannot be objected to. The second question, however, is certainly open to objection: "What difference do you make between a personal and impersonal being?" There are many persons, both in and out of college, who know the difference by intuition, but when you ask them to define the precise distinction, they are not able to give a clear-cut reply. Unless one has studied psychology—and doubtless many of these students had not—one has not yet learned the technical terms employed to define personality. Moreover, the most learned man would be greatly embarrassed if you were to ask him to tell you precisely what personality is. We know, but it is hard to define. You know what truth is; but define truth. You know what virtue is; but define virtue. The reply might be made that a person is any being who can say "I." True enough—but what is "I"? The things that we know by intuition are the very ones that it is impossible to define. So we think our professor took an unfair advantage of those "naïve" young folks when he asked them to give the distinction between a personal and an impersonal being.

But look at his third question: "Describe as fully as you can how, under what image, or images, you think of God. Distinguish here between what in your description is for you merely an image, a form of speech, and what is the reality." Now think of asking a number of young collegians to describe, and that "as fully as you can," the image they form of God in their minds when they think of Him! Why did not this astute professor require them to describe as fully as they could the image they form of the universal ether of space, or of an electron, or an atom? Why did he not ask them what is the shape of the mind, or the color of a thought, or the dimensions of heroism? Of every concrete or abstract truth we instinctively form a mental image; we cannot help it; but when we are asked to describe or define, in many, many cases we are unable.

So it is with our conception of God. Perhaps most of us conceive of Him as having something like a human form, but whether that is correct or not we do not know; perhaps we will not know until we receive the beatific vision. However, we need not trouble ourselves about the precise form of God, for we do not know even the shape of our minds or souls. We cannot tell what space is, nor time. What is electricity, Mr. Edison? Hear his modest reply: "With all my years of study and experimentation, I do not know whether electricity is a substance or only a force." Now think of a college professor asking a number of school boys and girls to describe the form of God!

The replies of the young people are quite interesting. Some of them are quite good; occasionally one of them is surprisingly profound; but, of course, a number of them are crude and indeterminate, showing that youthful minds must have time to develop before they are able to answer metaphysical questions. That the second question was too difficult is proved by the fact that some of the respondents declared that they believed God to be both personal and impersonal. All in all, the answers of the young collegians are not so far astray as might be expected. 82 per cent. of the women expressed faith in a personal God; a small number, perhaps 10 per cent., believed that God is impersonal; a smaller number yet were "doubters," and a still smaller number conceived of God as both personal and impersonal. The young men did not rank so high as the young women in theistic belief, only 56 per cent. of them holding the doctrine of a personal God, leaving 44 per cent. to be otherwise accounted. And here is the surprising fact: by far the larger number of the 44 per cent.—probably 31 per cent.—expressed belief in an impersonal God, which indicates just what clear conceptions they must entertain regarding personality. We should like to know under just what "image or images" these young men think of their impersonal God. Indeed, while we remember the point, we should like to ask Prof. Leuba "under what image or images" he conceives of that wonderful and inscrutable Power that works in the cosmos, and brings personal, rational, moral and spiritual beings like us men into existence. Is that supreme Power in the form of a man, or a globe, or a cube, or an ellipse? He surely must admit that there is such a Power.

Prof. Leuba tries to account for the fact that more women than men believe in God. He says: "This greater variation from tradition on the part of the men is one of the striking features of these records. It must be referred on the whole, I think, to a stronger impulse to self-affirmation and freedom, and to a correlated lesser need of affection and of moral support felt by the men."

This is a pretty cheap and superficial way of accounting for the difference. One might ask why women are so constituted as to have less self-affirmation and more need of affection and moral support than the men. As a rule, men are willing to admit that their mothers, sisters and wives are superior morally and spiritually to themselves, and they admit it, not out of mere gallantry, but because they know that it is true. If that is true, as it is, it is a cogent argument in favor of the conviction that belief in a personal God is a higher and nobler order of belief than are atheism and agnosticism. We should like to ask, too, whether the greater "need of affection and of moral support" felt by the women is creditable or discreditable to them. If the former, as every right-minded person must admit, it is another argument in favor of the superior moral character of theistic belief. Prof. Leuba cannot reply that woman is the "weaker vessel," and not endued with as strong intellectuality as man, for the replies which he publishes in his own book prove that the women exhibited just as much reasoning power and depth of thought as the men, and in some cases were more profound, and especially more definite. Once for all, we desire to say that it is to the credit of Christianity and theistic belief that more women than men accept them. As a rule, you will find more men than women in our penitentiaries! You will find more women than men in our churches! Significant, is it not?

In commenting on the replies of his respondents, Prof. Leuba usually betrays his own unbelieving convictions. He gives a special coloring to the remarks of the students, or makes his own glosses on them. As a rule, he tries to belittle the orthodox replies with disparaging remarks and explains every case of doubt as favorable to his own view. On page 218, in commenting on the *naïve* responses, he observes: "These figures would refute the accusation that some might be inclined to direct against colleges for indoctrinating their students. They indicate, rather, how distressingly uninterested and ignorant these 'cultivated' young people are regarding what is commonly considered a great religious issue. The preceding section shows that they are equally naïve with regard to the conception of God." On the next page: "We should hardly have expected to find 35 per cent. of the juniors and seniors in a Christian college unable to profess belief in immortality, and a considerable additional number evidently indifferent to it. This situation points to a very profound change now taking place in the convictions of our educated young people regarding a belief usually considered vital to Christianity."

Our reply is, Christianity is not a matter of mere intellectual opinion and ratiocination, but of deep inner spiritual experience that cannot be forced upon any one; and so, if parents, teachers and ministers fail to bring their young people into experimental relation to Christ, they will simply go on in their unspiritual way. The findings of Prof. Leuba ought to sound the note of warning to all our Christian institutions to make their teaching more positively theistic and Christian. That is one good thing that may result from our professor's questionnaires.

To show the author's one-sidedness in commenting on these answers, we quote the following from page 212: ''I shall merely remark that those who think their belief in God essential have not had occasion to test their conviction; whereas those who think themselves morally independent of the belief and who also disclaim the belief, that is, nearly the whole of the 43 per cent., may be said to have demonstrated their moral independence of the belief in God.'' To this inadequate kind of reasoning we would reply that it is not likely that young people from 18 to 25 have demonstrated anything of the kind. As a rule, there come experiences later in life when faith in God is felt to be a necessity, especially for those who have real moral earnestness.

We cannot help calling attention to a remark on page 188: ''Stupendous ignorance is the price paid by our youth for the absence of teaching and guidance. The situation cannot be improved until traditional and no longer teachable beliefs have been replaced in the confidence of public opinion by others in agreement with modern knowledge.''

And yet, as we have shown in a previous division of our argument, ''modern knowledge,'' according to Prof. Leuba's conception, has not led to any consensus among secular scholars on the two basic issues of God and immortality! To make this clear, let the reader remember that of the physical scientists 40 per cent. believe in immortality; about 18 per cent. reject immortality, and the rest—42 per cent.—are marked agnostics or doubters. How far will Prof. Leuba's marvelous ''modern knowledge'' go, at that rate, toward giving our young people clear and definite convictions? Well may they ask, ''Who are right, the 40 per cent., the 18 per cent., or the 42 per cent.?'' If these young people want to find a real consensus of conviction on God and immortality, they must go to true Christian people.

Value of the Specialist's Testimony

This will be our next inquiry—the value of the specialist's testimony respecting these great moral and spiritual problems. Instance the chemist, who deals with certain kinds of material data. If he does not take a thousand other facts into account, how much value would his researches into the constituent elements of matter be in determining great moral problems? How much morality would he find in oxygen, hydrogen and carbon? How much spirituality in H_2O? By his mere manipulation of chemical elements in retorts, crucibles and test tubes, would he be able to obtain a world-view, a cosmology, a theology? Chemistry alone, being only a small segment of the whole sphere of human knowledge, does not render a man competent to judge of philosophical and metaphysical matters. The same may practically be said of all the other specialists named in this symposium.

At this point another questionnaire might be pertinent: How many of these specialists have ever read and digested a first-class work on the theistic arguments, or a system of Christian theology, doctrinal or ethical? There are Flint's great works, "Theism" and "Anti-Theistic Theories," which are classics on the subject; and there is Samuel Harris's monumental work, "The Philosophical Basis of Theism;" how many of Dr. Leuba's catechumens ever mastered those works, or works of equal importance? How many of them have given serious attention to Ebrard's "Christian Apologetics," or Orr's "The Christian View of God and the World," or Fisher's "The Grounds of Theistic and Christian Belief"? How many of them have even seen or heard of Dr. Martensen's massive work on "Christian Ethics"? Until they have studied these or similar works of equal caliber to lift them out of their very much circumscribed specialties, their competency to pronounce final judgment on theological problems may well be interrogated.

The Theistic Arguments

Space will not permit us to unfold them and show their logical value. The usual theistic arguments are the General, the Teleological, the Cosmological, the Ontological, and the Moral (some theists add the Esthetic). In the interest of brevity we shall simply indicate the logical force of the Cosmological Argument, or the argument from causality. It is based on the fundamental principle that every effect or event must have an adequate cause, and that no effect can be greater than, nor essentially different from, its cause. These are principles that the mind accepts intuitively, though they are founded on the observation of sufficient empirical experimentation to prove the mind's intuitions to be correct. If you cannot trust the mind in such things, then no confidence can be placed in any of its operations, and the thinking of Dr. Leuba's specialists is just as futile as all other human thinking.

Now apply the causal principle to personality. There are persons in the world to-day. You and I are persons. We have self-consciousness; we can say "I." But the personal never could have evolved from the non-personal, because then the effect would be greater than the cause and essentially different from it. Therefore in order to have an adequate cause for the personalities that are in the world, you must put a personality back of and into the world to create or evolve them.

Apply the same principle to rationality. We are rational beings; but the rational never could have evolved, by means of merely resident forces, out of the non-rational, for that again would make the effect greater than its cause;

therefore the Power that brought rational beings into existence must itself be rational; but rationality can be predicated only of persons; therefore the Supreme Power must
be a Person.

Just once more, combining the Cosmological and the
Moral proofs: There are moral beings in the world to-day,
and have been for unknown ages. But the moral never
could have evolved out of the non-moral, for that again
would be contrary to the law of causality; therefore the
Power that gave existence to moral beings must itself be
moral. But you can predicate moral qualities only of
rational persons; not of mere things; therefore the Supreme
Power must be a Rational Person—God. Have Dr.
Leuba's eminent specialists ever canvassed seriously these
lines of thought, which penetrate to the foundation of all
realities? They must get out of their ruts; they must get
a world-view; they must make an induction of *all* the facts,
physical, mental, moral and spiritual, if they are going
to arrive at satisfying conclusions.

At the close of so long a chapter we cannot indulge in
preachment, although we feel almost in conscience bound
to do so. We will simply add that we believe it would be
a calamity to society and the nation if the majority of men
and women should turn atheists and agnostics. It would
speedily undermine the foundations of virtue and responsibility, because, if there is no moral Personality back of
and in the world, there is no proper ground for moral distinctions. We believe with that great and good man, Gold-
win Smith, who said: "The denial of the existence of
God and of a future state is, in a word, the dethronement
of conscience." Men may not realize this result at once,
but sooner or later moral deterioration must take place. "If
the foundations be destroyed, what can the righteous do"
(Psalm 11:3)? "Righteousness and justice are the foundations of His throne" (Psalm 97:2)—that is, of God's

throne. Eliminate God, and what becomes of the ethical foundations of the universe? Let us ponder long and solemnly as an American people before we give up our theistic faith, and open wide the floodgates of moral anarchy.

CHAPTER XIV

DOES NATURE MAKE PROGRESS?

A Criticism on Evolution

Now-a-days the idea of evolution seems to have taken a powerful hold on the scientific and popular mind, or, to be more accurate, the popular and scientific *imagination*. It is therefore patent to search into the matter, to see whether the natural realm which we know to-day possesses anything like a marked and irresistible tendency to make improvement, to pass from lower to higher forms. Is the law of progression plainly written on nature's pages as we may read them to-day?

None of us would dispute the general evidences of geology. We cannot and will not deny that in the geological ages there was a movement from the lower to the higher stages of existence. First came the oblique forms of life, which were obviously vegetable; then the primal forms of animal life; then the higher forms; lastly man himself, like a crown upon the pedestal of creation. That this general law of upward movement prevailed in the remote prehistoric past no one would be so foolish as to deny.

However, two things need to be said about this progressive movement in pre-historic times. First, the general law described is precisely in harmony with the Biblical narrative of creation, which outlines most graphically the process from primeval chaos, when the earth was waste and void, to the beginning of life and up to the finished product, man. Second, geology by no means shows a gradual and uniform scale of progress from the lower to the higher types. On the contrary, there are many leaps and gaps, some of them of tremendous width and depth. For instance, when the fishes first appear in the Devonian age, they are perfect fishes, not mere links in a graduated scale in which one form merges into another without leaving a distinguishable line of cleavage.* Many of the geological animals were great mastodons as perfect in organism as any animals we have to-day and some of them much more powerful. The first geological man ever found was, to all intents and purposes, a fully developed human being, physically considered, with a skull, as Mr. Huxley said, that might have been the skull of a philosopher. Note also the same admission by Mr. Roosevelt in his Oxford address in 1911.

Now, it is often said that Biblical interpreters change their explanations of the Bible to suit the facts as science discovers them. But Bible men are not the only ones—scientific men do the same thing. Seeing that nature in the geological cycles often made progress by leaps and bounds, the scientists have introduced a new term into their evolution theory—"mutation." And now this term is used for all and more than it is worth, just as the terms, "natural selection" and the "survival of the fittest," have been and still are employed. But no one has stepped forward to tell us why nature makes these tremendous saltations, or where the tendency comes from. Perhaps it is to balk the evolutionists in their desperate efforts to find the "missing links!" Permit me to ask, Does not this disposition of nature to bound along like a great kangaroo rather point to the Bible view of special creations than to the theory of

---

* There is no evidence, either in geology or in modern science, of what is known as the "transmutation of species"—that is, that one species is changed into another by an evolutionary process. See the admissions of scientists of all schools as recited in Kelley's "The Rational Necessity of Theism."

natural evolution? Indeed, is it not illogical to speak about evolution going by prodigious "mutations"? Surely, surely, a big leap from a lower form to a perfect higher form without any intermediaries cannot consistently be called evolution. It certainly breaks the continuity in natural processes that the evolution theory demands. Then why hold on to a term that has become antiquated?

Let us now look at nature as she is to-day and has been since the beginning of history. First, we would remark that the Bible tells us that when God had finished the creation, He pronounced it good, ceased creating, and "rested" from His creative work. This would point to a finished work so far as making new things is concerned—a work in which certain fixed laws would dominate; in which there would be reproduction of the types already created, in accordance with the fiat, "Increase and multiply," but in which new and higher forms would not appear. Does not this agree with nature as we know her to-day? Do we see the law of progress written large and plain on nature's domain? Do we not rather see the law of stability, of persistency of form and type? Which of these laws, we would insist, bulks the more largely and explicitly on the pages of nature's realm?

Looking at nature as we know her since the dawn of history, we find no law of progress clearly stamped upon her operations. If any new species have been introduced—and it is very doubtful—they have not been higher forms, but the low forms of insect pests. All animals in the natural state are just the same now as they were from three to six thousand years ago; the lion is still a lion, not an improved breed; the elephant still an elephant; the giraffe still the same long-necked beast; and even the monkeys of to-day are precisely like those pictured and described in Egypt three or four thousand years ago; moreover, certain forms of lower animal life are precisely the same to-day as

they were far back in the geological ages, as is indicated
by their fossil remains; no advancement, no progress, no
evolution; simply reproduction and the most stubborn persistency of type. Now this is our pointed inquiry: If the
law of progress is the palmary law of nature, why has it
become inoperative since the beginning of human history,
that is, since the era when it could be really tested by
human research? Surely a law which is made to account
for almost everything that we have at present in nature
ought not to be so shy and inactive to-day, and even so
obscure and elusive as to be incapable of empirical proof.
It ought to be writ large and plain everywhere on the pages
of nature's marvelous book. If evolution ever was the chief
law of the world, why did it resign its primacy?

There are *other* laws, however, that *do* stand out on
nature's pages like raised letters on a tablet. What are
some of them? The laws of stability, of persistency and
reproduction of type. There they are inscribed on the
surface, clear and plain, so that everybody may read as he
runs, scientist and layman alike. So far as we know, no
distinct species ever cross, or if there is one exception,
namely, the horse and the ass, the hybrid product, the mule,
becomes sterile—just enough of an apparent exception to
establish and emphasize the general rule. Nor is that all.
So anxious does nature seem to be to preserve and teach the
law of stability of type that, as soon as humanly cultured
breeds of animals and varieties of fruits and cereals are
left to their own way, they invariably begin to revert to
their original inferior forms. Let people simply neglect
their farms, gardens and orchards for several generations,
and note how great the retrogression will be. The same
would be true if their horses, cattle, sheep and farmyard
fowls were neglected. Let us imagine for a moment that
the whole human family were decimated. What then would
become of the natural world, so far as we know the proc-

esses of nature? After a time it would be converted—
nay, it would convert itself—into a howling wilderness.
Study nature where you will to-day, and you will find the
law of change written plainly, it is true, but nowhere the
law of progress. No; nature left to herself takes no forward steps. The invariable law, written plain as day
everywhere, is reproduction of species. growth to maturity,
then decay, by and by death, then reproduction again from
the seed or plant—a ceaseless round. If no new external
power touches nature, she will "go on forever," like Tennyson's brook, only to come back time and again to the same
point. We repeat for emphasis that, if progressive evolution is the preponderant law of nature, the great law or
force that has brought the cosmos to its present status,
it ought by all means to be in evidence to-day; nay, it ought
to be the most conspicuous force now in operation. But
what do we see at the present time? Instead of holding
that position, it is so negligible a power that even many
of the most competent physical scientists to-day cannot
discern it, and nobody can prove that it is operative.

And now I wish to present an argument—one that, so far
as I know, is new—why evolution *ought* not, in the divine
economy, to have been made the dominating law of nature.
Had it been the regnant principle, nature would have been
in a state of flux, of instability, of constant change, so that
man could never rely upon her. The farmer could not be
sure, when he sowed wheat in the autumn, that his field
would produce wheat the next harvest. The same would
be true of every effort he made to reproduce his grain, fruit,
vegetables and stock. But as nature has been constituted,
he can depend upon her uniform laws; he can plan for the
future; he knows that nature, being stable, will be true to
herself, and will abet his efforts. So firm is nature, so much
is she his friendly co-operant, that she will even preserve
the specific variety of beasts, fruits and grain that his in-

genuity has produced through selective inter-breeding and crossing. So beneficial to man, therefore, is this law of stability of type in nature's fecund processes, that it affords strong evidence of a divine teleology in the plan of the world. Thus facts agree with the teaching of the Holy Scriptures, which declare that, in the creation of the cosmos, God made all vegetables and animals to reproduce "after their kind." How much more benign are God's ways than the ways of speculative science!

And now, in the interest of thoroughness, we must reply to a counter-argument that a thoughtful student once brought forward in our college class-room. No difficulty ought ever to be evaded, for truth should always be the desideratum. After we had declared that science had not yet proved by empirical experiment or observation that one species had ever been transmuted by natural processes into another, our student rejoined acutely: "You cannot prove the theory of special creations empirically, either." We recognize the force of this reply. It must be dealt with; it cannot be evaded.

Let it be frankly admitted that the doctrine of special creations cannot be proved by physical experimentation. We have no means in our laboratories of demonstrating that there ever were special creations or that there are at present. The theologian and the scientist must join in admitting this fact. Therefore, to be entirely frank and open-minded, we must admit that physical science can demonstrate neither the doctrine of special creations nor the doctrine of the evolution of species by resident forces. So far as science can carry us, both of these views are only hypotheses. There is no more empirical evidence of the transmutation of species than there is of divine creation. Thus science can make no assertions either way.

What shall be done in such a case? For one thing we must try to discover which method is the more reasonable, creation or evolution. Let us see. The exponent of evolution holds that in nature the all-dominating law is progressive development by means of resident forces. If that is true, it is reasonable to believe that this law should be the dominant law to-day, because, the evolutionist maintains, it has brought the cosmos to its present status. But, as has been seen, stability of type is the most powerful law to-day—the law that is written most plainly on the face of nature. Now, no good reason, either ethical or otherwise, can be given why this law should have resigned its suzerainty as soon as human history and science began, at the very time when men have an opportunity to test it.

With regard to the doctrine of the special divine creation of species and types the same kind of reasoning does not hold. No advocate of this doctrine contends that special creation is the *one and only* law that prevails in the cosmos. On the other hand, we hold that God in the beginning created the world, and after that ceased the work of creation, but *unfolded* the cosmos that He had brought into being. Therefore, according to this view, no one expects to see the law of new creations the dominating principle to-day. On the other hand, that very theory itself teaches that to-day the outstanding law is the stability and reproduction of the types originally created. This view takes its stand on the position that each species produces "after its kind," just as the Bible, in its great first chapter, declared should be the case, and just as we see nature operating to-day.*

* Note Gen. 1:11, 12: "And God said, Let the earth put forth grass, herbs yielding seed, fruit-trees bearing fruit, after their kind, wherein is the seed thereof, upon the earth: and it was so. And the earth brought forth grass, herbs yielding seed after their kind, and trees bearing fruit, wherein is the seed thereof, after their kind: and God saw that it was good." Verse 21: "And God created the great sea-monsters, and every living creature that moveth, wherewith the waters swarmed, after their kind, and every winged bird after its kind: and God saw that it was good." Verse 25: "And God made the beasts of the earth after their kind, and the cattle after

And for this view good scientific and ethical reasons can be given. Was it not a wise provision of the Creator first to bring into existence the various types of vegetable and animal life, then stabilize them, so that man, His highest creature, endued with rationality, might have a dependable and uniformly governed dwelling-place? Thus we can see that God had good reason for creating the world as it is, and then "resting from all His work which God had created and made" (Gen. 2:3). The Bible, therefore, gives the most rational explanation of the present status of the world.

Should the opponent reply that evolution, too, worked toward the stabilizing of type and ceased its operations when it had accomplished that purpose, we would rejoin that no evolutionist, so far as we know, has ever taken that position. Evolutionists constantly contend that progressive evolution is still in the saddle. If these theorists desire to be rational, let them admit that evolution was once operative, but has now resigned its place in favor of persistency and reproduction of type. Then they can devote all their energies to an investigation of the geological ages to see whether there is any solid proof for their doctrine of the evolution of life by means of physical and chemical changes and of the evolution of higher types from lower forms.

Well may we ask, too, if evolution was once the law of the world, why she aimed to bring about the stability of type in order to make the world a habitable residence for man. Was there teleology in evolution? Did it work with a distinct purpose? If so, evolution must have mind; and if it has mind, working with a distinct purpose, it must be a person. But all such reasoning is the height of ab-

their kind, and everything that creepeth upon the ground after its kind: and God saw that it was good." Permanence of type, just as we see in nature to-day!

surdity. If there was purpose in the evolutionary process, there must have been a Mind back of that process, and that would lead us to the theistic view. Then evolution was only God's *modus operandi*. The idea advanced by some materialists (Haeckel) that mere naturalistic evolution works with a purpose, and therefore is endued with "mentiferous ether," is too far-fetched and preposterous a theory to merit serious consideration. All empirical observations prove that wherever there is sufficient mentality to amount to purposive action there must be personality. A mind that can design anything, even the simplest piece of mechanism, can also say "I," and therefore must be a self-conscious person. If all evolutionists were theists, there might be some reason in their contention. In that case the only duty for them to perform would be to investigate God's world to discover whether evolution was His method of operation in bringing the world to its present condition and whether He still operates according to that law. Later on in this chapter we shall have some pertinent remarks to make regarding the theory of theistic evolution. Our contention here is simply this, that it is more reasonable to believe that God first created the various types of life, making them stable for the sake of the rational beings whom He intended subsequently to bring into existence, than that pure evolution was and is the dominant law of the cosmos. We may add that the exponents of the view of special creations do not contend that God is now inoperative in the world of nature. No; He still holds sway; He still is in His world, ruling over it; but for wise and beneficent purposes, He has ceased creating *ex nihilo*,* at least for the present epoch, and now governs the world by preservation, provi-

* We know of no book in which the doctrine of divine creation is more fully and cogently set forth than Dr. L. F. Gruber's work, "Creation ex Nihilo," in which he proves that the universe is "a finite and temporal entity."

dence and redemptive grace. Should physical science respond that the above propositions cannot be proved by empirical tests, we reply that, even though that may be true, the view advocated is according to reason, and we certainly ought to be rational beings. Is it not reasonable that God should create a cosmos, make it stable and uniform for man's benefit, and then exercise beneficent control over it, and finally bring His highest creature to the noblest and happiest destiny? If this is not true, then the universe does not have a rational basis; in which case all the reasoning of even the evolutionist would be null and void—another story, and a tragical one, of "love's labor lost."

Does some one ask how a man can be absolutely assured that God's plan for the world and mankind is a kindly and beneficent one? We reply humbly, gratefully, and positively, by a Christian experience of the redeeming grace of God in the soul. We are aware of no other way by which *certitude* on the crucial problem can be reached. Let us now return to our argumentation on the uniformity and stability of nature.

"But there is progress in the world!" some one exclaims. Yes, my friend, there is progress in one realm; but in only one—the human realm, among the races of men. Here in many instances the law of progress is written in bulking letters of gold. Progress, sometimes all too slow, yet clear as the noonday. Though we do not breed a new species of men, we do produce a higher grade of men. Even here the progress is not universal, and, sadly enough, there have been many cases of degeneration. There are heathen peoples that are the same now as they have been from time immemorial, while others have slid backward in the scale of progress. But note, wherever Christian civilization truly touches man, there is advancement. Does not this agree with the Biblical conception of man? Made in the divine image, endowed with mind and soul and therefore with rational powers, he is capable of improvement, yea, of endless progress, by his own initiative and volition, aided by the power and grace of God. Nature is not rational; therefore in and of herself she cannot advance; her own inertia keeps her what and where she is. There is only one thing in all the world that has the divine gift of initiation and self-movement; it is mind with a will.

And mind you, too, that wherever in nature's realm there has been improvement, since the dawn of history, since men have been able to investigate and test, it has come about only through the uplifting touch of human genius. All our blossoming gardens and orchards, all our fertile fields, all our highly developed breeds of fowls and animals, all our multitudinous inventions—which are simply pushing nature beyond herself—bear witness to the advancing faculty of man. Nature never could have made an electric trolley car. She was never intended to do such things, but simply to furnish the materials for man's genius to work upon and push to new conquests.

How unmistakable is nature's teaching here! She stands still, waiting for the transforming touch of her master, man. How beautifully this harmonizes with Holy Writ, which tells us that man was created to till the ground and to have dominion over the animal creation!* Yes, there is progress in the world to-day; but it is found only where there is a rational mind, and even there it becomes really marked and extraordinary only where it is kindled and fostered by the Gospel of Christ and the arts of Christian civilization.

Some time ago a correspondent took us to task for an article opposing the evolutionary doctrine by saying that

---

* Gen. 1:26-31. Most significant is the language of verse 28 in this passage: "And God blessed them; and God said unto them, Be fruitful, and multiply, and replenish the earth, and *subdue* it." The word "subdue" has a world of meaning in it; it connotes that man was to bring the natural cosmos to higher states and forms.

we made the mistake of identifying evolution and progress.
His contention was that evolution, as now held, does not
always mean progress; it also includes retrogression. That
is, sometimes a thing evolves the wrong way, or backward
like the crawfish. This surely is a violent stretching of the
word evolution. Spencer declared that evolution is a
process of unfolding from the homogeneous to the hetero-
geneous by means of resident forces. Joseph Le Conte
defines evolution in this way: "A continuous progressive
change, according to certain laws and by means of resident forces." We hold that men have no right, in the very
midst of a discussion, to change the primary word in the
dispute to a different sense. In that way you can make a
word mean almost anything, and you get nowhere in your
discussion. If the word evolution has as yet no stabilized
meaning, that very fact proves that it stands for an un-
proved theory. We dislike a term that flits to and fro like
a will-o'-the-wisp. To our mind, evolution backward is a
queer kind of evolution. Surely the etymology of the
word itself would indicate something progressive (e, out,
and *volvere*, to roll). For instance, when highly cultivated
strawberries are neglected, and reversion takes place according to a dominant law of nature in the vegetable sphere,
would you call such a backward movement by the term
evolution? If you would, then the term is a ludicrously
elastic one, and has too indeterminate a meaning for a
scientific term. Are evolution and degeneration the same
process?

And right here is the difficulty with the evolutionists—
they use their capital term in such a variety of senses that
nothing is fixed, nothing is definite in their philosophy.
If something progresses, that is evolution; if retrogression
occurs, that is evolution, too; if nature goes by big saltations, or leaps, lo! that also is evolution; if, as is the case
in geology, a new species, fully formed, appears suddenly

and without graduated antecedents, still it is all evolution! Some men speak even of the "evolution of a jack-knife," in spite of Spencer and Le Conte, who said that evolution is a method of unfolding by means of *resident* forces. So, according the rubber-like use which some men make of the term, you might say that evolution is that power that makes everything that is made and does everything that is done! It is a blanket-sheet term; it covers everything. It is some men's god, and should always be written with a capital "E." But do not logical thinkers realize that a word that means anything and everything means nothing?

At this point we wish to interject this thought. For our part, we can think of only one Power that was adequate to bring this universe into being and carry it to its present status of development; and that Power is an all-wise and all-powerful personal God. Put Him back of and in the universe, and you have assigned a sufficient cause for all that is and all that our aspirations lead us to hope may yet be. And when we come to study the universe largely, comprehensively and adequately, not in a partial and *ex-parte* manner and spirit, we find that He works in various ways "His wonders to perform"—now by creation, bringing new things into being; now by miracle, putting some new force into operation for a high purpose, and now by gradual development through the laws He has established. Whatever else may be said about it, this is an adequate hypothesis, and takes all the facts into the account. It does not convert one set of facts into a hobbyhorse, and then ride them to death. The indictment we bring against the hypothesis of evolution is, it makes an elastic and indeterminate use, and therefore a misuse, of the capital term it employs, making a talisman of it rather than a scientific factor. Our argument here for the theistic world-view is not the so-called argument *Deus ex machina,* but a legitimate induction from all the facts in the case.

An illuminating article by Dr. L. T. Townsend appeared in the December (1918) number of *The Bible Champion*. Its title was "Prehistoric Peoples of the Western Continent." Dr. Townsend's contention is that the high civilization indicated by the ancient cities exhumed in Mexico, Yucatan, and Central America, compared with the present inferior civilization of many of the people in the same regions, is absolute proof against the theory of evolution, whatever adjectives may be put before the term. Let us quote in proof of this position:

"Of the wonderful prehistoric cities of Mexico much has been written, but none too much. Where once were cities having a hundred thousand or more inhabitants, adorned with parks, palaces and temples, are now to be seen the outlines only of deserted streets and ruins of palaces that had been built and were in ruins long before the Aztecs and Toltecs had settled in the country. In Yucatan alone there are ruins that were once large and flourishing, where now silence reigns; and noblemen who lived in royal palaces have given way to half-clothed and half-fed peons living in adobe huts."

What shall we say of evolution in those countries? If there was evolution of any kind, it was obviously evolution downward. This is the question we should like to ask: If evolution is the outstanding and dominant principle in the world, why is its working not more strikingly displayed both in the past and in the present? There is not one scintilla of evidence that animistic and polytheistic people have ever risen into monotheism by means of purely "resident forces." When such degenerate people *have* been lifted to a higher level morally and religiously, it has always been because they have been touched and uplifted by forces outside of themselves; and in every such case it has been the Bible and Christianity that have thus lifted them out of their pitiful condition. But that is not evolution; it is the adding of a supernatural force. In the world of nature and of man there is the most tangible and striking evidence of the operation of two principles: one is a ceaseless round without progress; the other is degeneration. The proof of progressive evolution by means of merely resident forces is conspicuous for its absence.

Dr. Townsend speaks by the book of the status of affairs in the countries named, for he has himself been on the ground, has personally examined the ruins, and has made extensive collections of relics from the marvelous ancient cities which furnish indubitable evidence of a high civilization in a remote antiquity. In view of these things, it is useless for certain classes of would-be scientists to continue to go along in smug assurance that their evolutionary theory has been proved and that no more is to be said. That is conservatism gone to seed; it is not science, which always has its mind open to truth and reality.

In another number of the above-named magazine (July, 1919) Dr. Townsend points out the impossibility of accounting for the wings of a bird on the theory of evolution. We quote *verbatim*:

"They (the bird's wings) were not evolved from the lower orders of animal life by any recognized theory of evolution; for, if evolved, they must have come through variation from some non-winged animal. But, according to the theory of evolution, the first variation of that non-winged animal must have been an incipient wing, or the stump of a wing, on some of the reptile or other families. That, however, could not have been the case, for such a stump would have been an awkward and burdensome appendage, really a monstrosity on the reptile or other non-winged creature—a thing that nature does not like to tolerate, and will not tolerate. Indeed, it is one of the fundamental teachings of evolutionists that nature's purpose is to stamp out all disadvantageous characteristics; and clearly the stump of a wing would be such (an encumbrance), as it would afford no advantage over a companion that had no stump. And more than that, Mr. Darwin's natural selection could not *originate* a wing; all it could do would be to cultivate a stump of a wing after it had been made.''

We may add a thought or two to this argument. How could the stub of a wing ever get started on a non-winged animal like a reptile? What would have caused such a stub to start when, as yet, there was not the least use for it? After it had gotten started, how could it have developed? For, as Dr. Townsend says, it would have been an encumbrance instead of an advantage. A mere stub could not have been used for flight. Surely, according to the theory of evolution itself, such a useless bulge on the side of a reptile, even had it arisen by some accident, would have soon disappeared by virtue of the very fact that it would have been of no use, but rather a handicap. Moreover, why did nature want to convert a reptile into a bird? What was her motive or purpose? If there is an advantage in wings, nature must be gifted with the idea of teleology in conferring such an advantage on a non-winged creature. But if there is teleology in nature, there must be a Mind back of nature which pushes her forward along the line of progress. But that would give the theistic view of the world as opposed to the naturalistic. But we go further: If nature saw that there was a decided advantage in wings, why did she select only one reptile, or possibly a few reptiles, as her favorites and give them so great an advantage over their fellows? Or did wings evolve purely by accident? Considering their marvelous and complicated mechanism and their wonderful adaptation to the specific purpose which they serve, such a supposition is irrational. Thus the hypothesis of evolution falls to pieces on the lightsome wings of a bird. It seems to be pretty easily shattered! On the other hand, creation by an all-wise God gives an adequate and rational cause for the marvelous effect. No other view does.

Another citation from Dr. Townsend's article is germain. He asserts that he is willing to stake his conception of divine creation as opposed to natural evolution on the structure of a man's eye or ear as well as on the feathers and wings of a bird. To quote: "There has been found occasionally an anatomist who has pointed out two or three imperfections (from his point of view) in the construction of the human eye. But for all that, the eye is an astonishing piece of mechanism. There are no fewer than 438,000 optic nerve fibres, nor fewer than 3,360,000 retinal cones, all of which are nicely correlated. There are seven matched bones forming the eye socket, and six outer muscles attached to the ball of the eye, and one of them is geared through a pulley. There are oil and water supplies, with a tube for carrying off any over-supply. There is also an expanding and contracting pupil that adjusts itself automatically to the surrounding light. There is a marvelous network of nerves, three sets of which are quite different in the services rendered—those of vision, of sensation and of motion, and one of these nerves is unlike any other in the entire human body, without which sight would be impossible. There are also contrivances for adjusting the focus to different distances, so that the eye is both a telescope and a microscope, the same eye being able 'to sight a star or thread a needle.' There are other contrivances for the correction of the spherical and chromatic aberration; also the mechanism of lids and lashes for the protection of the eye against what might otherwise be injurious to it. And all these different parts are perfectly co-adjusted for a specific purpose: that of reporting to the brain things from the outer world."

In view of these facts, we are constrained to say that the person who can believe that the human eye is the product of mere chance or fortuity is afflicted with blind credulity akin to superstition, and has surrendered the elements of reason.

One of the outstanding arguments of the evolutionists is the fact that the human embryo and fetus in their development seem to recapitulate the natural history of the animal world from the lowest forms to the human form. At first blush, this reasoning seems to be quite plausible. However, after more thought, it is, after all, far from convincing. The mode and circumstances of the development of the human fetus are very different from those surrounding the evolution of animals by means of both immanent forces and external influences. The fetus unfolds entirely within the womb, while plants and animals have evolved largely by means of external circumstances and forces. Moreover, the facts cited can easily be accounted for on the theory of creation according to the Holy Scriptures; for God created the vegetable and animal kingdoms, and then made man akin to them in many respects, so that he might be "at home" in the cosmos in which he was placed by his Maker. Hence it was perfectly natural and rational that the human babe's development in the womb should be a recapitulation of all that God had previously done. How else, we would ask, in the name of common reason, could God have connected man *organically* and *structurally* with the natural cosmos which was to be his dwelling-place? Thus the facts of biology as known to-day tally best with the view of divine creation. The ways of God are all "sweetly reasonable." If man had not been created with organic kinship with the mineral, vegetable and animal kingdoms, he would have been an alien, not a citizen, in the world. He was the crowning work of God, but nature's crown was vitally conjoined with the nature it glorified. What a beautiful unified scheme the Word of God depicts!

We desire now to present another idea for the earnest

consideration of thoughtful people. If the universe was not created by a divine Person, but is eternal, then the universe *as a whole* is incapable of evolving; it is and must be a closed system; for, being eternal, and there being nothing else besides itself in existence, no new material or force could be added to it. Therefore it follows logically that, as a totality, it must have always been what it is now, and must remain so forever. Of course, some parts within the universe are capable of development. But observe the conditions under which alone development is possible: there must always be an *environment of available material that can be manipulated by the embryo, and added to the first plasmic substance.* Take an acorn for an example; there lies the unfolded germ within its kernel. Now what is absolutely necessary in order that it may develop into an oak? A suitable environment. It must be planted in the soil, and must have moisture and warmth. The embryo can unfold only when it can add to its own substance the fitting material from the surrounding soil and water. Let the acorn lie out in a dry open space, and it will never evolve into a tree. The same is true in the whole realm of embryology, vegetable, animal and human; all germs unfold only when they can assimilate and add available substances from their environment. Therefore, while it is true that development is possible under proper conditions of some parts of and within the universe, the universe itself as an entirety, if it is eternal and uncreated, is a fixed system and incapable of progress. There is nothing from the outside to be added to it.

However, if the universe is not eternal, but was created by a divine Being, a personal God, then it is evident that He could have so constituted it that it would be capable of further development by the injection of new forces through acts of His will. However, He Himself cannot undergo the process of development, because He is eternal, and therefore must be unto eternity what He has been from eternity. It is an absurdity to say that the eternal can be unfolded progressively. Only that which is temporal, only that which had a beginning in time and which is finite, can be developed. So we maintain that, if the universe is a developing universe, it must have been brought into being in time and must be finite. That there has been progress in the history of the cosmos there can be no doubt; both astronomy and geology afford empirical proof of that fact. Therefore reason itself drives us to the theistic world-view.

It will be noticed that in the foregoing argument we have refrained from using the term "evolution," but have used 'the words "development" and "unfolding." This has been done advisedly. As has been previously said, the word "evolution" is so elastic that at the present time it has come to have only an obscure meaning, and therefore stands for nothing in particular. For this reason we are bound to say that we think the term "theistic evolution" is a misnomer—in fact, a contradiction. If the term "evolution" has any clear and definite meaning, it must be, as Spencer and Le Conte defined it, an unfolding "by means of *resident* forces;" then it would follow logically that there would be no room for God's immanency in the world; that is to say, if God in the original creation put into the cosmos all the potencies ("resident forces") necessary for its evolution, then, having created it, He must have retired from the cosmos in favor of secondary laws, and that would make Him the God of Deism, not of Theism. We repeat, if the universe evolves by means of resident forces, there is no need of God's immediate action in it. It is a self-perpetuating machine set going once for all. God is transcendent, not immanent. Therefore the term "theistic evolution" is a contradiction.

Let us look at the problem from still another viewpoint. If God is immanent in the creation, if He is active therein, and if the creation is unfolding progressively, as the evolutionists maintain, then God must be continually *adding new forces* from His omnipotence in order to produce the forward movement; otherwise it is plain that there could be no progress. But if God is constantly injecting new energies into the creation, *that* is not *evolution;* for evolution means unfolding by means of *resident* forces, and not by the introduction of *new* forces. Therefore, as we have said, development through resident forces makes God's immediate action, or, in other words, His immanency, superfluous. Thus the doctrine of theistic evolution leads logically and inevitably to the deistic view of the world.

The law of the conservation of energy, to which modern evolutionary science is committed soul and body, also makes theistic evolution impossible, because it crowds God out of the cosmos. This law is thus described by one of its advocates: "All physical energy becomes kinetic energy, or the momentum of masses, and the law of the conservation of energy asserts that the kinetic energy of the universe is a constant quantity." On this statement Canon McClure, in his "Modern Substitutes for Traditional Christianity," offers the following pertinent remarks: "This means that every form of physical activity is an instance of motion caused by other motion only, and the sum total of the energy causing all motion is constant; it cannot be added to or diminished. Every motion taking place in the universe comes under this law. There is seemingly no room for miracles here. For if any *spiritual* influence, it is contended, were supposed to change the rate of motion of the least particle of matter, it must increase or diminish the existing quantity of kinetic energy in the universe, and would thus be a contravention of this law."

Thus our point against the doctrine of theistic evolution is established. The law of the conservation of energy, which is constant, renders the divine immanency unnecessary and even impossible; for if God is *active* in the cosmos, and not merely a transcendent spectator, He must constantly be injecting new energy into the process.

Since the word "evolution" has come to have an indeterminate and over-elastic use, so that it is practically made to do duty for everything that happens, we would frankly propose a change of terminology. Instead of forcing a single term to account for every process in the cosmos, let us employ several terms; for true science and philosophy require that we hold a hypothesis and use a terminology that are adequate to the situation. The three terms that we propose are "creation," "miracle" and "development." Let the word "development" describe all the *gradual* processes that the Divine Being employs in carrying forward the movement of the creation. The word "development" has not been used, like "evolution," to describe a forward movement merely by means of *resident* forces, and therefore can include unfolding by means of such forces, if God wills, and at the same time the injection of new forces when required. In this way God's immanency and activity in the cosmos are preserved. But God does not always work in the way of gradual unfolding; He has other ways of carrying forward His plans; therefore the word "development" needs to be supplemented by other terms. So the words, "creation" and "miracle," should be employed to describe those works of God by which He brings something new into being, or makes some especial manifestation of His power, grace and righteousness. No; you cannot fathom the whole depth and measure the whole plenitude of the divine operations by a single term. God moves in divers ways "His wonders to perform," and we must use divers terms to depict them. Of all the inadequate and inept terms that have been used to sum up the divine energies and processes, we look upon the word evolution as the most perverted and misemployed. Nor would we even venture to assert that the three words, "creation," "miracle" and "development," exhaust all the divine plans, purposes and operations; but they certainly do account for more things, *toto coelo*, than does the narrow, limping, obscurantist term "evolution."

Before bringing this chapter to a close, we must add some reflections on a recent book which came into our hands after the foregoing was written. We refer to the Right Reverend J. E. Mercer's work (1917), "The Problem of Creation." It certainly is a work of much profundity of thought, and deals with all the scientific and philosophical problems involved. In many respects we would commend the book. Its theistic position is, to our mind, unassailable. The author's restatement of the teleological argument is fine and convincing, and supplies what was lacking in Paley's presentation to bring it up to date, to correlate it with modern science, and make it convincing to the modern mind.

However, we are bound to say that the author has not convinced us on two points: eternal divine creation and the evolution doctrine, both of which he stoutly tries to uphold. To answer him thoroughly would require a book, but we cannot avoid making a few suggestions in the way of reply. Regarding God's being an eternal Creator, the author's argument goes limping; for, after all, it is impossible to grasp clearly the proposition that the universe has always been and yet has been created. It requires a winding dialectic to get even a vague idea of an eternal process that can be called creation. On the other hand, when you speak of creation *ex nihilo*, you feel intuitively that such an act is a real creation—a bringing into being of something that had no previous existence. There may be insoluble mystery as to how God did and could create, but the idea that it was a real creation stands out before the mind like a clear-cut cameo.

Again, if the material universe is eternal, it either must

be a part of God's being (which would be the old theory of emanation *redivivus*), or else you are plunged into the absurdity of believing in two Eternals lying, as it were, side by side. The former error surely was rejected by right philosophy long ago, while the latter leads to the error of Plato that matter is an eternal limitation and burden to God. Moreover, our author, while he refers a great deal to science, and is constantly quoting the scientists, makes very little reference to the teaching of the Holy Scriptures. We do not see how any one can read the first verse of the Bible reflectively, and still believe in an eternal process of creation. "In the beginning God created the heavens and the earth," surely says expressly that there was a beginning; and if God Himself is eternal, as Dr. Mercer rightly maintains, then it must have been the heavens and the earth that had a beginning; otherwise that majestic first verse of the Bible would be devoid of sense. Still more, Dr. Mercer holds that the universe has always been an evolving universe. If that were so, and if it were eternal, it should have reached its present status long ago, because it has had eternity in which to unfold. However, if it was created in time, and so had a beginning, we can readily see why, in the wisdom of God, it has only now attained to a certain stage of development. That which had a beginning in time can be unfolded progressively; that which has been from eternity must ever be what it ever has been.

In many places in his book Dr. Mercer seems to reduce matter to force or energy, although we do not think he makes himself quite clear on that point.* If that is his view, it is untenable, because force is a quality of a substance and not a substance itself. You must have an entity,

---

* "I myself am prepared to see in matter the potentialities of mind. But that is because, as I have shown, I conceive matter to be mind from the very start. I hold matter to be Energy, and Energy to be Will." So says our author on p. 175 of his book.

a thing in itself, in order to have a quality; you must have the *noumenon* in order to have *phenomenon*. Something that does not exist cannot have quality. Nothing can manifest nothing. If Dr. Mercer's talismanic energy in the material world is only the Divine Will in action, and if God impinges that energy upon the human consciousness as if it were real material substance, then it follows that God imposes a universal delusion upon the human family; for, with the exception of a few highly speculative idealistic philosophers, everybody believes in the reality of matter. We cannot bring ourselves to believe that God has put His rational creatures in a phantasmagorical world like that. Again, this view comes very near being idealism (used here in the philosophical sense)—a system of philosophy that is discredited by the common-sense of mankind. We hold to the doctrine that there must be both quiddity and quality in order to have a real world such as the one which we inhabit.

We must give attention to Dr. Mercer's theory of evolution. Beginning with the Ether of Space, he traces the evolutionary process without a break through the vortex whorls, ions, electrons, atoms, molecules, palpable material, life, sentiency, personality, consciousness, morality, and spirituality, and it is all evolution without a single place of cleavage in the continuity; even the "mutations" or "saltations" of the scientists are included. In no place is there the injection of anything new either by creation or miracle. Let it be said, however, to the author's credit, that the energy that carries out this marvelous process is the Divine Will; not the "Unconscious Will" of the German philosophers, but the Will of the Divine Being, who, because He has Will, must also have Intelligence and hence Personality. We must acknowledge that in this essay the proponent of evolution has "put his best foot forward." Our author demolishes the atheism of such crass materialists as the Frenchman, Le Dantec. He also 'indicates the inadequacy in Bergson's ''Creative Evolution,'' by showing that such a process would be impossible without the directive purpose and will of a personal God. In many ways, therefore, our author has done excellent service to the cause of Theism.

However, so far as regards the theory of evolution as here upheld, we feel that we must dissent. First, as we have already shown, if the universe is eternal, it is incapable of being evolved. Second, the author's theory does not correlate well with the Bible, which certainly includes both creation and miracle in its scheme of the world. The fact is, our author appeals very little to the Bible for his theory, but delves almost solely into the depths of speculative science and philosophy. Third, the progress of the world up to its present state of stability is, to our mind, most rationally accounted for by simply taking the Genetical narrative as it stands and according to its simplest *prima facie* construction. In the sublime cosmogony of the Bible all the facts are amply accounted for, and there is no danger of idealism, on the one hand, or of pantheism, on the other. And, lastly, while no one will deny that in prehistoric times there is evidence in both the Bible and science that the world was being prepared progressively, and brought to its present status, Dr. Mercer must admit that it is now stabilized, so as to make it a fit and reliable dwelling-place for man, and that to-day we do not find chemistry and physics running over into biology, nor one species of plants or animals merging into another, nor any of the plants and animals making improvement by inherent forces, nor any of the lower forms of animals evolving into men. Even if it were admitted that God has developed the world to its present status by a process of continuity, it is evident that the process has stopped now, in order to give man a habitation of stability and uniform law. But we think that the simple Bible way is the most rational—that in six days or periods God created and unfolded the universe to its present condition, and then "rested from all His works which He created," and now operates through the laws that He established. No; the cosmos is not in a state of flux; it is a régime of fixedness in the realm of nature, and whatever progress is made must be made by man, whom God created to be the head and crown of His handiwork and delegated him to "multiply and replenish the earth and to subdue it." Slowly it yields to his efforts, and if he will continue to do God's righteous will, by and by he will succeed in Edenizing the earth. Perhaps by and by God will introduce a new dispensation, and then we shall have the "new heavens and new earth wherein dwelleth righteousness," so comfortingly promised in Sacred Writ.

Our duty would not be wholly done did we not point out the danger accruing to the evangelical faith from the theory of evolution. Just now we will not argue the question as to whether this hypothesis can be reconciled with the teaching of the Bible or not, but will simply point out its practical effect on almost all classes of people, educated and uneducated alike. According to Dr. George Henslow ("Present Day Rationalism Critically Examined," pp. 17-27), the rationalism and materialistic monism of Great Britain are "professedly based on Darwinism." Nearly all the various classes of secularists, freethinkers and latitudinarians of England and America accept outright the evolutionary hypothesis. So to speak, they are "obsessed" by it. It is a well-known fact that the rationalism and materialism of Germany are founded on Darwinism, which was transported to that country from England. Vogt, Buechner, Feuerbach, and Haeckel—all are materialists and all champions of evolution. Graf, Wellhausen and Kuenen, destructive Biblical critics of the most radical type, held to this theory, and made it the foundation stone of their dissecting treatment of the Bible. The principle involved in the magic phrases, "the struggle for existence" and "the survival of the fittest," lie at the basis of the "superman" and "might-makes-right" philosophy of Nietzsche, who simply changed the doctrine of "the will to live" to that of "the will to power."

The author was once drawn into a debate with a secularist, who was violent in his denunciation of the Bible, and who also denied the existence of a Supreme Being. When we asked him how he would account for the world with all its evidences of design and beneficence, he declared that "evolution will account for everything that is." Only a few days ago one of our students reported to us that he had had a dispute with an unbeliever who declared that "every informed and up-to-date person to-day believes in evolution." When he was asked how he would account for the evolutionary process itself, for the force that operates through the law and that pushes on to higher and better forms, his wise reply was: "Well, I never thought of that!" How profound! The very thing that he ought to have considered first of all had no place in his superficial world-view.

For the reasons given, and many others that might be adduced, we feel constrained to register our firm belief that the theory of evolution, by whatever adjectives qualified, is inimical to the evangelical faith, and lacks scientific verification.

CHAPTER XV

SCIENTIFIC THEORIES THAT CHALLENGE FAITH

IT is a mistake to think that the only subjects of thought that put a strain upon faith are religion and theology. Some persons aver that they cannot accept the doctrines of the Christian system because they are so mysterious. These people declare that they cannot understand God; that He is the inscrutable, unknowable Being, if He exists at all. Neither can they conceive how God can be a Trinity; how He could create the universe *ex nihilo;* how He could become incarnate in the person of Jesus Christ; how He could have been "conceived by the Holy Ghost, born of the Virgin Mary"; how He could personally take man's sin and moral task upon Himself, and make expiation for iniquity; how the soul can perdure after the atoms and molecules of the brain have been dissolved.

It shall be the purpose of this chapter to show that the scientists of the day also accept certain hypotheses that challenge and stagger faith, and even strain it to the breaking point—to the point, indeed, where it becomes little less than blind credulity. We have, in fact, often been both amused and amazed at men who have protested that they could not believe in the supernatural, and especially in miracles, and then in almost the next breath they would declare their faith in scientific theories that border on the grotesque, that are utterly beyond scientific verification, and that require the most childlike credulousness.

Just for the sake of comparison, let us consider one of

the outstanding mysteries of Christian theology—namely, the doctrine of the Trinity, which some people reject because they think it utterly inexplicable. We believe that just as rational a vindication of this doctrine can be made as of the theory of the atomic or corpuscular composition of matter. This is the process of reasoning.

God is a Trinity—that is, He is both one and three. But remember He is not both one and three in the same respect. There are many things right around us that are one in one respect and three in another respect. So God is one as to His essence or being, but three as to hypostases, persons, and modes of life and functioning.

Mr. Ingersoll used to make great sport of the theologians because, he said, they did not know as much about arithmetic as a small boy in the country school; for the schoolboy would say, "One plus one plus one equals *three*"; but the theologians declare that "one plus one plus one equals only *one*!" Then he would smile patronizingly, and his audiences would applaud. Well, suppose we look for a moment at this simple sum in mathematics. Put the formula on the black-board: "One plus one plus one equals three." How many figures have you at the right end of the equation? Why, only one, the figure three. So, after all, in one respect, one plus one plus one equals only one, while of course in another respect it equals three. So with God. But some one says that is only a manipulation of figures. You cannot make good your claim when you take three actual objects and add them together. Let us see. Here are three apples lying on different parts of the table. I want to add them together. So I pick up one and set it down here; then the other and set it down right by the side of the first one; then the third by the side of the second. Now what have I? I have three apples, true enough; but how many *groups* of apples have I? Only one. That collection of apples is one in one respect and three in another.

So with the Triune God; one as to essence or being; three as to persons, or *foci* of self-consciousness.

However, no trained theologian has ever contended that God is a mathematical material Trinity. No; God is a psychical or spiritual Trinity. The Bible itself says, "God is a Spirit." Therefore our best illustrations of this doctrine are to be found, not in the material realm, but in the mental or psychical. Have you ever thought about it that in a very inner sense the human mind has a triune constitution. It is made up of the Intellect, the Sensibility and the Will—that is, the cognitive, the emotional and the volitional functioning powers. Yet they do not constitute three minds, but only one mind. More than that, the mind is a unitary entity, and is not made up of parts as a lump of material substance is. Therefore the Intellect is the whole mind, the Sensibility is the whole mind, and the Will is the whole mind; each and all are identically the same substance or quiddity. Each in substance is equal to all, and yet all together are equal to each. Thus we see again that an entity can be, in a very mysterious and profound way, one in one respect and three in another. Remember, we do not hold that this is an analogy; it is only an illustration of the point I have stated, that the mind is one in one respect and three in another. So with the Triune God. Only God is *personally* triune, not only *functionally*. This distinction must be made to avoid the old heresy of Modalism, advocated by Sabellius and others in the early days of the Christian Church.

A still profounder illustration of the Trinity may be found in the process of self-consciousness in the human mind. The self, the ego, the mind, can objectify itself—that is, the mind can think of itself, make itself its own object; it can, as it were, set itself out before itself. There, then, are two, the subject and the object, and both are the same ego and substance. But the circle of self-consciousness is not complete; another step must be taken: there must be another ego set off to one side, as it were, by which the subject cognizes the object as itself, and the object cognizes the subject itself. Now when you have these three acts of the soul, and only then, do you arrive at complete self-consciousness. So with the triune God, who is eternally and perfectly self-conscious, and therefore knows Himself in the Father, the Son and the Holy Ghost. This is the profoundest illustration of the Trinity that can be given, because it is an analysis of that deep and inner synthesis which we call self-consciousness; but let us remember that, after all, it is still only an illustration, not an analogue; it designates three modes of life in God, but does not lead us to comprehend how there can be three *foci* of self-consciousness, or three persons, in the one Godhead.

Yet I believe we can press thought still a little further into the wonder and depths of the eternal Trinity by this mode of speculating: If God is the perfect, infinite and absolute Being, we may conceive that, since He must be absolutely and perfectly self-conscious, He may exist as three egos, three *foci* of personality, in the same being or substance, each of which knows the others with absolute perspicacity; so that Christ could say, ''The Father knoweth the Son, and the Son the Father,'' and Paul could write by inspiration, ''Who knoweth the mind of God save the Spirit of God?''

Thus we can, in a measure, at least, vindicate the profoundest doctrine of the Christian religion by a rational process; and we maintain that we can come as near doing this as we can prove many of the theories of physical science, as we shall now proceed to show. There are inscrutable mysteries and insuperable difficulties in the material world as well as in the spiritual sphere. Our Lord said to Nicodemus: ''Marvel not that I said unto thee, Ye must be born again. The wind bloweth where it listeth, and thou hearest the sound thereof, but canst not tell whence it cometh and whither it goeth. So is every one that is born of the Spirit.'' As much as to say, ''Do not stumble over the mystery of the new birth. Why, you cannot understand the mystery of the blowing wind. Why should you expect to fathom all the mysteries of the spiritual life? You need not comprehend them; all you have need to do is to experience them, just as you experience the action of the wind itself.''

Our purpose now will be to consider some of the modern scientific hypotheses, some, too, that the writer himself accepts. We shall show that they carry in their very nature such absolute difficulties as to stretch both faith and reason almost to the breaking point. We shall begin with the Copernican theory of the universe, or at least of the solar system. Up to the time of this great Prussian investigator, the Ptolemaic view mostly prevailed—the view that all the old astronomers practically held. This view was that the earth is the central orb, and the most important, and that the sun, moon and stars revolve around it. It is called the geocentric view. The theory was wrought out in a wonderful way by means of cycles and epicycles; but of course it was encumbered with insurmountable difficulties. Then came Copernicus, who lived from 1473 to 1543, and who taught that the sun is the greater orb of our system, and that the earth and the other planets swing in vast orbits around it. This is called the heliocentric view, because *helios* means the sun. A century later—1564-1642—lived Galileo, who laid special emphasis on the theory that the earth is round and revolves once in twenty-four hours on its axis. For his advocacy of this view he was persecuted by the Church and condemned and abused by his fellow-scientists; all of which, of course, was very wicked.

I suppose all of us accept Galileo's hypothesis; the writer most certainly does; but think for a moment what a tremendous demand is made on our faith in holding this view. The earth completes a revolution on its axis in twenty-four hours. The earth's circumference at the equator is 25,000 miles. Therefore we who live in the temperate and torrid zones must be traveling at the astounding velocity of 700 to 1,000 miles an hour. Have you ever been on an express train that was rushing along at 60 to 70 miles an hour? You well remember what your feelings were. But that is a mere trifle compared with the rate at which you and I are at this moment speeding along on the earth's surface. Here we sit quietly and unconcerned, and to-night we shall go to sleep without a twitch of uneasiness; and yet we are swinging along at nearly a thousand miles an hour, almost 17 miles a minute, almost one-fourth of a mile a second. Now we are here; presto! we are yonder, a mile away. Yet we are not conscious of any movement at all. We seem to be perfectly at rest. This is most astonishing—that we should be rushing along at such an inconceivable speed, and yet are not in the least aware of it. Does not such a theory tug mightily at the strings of faith?

But I have not yet stated the greater part of the difficulty. The atmosphere, so light and volatile, goes with the earth in its impetuous onward rush; so do the clouds and vapors and all the gases of the earth, no matter how light they may be.

But a still more inconceivable thing is that the earth in its mad whirl never *wobbles;* never is deflected a hair's breadth from its strictly spherical revolution on its axis. If so tremendous a sphere were to get out of plumb the diameter of a needle, it would surely fly into chaos, and we —well, deponent sayeth not where we would be. But how can the earth keep from wobbling in its swift rotation? How can it go without the slightest jar? It has no real axis, no spindles projecting out at the north and south poles and resting on something solid. No, it is simply out here in space with apparently nothing but the subliminal ether around it to hold it in place. How does it keep its equilibrium? Why does it not wobble?

When you consider the character of the earth's surface, the difficulty is accentuated. The earth is far from being a perfect sphere. It is broken up into oceans and continents, hills, mountains, valleys, plains. The eastern continent is much larger than the western. In both the arctic and antarctic regions there are vast uneven mountains of snow and ice. Note the vast mountain ranges, the Rockies, the Andes, the Alps, the Himalayas, great excrescences on the earth, broken up here and there without any discernible order, with no apparent attempt to preserve the earth's balance on its imaginary axis; and yet the earth goes on gyrating at the rate of a thousand miles an hour, and never veers a hair's breadth from its appointed place. Well may we exclaim with Nicodemus, "How can these things be?"

The writer confesses that sometimes, in thinking over this theory, he grows rebelliously skeptical, and declares, down in his inner consciousness, he does not believe it. The whole theory of Galileo and Copernicus may be a scientific blunder, a huge mistake, and we may be entirely on the wrong track. There must be some other way of explaining the phenomena of the solar system. But what other hypothesis is there to believe? The earth must be round, or people could not go around it by continuing in the same direction; and if the earth is a globe, it must revolve on its imaginary axis, or there is no way of accounting for the diurnal successions. So there you are—you must believe *nolens volens*. It is a case of Hobson's choice.

We have already indicated that we are very swift travelers with the earth in its daily revolution. But the half has not yet been told, if good old Copernicus was right. Would you believe it, we are also voyaging on our planet around the sun? We are being hurled at more than a breakneck speed in the earth's annual journey in its orbit. And here is still a greater challenge to faith, coming again from the scientists, not from the theologians. We are traveling—remember, this is what the astronomers say—at the rate of 66,600 miles an hour with our planet around the sun, or 1,112 miles a minute, or 18½ miles a second. Let us note the demands that science makes on our faith while we are cultivating the fine art of traveling: we are moving this moment in one direction at the rate of nearly 1,000 miles an hour, and in another direction at the rate of 66,600 miles an hour! If any one doubts my figures, and thinks I am jesting, I refer him to any modern astronomy, like Todd's manual, and he will find that the astronomers are seriously teaching our boys and girls in the high school and the college these very theories as scientifically established facts. You can figure it for yourself. The earth's elliptical orbit is 584,600,000 miles in circumference; our mundane sphere has to travel all that distance, from perhelion to aphelion and back to perhelion again, in 365 days, 6 hours, 9 minutes and 9 seconds, arriving at every station on schedule time. So you can make the division, and find out that you are going leisurely along at the rate of 18½ miles per second without feeling dizzy or growing excited. Even though hurled at this rate, the earth never vacillates the diameter of a hair from its course; and it also carries its atmosphere with it without the loss of an atom, so far as we know. Does not all this seem incredible? Does it not stretch the faith even of a scientist to the breaking tension? I confess that sometimes in my weaker moments I whisper to myself: "There isn't a word of it true. We are utterly on the wrong track." At all events, the man who can bolt this hypothesis ought not to strain at the doctrine of the Trinity or the Incarnation, or balk at the story of the fish that swallowed Jonah.

Perhaps you will think that all the difficulties have been

mentioned; but the physicists join with the astronomers in imposing still another burden on our tottering faith. They tell us about the "ether of space"—that is, a fine, ethereal substance, an almost *thingless* something, that fills all the interspaces among the planets, that bears the light and heat of the sun and other orbs on its lightsome wings, and holds all the planets in their orbits. They say it is thousands of times lighter than the air, is perfectly ductile, mobile and elastic, and yet it is the source of that tremendous power we call gravitation. Now note: the earth, speeding at the rate of 66,600 miles an hour, plunges through this ether; and yet, so light is it, that not enough resistance and friction are met with to retard the globe one second in all the millenniums. What! and that frictionless ether is the force of gravitation that holds Neptune, Jupiter, Saturn, Uranus, Sirius and the Pleiades in their orbits! Does not your faith snap at such a proposition? If it does not, it must be made of elastic material.

Next, we shall treat of some scientific hypotheses that do not deal with things on so colossal a scale, but that are no less mysterious. Let us look at matter itself. Some people cannot believe in mind as a distinct quiddity because, forsooth, they cannot understand what mind is. We are disposed to inquire first what matter is. What is matter, anyway? Of what is its substance composed? Or is it really substance? Is it only force? No one has ever seen an ultimate particle of matter any more than he has seen an ultimate element of mind. At the *ultima thule* one is just as mysterious as the other. All we know anything about is the *phenomena* of both mind and matter; we do not know the *noumena*—the things in themselves, just as the philosophers have said for centuries. Here is an old saw we used to hear in our boyhood days: Some one would ask you, "What is mind?" You would answer, "No matter." Then he would ask, "What is matter?" and you would reply, "Never mind." But that is no explanation; it is only a quip, an evasion.

Some people are greatly puzzled about the infinite. They cannot understand at all what the infinite is. However, they never seem to reflect that the infinitesimal is just as mysterious. Take matter, and say, as many scientists do, that it is composed of atoms. If you ask them, What is an atom? they reply, It is a particle of matter that is so small and so constituted that it cannot be made any smaller. But how can that be? Can you conceive of a particle of matter that could not be halved or quartered? Then why cannot these diminutive particles be subdivided, and so on and on, *ad infinitum?* You can think, but you cannot think the problem through. At last you must simply give it up. Yes, the infinitely tiny is just as baffling to thought as is the infinitely immense. Yet the physicists and chemists insist that we must believe in atoms or atomies, or at least in something ultimate.

Suppose, now, we take a still deeper look at the modern theory of matter. But to go back: Democritus, the Greek philosopher, is usually called the father of the atomic theory of matter. He made some advance in refinement over his predecessors, whom we cannot take time to mention. But when some one asked Democritus how the atoms held together, he said they had *hooks.* But that simply throws the mystery back a little further, for the next question would be, What are the *hooks* made of? Epicurus and Lucretius, the former in prose, the latter in verse, developed the doctrines of Democritus, and the three together were the founders of the materialistic theories that have come down through the centuries and are in the world to-day.

The modern theories, however, hark back a good deal further into.the constitution of matter than did their predecessors of the olden times. Atoms no longer are satisfactory. They are too big and ponderous, too coarse and lumbering, and in themselves explain little, while they themselves must be explained. Of course, the Greeks knew nothing scientifically of electricity and magnetism, nor of radium, helium, uranium, thorium, actinium, etc. So to-day the scientists must get back to something a great deal finer and more pliant than atoms. Therefore they presuppose the universal ether, the substance that fills all space not occupied by suns, stars, planets and comets, and that is the substratum and source of all the ponderable and palpable matter of the universe. This ether is the primordial material. Sometimes it is called "the eternal receiver and transmitter of force." Note the attributes assigned by science to this marvelous substance. It is most highly refined and sublimated, perfectly ductile, mobile, continuous and elastic, not made up of atoms or particles of any kind.

Here is a breaking test of faith again. How can a substance exist without having parts and being composed of atoms. How can anything material have perfect continuity? How can such attenuated substance be so elastic and strong that it can be indefinitely stretched by the flying stars and planets without breaking? These are hypotheses that seem to be utterly untenable. Nor is this all. The ether is, after all, slightly inert, say the physicists, because it offers enough resistance to the light waves to retard them eight minutes in traversing the distance from the sun to the earth, which is 93,000,000 miles. But if it has enough weight and inertia to retard the waves of light, how can the earth, with its vast bulk, slip through it at the rate of 1,100 miles a minute without friction? This theory stretches one's faith about as much as the racing planets stretch the ether! Surely if the ether has the least resistance and inertia, it would scale off our mundane atmosphere, and perhaps convert the earth itself into an incandescent ball by the friction caused by its velocity.

The scientists assume the existence of the primordial ether. They do not presume to tell how it came into existence. If it just happens to be, that is again a breaking pull on our faith. However, assuming the ether to be a real entity, its original condition was that of pure homogeneity and quiescence. If that is so, how·could it ever get into motion and convert itself into heterogeneity? Can you get diversity out of pure sameness without an outside force? If so, how? Can absolute quiescence ever bring about motion with no external help? How did motion ever begin? There can be no motion without force, but where did the force come from? Of course, it may have just happened to come along at the fortuitous moment, but some of us who are troubled with skepticism cannot help wondering how it could just happen to come along, and if it did just happen, how it could have produced such a wonderful cosmos of order and law and intelligence as the present universe is.

Well, to continue the story: In some way, no one knows how, and at some place, no one knows where, the ether was thrown into vortices—that is, infinitely small whorls or whirlpools; these eddies formed ions, which were charged with electricity both negative and positive, thus making electrons; and these coming together in just the fortuitous way, formed atoms; the various atoms, being combined in divers ways, formed molecules, which in turn combined into all the various known palpable substances. There you have it in a nutshell—the program of the production of the material universe.

However, here again a sore strain is imposed on our faith. Of course, we can see how God, if He created the pristine ether, could very easily have set it here and there into whorls, and thus given it motion; for mind, as we know, has the power of auto-action and auto-determination. But what we cannot understand is how these vortices in a continuous and atomless ether could have formed the particles of matter called ions. We repeat, if there were absolutely no particles there in the original ether, we do not comprehend how *whirlpools* could have produced *particles*. If you were to set a number of eddies to going in water, you would rather spread the water out further and further than cause it to come together into solid lumps. If the scientists will let God come into the process at all, we would think He would not have produced ponderable material from the ether by means of whorls, but would rather have pressed the ether here and there into solid particles, then made electricity and charged the ions with it, thus forming electrons, which He combined into atoms and molecules. But without supernatural power back of and in the process, we certainly cannot see that the assigned causes are adequate to produce the assigned effects.

Physical science multiplies difficulties in its many assumptions and theories. It has pushed the mystery back from the atom to the ion, which it now hails as the smallest particle of matter, the nucleus of the atom. Some hold the atom to be a "closed" system with its electricized ions whirling about within it. There are both negative and positive ions. The negative ions are the more important, and are called corpuscles. We quote here from Dr. R. W. Micou, who has given special study to the new theory of matter. He says of the infinitesimal corpuscles: "They are all alike in nature and size, and constitute actual parts of the forms of matter from which they fly. Their velocity is between 10,000 and 90,000 miles a second, or about half the velocity of light. They are almost inconceivably small, being about one-thousandth part of a hydrogen atom, which has heretofore been considered the smallest particle of matter." At another place this author says that the *beta* corpuscles produced by radio-activity "move with very nearly the velocity of light"—that is, they fly off at the marvelous speed of almost 186,000 miles a second. Let us bear in mind that even an atom is a microscopic particle of matter. No one has ever seen an atom or a molecule, not even with the most powerful microscope. The scientist, Kauffman, a recognized authority, tells us that an electron is to a bacillus as a bacillus is to the earth. There are millions of atoms in a drop of water, and it takes a thousand ions to make the smallest atom known, that of hydrogen. Yet the ion is flying at the rate of 186,000 miles a second! There! in that second an ion has traveled 186,000—if there was nothing to obstruct its progress! This is one of the serious contentions of science. When we read of such speculations, we wonder whether the scientific guild are aware of the terrible burden they are imposing on a layman's faith. We do not mean to say we reject the scientist's guess, or that we have a better theory to propound, for we have not; but we confess that it is easier for us to believe that God caused the sun and moon to stand still over Ajalon in answer to Joshua's prayer than it is to believe in the amazing exploits and athletic feats of those infinitesimal ions of the scientists. We are not making fun; we are very much in earnest; and therefore we must confess frankly that there is no doctrine of theology that so strains our faith as the gymnastics of the ions and electrons.

The scientists tell us that no particles of matter are at rest; all are dancing and whirling in even the solidest substances. They tell us that heat is only a mode of motion; that the reason an object feels hot is not because there is any real heat there, but because the waves of ether have pushed the atoms farther apart, and given them a swifter motion and a wider orbit; and thus, when you touch a so-called heated substance, these tiny whirling dervishes strike your hand with enough force to raise a blister! Of course, in some mysterious way—not explained by science, as far as we know—the increased rapidity of the motion of the atoms turns the heated iron red, so that we call it "red hot." We do not for a moment mean to say that we reject these theories; yet we confess that at the bar of reason they seem to be sadly inadequate, and really create more difficulties than they explain.

The science of the day appears to have accepted without demur the undulatory theory of light. Perhaps it is the true view. At all events, we have no better one to advance. However, we must say that sometimes we grow rebelliously agnostical. Let us examine the modern scientific theory of optics, and see how many difficulties it imposes on both our faith and our reason. First, according to this view, there is no *luminous* ether or substance, but light is simply and solely the result of the wave-like movements in the universal ether. Even the sun is not in itself luminous; but for some cause its atoms and molecules have been set into such violent motion, and their orbits extended so greatly, that this very rapidity of motion, in some way, produces light; or in reality not light in the sun itself, which is as dark as Erebus, but the accelerated motion of its atoms sets the ether into undulations, which spread out through space like waves of the sea, until finally some of them strike the eye of a human being or an animal, and then, in some mysterious way not explained, they are converted into luminosity through the optic nerve in the brain and the consciousness.

Now, anent this seemingly beautiful theory, we want to raise this fundamental question: If the ether is entirely dark, and if the human eye, with its iris, crystalline lens, aqueous and vitreous humors, its retina and optic nerve, is also dark, how can the black waves of the ether falling on the black organs of the eye be converted into the sensation of light *merely by motion?* Will anybody arise and explain how these things can be? How can nature get light out of darkness without a luminous ether? Sometimes, as we ponder these matters, we almost feel like declaring that the undulatory theory of light is all wrong, and that the old theory, that light is really a luminous ether, is the true one; so that, when it penetrates the eye, the sensation of luminousness is easily produced.

Nor is the mystery of light and color lessened when we are told that the different colors of the spectrum are due to the variation in the length of the ethereal waves; that ultra-red is produced by the longest waves, and ultra-violet by the shortest waves. What is there, we would humbly ask, about a long wave of a dark substance that it should produce a dark-red sensation, and about a short wave that it should produce extreme violet? If some one should explain that the sensation of light is due to the action of electricity in the ether when its waves strike the visual organs, we would reply, "Then you have introduced another ether besides the universal ether to help you out of your difficulty, and that only increases the mystery as to how the earth in its revolution and its course about the sun can slip through *two* ethers without creating friction!" Besides, most scientists tell us that electricity is itself only a mode of motion, or at least the result of motion, and so we come back to our first inquiry, how the wavelets can convert a dark substance into light. The conversion of a sinner into a saint is no more mysterious than that.

And now, in the language of Holy Writ, "Behold, I show you a mystery." The various colors depend on the rapidity of the ether vibrations. And what, according to science, is that rapidity? I quote from a recent work of science, used in high schools and colleges, Hinman's "Eclectic Physical Geography": "When the rate of vibration is 392 trillions a second, the sensation of *red* is produced upon the eye. As the vibrations increase in rapidity, they give rise successively to each of the color sensations of the spectrum. If the rapidity of vibration increases beyond that which produces the sensation of violet (757 trillions to the second), the eye is not affected, and they cease to be luminous. A ray of sunlight is composed of vibrations of all degrees of rapidity, which collectively produce a white or colorless sensation.''

There you have the theory all as clear as midday! For convenience we will strike an average between 392 trillions, and 757 trillions, which is about 574 trillions. Now, in order to produce in the eye the sensation of white light, the ether pulsations must strike the retina and optic nerve at the rate of 574 trillions per second!! I have placed two exclamation-points after that statement. What becomes of the miracle of the fish swallowing the run-away prophet in comparison with this optical miracle propounded to us in all seriousness by modern science? Just ponder the supreme miracle for a moment. The ether pounds on your eye 574 trillions of times a second in producing light, and yet you are not aware of any motion or impact whatever, but have, on the other hand, a sensation of perfect immobility. "How can these things be? How can a man be born when he is old?" Note the difficulty and the contradiction of science. It holds that the ether is slightly inert— that is, has a slight degree of weight, else it would not require eight minutes for light to travel from the sun to the earth. We maintain that, if the ether has any degree of weight, even the slightest, 574 trillions of vibrations a second beating upon the eye would pound that delicate organ to pieces. But the scientists do not think so. They have a stalwart and boundless faith. Nothing staggers it— at least, no wonder in the physical realm. It is only when men like Haeckel, Tyndal, Huxley, Ward and Mains come to consider such Biblical mysteries as the miraculous conception of Christ that they balk, and their faith cannot or will not bear the strain!

We propound still another enigma in the modern scientific theory of optics. It relates to the very common function of physical sight. How do we see? The present theory is that yonder tree, green and symmetrical, throws back the waves of the ether with inconceivable velocity upon my eyes. They penetrate the iris, dash through the lenses and humors, form an inverted image of the tree on the retina, and then, in some mysterious way, the optic nerve bears that image back into the proper brain center, where, in a still more mysterious way, it blossoms out into my consciousness, and, behold, I see a tree out there on the lawn. A beautiful hypothesis, in very truth, and I confess that I myself believe it. But how mysterious! how inexplicable! Observe the *lacunae*, the dark places, in the process. How and why does the tree set the ether in motion? How can the transverse oscillations of the ether bear to the eye the image of the tree? What is the precise connection between the ethereal undulations and the color, shape and size of the object? If the mind, through the optic nerve, simply perceives the image of the tree on the retina of the eye, how comes it that I see the tree out yonder on the lawn and not within my eye at all? Centuries before modern science knew that the eye had a moving-picture curtain on its rear wall, men had been seeing objects just where they were out there in space, and had not the slightest suspicion that they were merely perceiving pictures on optical screens. Thus we see that our consciousness and our scientific theory do not agree; and that is another strange mystery. Why should we be so constructed that we think we see objects when we really see only images?

In order to prove that my perception and awareness are correct, whether the scientific hypothesis is or not, I simply walk out to the spot where I think I see the tree, and, behold, I find it *there*, and not in my eye. How inscrutable! How past finding out!

Thus we might continue to point out the many dark, inexplicable riddles in the theories of modern science.

There is the hypothesis of gravitation—is it a push or a pull? Is it some kind of an attractive power that matter possesses toward its fellow-matter all through the universe? If so, how can one body draw another through the space between the planets without any ropes with which to pull—without any strong and unbreakable substance that will endure the strain? Or is gravitation due to the universal ether, as the most recent pronouncements of science would have us believe? Then how can that light, ductile, subliminal substance, which permits the earth to slip through it at the rate of 66,600 miles an hour without friction and retardation, be so strong as to hold the planets and suns in their orbits? It is all very, very mysterious. The doctrines of the Trinity and the Incarnation are not more so.

Note a whole catalogue of scientific riddles of the universe: the theory of evolution producing a cosmos without an Involver or Evolver; the theory of the fortuitous concourse of vortices and atoms producing an orderly world and "the reign of law"; the theory of an unconscious intelligence and will operating in all things; the conception of a "power that makes for righteousness," and that still is impersonal; the view of design and adaptation without a conscious, designing intelligence; the proposition that the atoms are endowed with mentality, and when enough of these infinitesimal minds come together in a conference-meeting in the human brain, presto! they produce the human mind; the hypothesis that human sentiency, consciousness, morality and spirituality have evolved by purely resident forces from material substance, making the effect greater and nobler than its producing cause; the theory of parallelism in psychology; the theory of pluralism and pragmatism in philosophy, ethics and theology; and so on and so forth. But we must forbear.

Our purpose in presenting this thesis has not been mere art for art's sake. We frankly concede that our primary

motive has been a moral one. Our aim has been to show
that, in science as well as in religion, we must often walk
by faith and not by sight; that we cannot always find our
way by pure reason or purely logical processes; that the
science of the day makes as strenuous a demand on our
belief as do the doctrines of theology and religion; that
theology and religion have no monopoly of the mysterious;
that general skepticism never gets anywhere nor achieves
any success, but that faith is necessary for constructive
work and advancement in any realm of the worth while.
How many things in this life we must take by faith! Yes,
"faith is the substance of things hoped for, the evidence of
things not seen." Call the roll of the heroes of faith; they
have all been men who have achieved success and have
pushed along the car of progress. The inspired writer
looked into the very heart of things when he penned the
line, "Without faith it is impossible to please God."

Our theme teaches us another needed moral and spiritual
lesson—that of humility. How little we know! How little
we can know! The sum of human erudition sometimes
seems to be large; yet the more we advance and discover,
the more we realize the limits of human knowledge. Therefore we may well heed the admonition of Holy Writ, "Be
not wise in your own conceits."

We think we may bring this chapter and our entire book
to a close by apt quotations from two sources—two from
Tennyson's "In Memoriam" and two from Holy Writ:

> "Our little systems have their day;
>   They have their day and cease to be:
>   They are but broken lights of Thee,
> And Thou, O Lord, art more than they.

> "We have but faith: we cannot know;
>   For knowledge is of things we see:
>   And yet we trust it comes from Thee,
> A beam in darkness: let it grow.

"Let knowledge grow from more to more,
But more of reverence in us dwell;
That mind and soul, according well,
May make one music as before.

And again:

"Oh, yet we trust that somehow good
Will be the final goal of ill,
To pangs of nature, sins of will,
Defects of doubt and taints of blood;

"That nothing walks with aimless feet;
That not one life shall be destroyed,
Or cast as rubbish to the void,
When God hath made the pile complete;

"That not a worm is cloven in vain;
That not a moth with vain desire
Is shriveled in a fruitless fire,
Or but subserves another's gain.

"Behold, we know not anything:
I can but trust that good shall fall
At last—far off—at last, to all,
And every winter change to spring."

1 John 5:4, 5:

"For whatsoever is born of God overcometh the world: and this is the victory that overcometh the world, even our faith. Who is he that overcometh the world but he that believeth that Jesus is the Son of God?"

Heb. 11:6:

"But without faith it is impossible to please Him; for he that cometh to God must believe that He is, and that He is a rewarder of them that diligently seek Him."

SELECTED BIBLIOGRAPHY

ALTHOUGH the following list of conservative works along apologetic lines has grown to a considerable length, the author has not attempted to make it exhaustive. The field is a wide one, and no one can hope to be omniscient even in his own specialty. Indeed, the writer is haunted by the fear that some excellent works may have been inadvertently overlooked, so that some reader will wonder why they were not included. As has been suggested, this is a list of conservative works. We do not know that so extensive a roster has ever been printed previously, and therefore we hope this one will be of real value to those who desire to pursue further investigations.

We commend all the books here listed. Nearly all of them will be found to be of real value in eliminating doubt and fortifying faith. True, a few of them make, as we think, unnecessary and even dangerous concessions to the liberal side, but in the main they stand firmly for the fundamentals of "the faith once for all delivered unto the saints." Some of these works deal a little too liberally in epithets, and do not always display as calm a temper as they might, but even these often contain sound and convincing arguments, and the drastic words are due rather to earnestness of conviction and concern for the truth than an unjudicial frame of mind. In these cases let the reader weigh the reasoning and overlook the slashing style.

It may be asked why so formidable a bibliography has been presented. Frankly, we have had a motive. In the last two or three decades many people—some, too, who pretend to scholarship—have been reading only one side of the religious controversy, especially in the case of Biblical criticism, and are not aware of the large and erudite body of literature that has been produced by competent scholars in favor of the evangelical view of the Holy Scriptures and the doctrines of our religion. To these persons this citation will, we trust, be informing and helpful; and certainly to all persons the proportions of our list must be morally impressive, proving that the evangelical faith has not lacked capable championship. In the great contest the conservative party has been able to meet argument with argument and to match scholarship with scholarship.

Our purpose has been to cite only works bearing distinctively on the science of Christian Apologetics. There are many other works, such as Biblical commentaries and books on Christian and natural theism and Christian and general ethics, that also carry a strong apologetic element, and may be read with much profit by all concerned. We could not add to our pages by citing such works. For selected bibliographies on the relevant subjects we would refer the reader to our two books, "A System of Natural Theism" (1917, pp. 12, 13) and "A system of General Ethics" (1918, pp. 276-278).

Perhaps it will be said that, in order to be fair, we should have also presented a catalogue of liberal books. However, in the body of this volume many of these works are referred to again and again, and an attempt is made to refute their arguments; so that it does not seem to be necessary to burden our pages by citing titles. Yet, to be as "broad" as possible, we will frankly indicate where lists of liberal authors may be found. First, the following great conservative works cite, along with evangelical books, also numerous works by liberal authors, thus showing themselves eminently fair: William Henry Green: "The Unity of the Book of Genesis," pages 15-17; Edwin Cone Bissell: "The Pentateuch: Its Origin and Structure," pages 410-475: Samuel

Colford Bartlett: "The Veracity of the Hexateuch," pages 393-398; James Orr: "The Problem of the Old Testament," pages 543-547; Franklin Johnson: "The Quotations of the New Testament from the Old," pages 396-405. Besides, many of the other works in our list (e. g., Ebrard, Fisher, Fairbairn, Sheldon, Robertson, Cave, McKim, Wilson, Wiener) constantly refer to liberal authors, citing titles and pages. The following books are liberal. They also give lists, but, with very few exceptions, they call the roll of authors that belong only to the liberalistic school: William Frederic Bade: "The Old Testament in the Light of To-day," page 88, footnote, and numerous other footnotes throughout the book; Ismar J. Peritz: "Old Testament History," pages 334-336; Frank Knight Sanders: "History of the Hebrews," pages 337-353; Charles Foster Kent: "Heroes and Crises of Early Hebrew History," pages 233-251. Dr. Kent's other works also for the most part give only the titles of liberal authors. The ignoring of conservative books by the authors just named and others of their ilk seems to be studied. Why?

As a foil and antidote to their *ex-parte* method we give a list of authors who uphold the evangelical and orthodox positions. Some of these works run back into the nineteenth century, while others are very recent. Both classes are valuable, for the student will desire to note how, all along the years, capable defenders of the faith have heeded God's call to the great and vital conflict. These men, too, have been "heroes of the faith."

The author desires to add that he will welcome suggestions from any of his readers relative to effective conservative works on Apologetics that may have been inadvertently omitted from the following list. The more stalwart defenders of the faith, the more will Christ's kingdom be advanced.

GENERAL APOLOGETICS

AUBERLEN, C. A.: "The Divine Revelation: An Essay in Defense of the Faith."

BEATTIE, F. R.: "Fundamental Apologetics" (Vol. I).

CHRISTLIEB, T.: "Modern Doubt and Christian Belief."

EBRARD, J. H. A.: "Christian Apologetics, or, The Scientific Vindication of Christianity," 3 Vols.

FAIRBAIRN, A. M.: "The Philosophy of the Christian Religion."

FISHER, GEO. P.: "The Grounds of Theistic and Christian Belief."

FRANK, F. H.: "A System of Christian Certainty."

GIBSON, J. M.: "The Inspiration and Authority of Holy Scripture."

ILLINGWORTH, J. R.: "Reason and Revelation."

LA TOUCHE, E. D.: "Christian Certitude."

LINDBERG, C. E.: "Apologetics: A System of Christian Evidence" (1917).

LORIMER, G. C.: "The Argument for Christianity."

LUTHARDT, C. E.: "Fundamental, Moral and Saving Truths of Christianity," 3 Vols.

MAIR, G. E.: "Studies in Christian Evidence."

MEAD, C. M.: "Supernatural Revelation: An Essay Concerning the Basis of the Christian Faith."

McGARVEY, J. W.: "Evidences of Christianity" (1912).

MULLINS, E. Y.: "Why Is Christianity True? Christian Evidences."

ORR, JAMES: "The Christian View of God and the World."

PHILLIPS, L. T. M.: "Cumulative Evidences of Divine Revelation."

PIERSON, A. T.: "Many Infallible Proofs."

RISHELL, C. W.: "The Foundations of the Christian Faith."

SHORT, F. B.: "Christianity: Is It True" (1917).

STEARNS, L. F.: "The Evidence of Christian Experience."

STORRS, R. S.: "The Divine Origin of Christianity: Indicated by Its Historical Effects."

SWEET, L. M.: "The Verification of Christianity" (1920).

WRIGHT, GEO. F.: "Scientific Aspects of Christian Evidences."

MANUALS

FISHER, G. P.: "Manual of Christian Evidences."

KENNEDY, J.: "Popular Handbook of Christian Evidences."

KNOX, G. W.: "The Direct and Fundamental Proofs of the Christian Religion."

ROBINSON, E. G.: "Christian Evidences."

ROW, C. A.: "A Manual of Christian Evidences."

STEWART, A.: "Handbook of Christian Evidences."

WELLS, AMOS R.: "Why We Believe the Bible."

SPECIAL APOLOGIES

BETTEX, F.: "The Miracle" (revised edition, 1918); "The Word of Truth" (1914); "The Glory of the Triune God" (1911).

BLACK, S. C.: "Plain Answers to Religious Questions" (1910).

BLANCHARD, C. A.: "Visions and Voices, or, Who Wrote the Bible?" (1917).

BROCKINGHAM, A. A.: "Old Testament Miracles in the Light of the Gospel" (1907).

BROOKES, J. G.: "God Spake All These Words."

BURRELL, D. J.: "Why I Believe the Bible" (1917).

CHRISTIAN HERALD: "555 Difficult Bible Questions Answered" (1920).

D'ARCY, C. F.: "Christianity and the Supernatural."

DORCHESTER, D.: "Christianity Vindicated by Its Enemies;" "Concessions of Liberalists to Orthodoxy."

DRAWBRIDGE, C. L.: "Common Objections to Christianity;" "Popular Attacks on Christianity" (Fifth Thousand, 1914).

FAUNCE, D. W.: "A Young Man's Difficulties with His Bible;" "The Mature Man's Difficulties with His Bible;" "Hours with the Skeptic."

FITCHETT, W. H.: "The Beliefs of Unbelief" (1907).

FLEWELLING, R. T.: "Christ and the Dramas of Doubt" (1913).

GODET, F.: "Studies on the Old Testament;" "Studies on the New Testament."

GREGG, DAVID: "Facts that Call for Faith."

HALEY, J. W.: "Alleged Discrepancies of the Bible."

HALL, A. C. A.: "The Virgin Mother."

HAY, C. E.: "The Truth of the Apostles' Creed" (by twelve German theologians, translated, 1916).

HEAGLE, DAVID: "The Bremen Lectures on Great Religious Questions of the Day" (translated from the German).

HENSLOW, G.: "Present-Day Rationalism Critically Examined."

HITCHCOCK, F. R. M.: "The Present Controversy on the Gospel Miracles" (1915).

KNOWLING, R. J.: "The Testimony of St. Paul to Christ" (1905); "Our Lord's Virgin Birth and the Criticism of To-day" (third issue, 1907).

LAMB, F. J.: "Miracles and Science."

LEWIS, HENRY: "Modern Rationalism: As Seen at Work in Its Biographies."

LILLEY, J. S.: "Was the Resurrection a Fact? And Other Essays" (1916).

MACARTHUR, R. S.: "The Old Book and the Old Faith."

MACKENZIE, K.: "An Angel of Light" (1917).

MARGOLIOUTH: "Lines of Defense of the Biblical Revelation."

McCLURE, E.: "Modern Substitutes for Traditional Christianity" (1913).

McPHERSON, G. W.: "The Crisis in Church and College" (1919); "The Modern Conflict Over the Bible" (1919).

MUIR, P. M.: "Modern Substitutes for Christianity" (second edition, 1912).

MULLINS, E. Y.: "Freedom and Authority in Religion" (1913).

ORR, JAMES: "God's Image in Man;" "The Virgin Birth of Christ;" "The Bible Under Trial;" "The Resurrection of Jesus;" "Revelation and Inspiration."

PIERSON, A. T. (editor): "The Inspired Word: Papers and Addresses."

QUACKENBOS, J. D.: "Enemies and Evidences of Christianity: Thoughts on Questions of the Hour" (1899; second printing, 1909).

REMENSNYDER, J. B.: "Reason, History and Religion" (1907); "The Post-Apostolic Age and Current Religious Problems" (1909).

RILEY, W. B.: "The Menace of Modernism" (1917).

SAPHIR, A.: "The Divine Unity of the Scriptures;" "Christ and the Scriptures."

SCOTT, E. F.: "The Apologetic Element in the New Testament" (1907).

SEEBACH, J. F.: "The Book of Free Men: The Origin and History of the Scriptures and Their Relation to Modern Liberty" (1917).

SHEBBEARE, C. J.: "Religion in an Age of Doubt."

SHINN, G. W.: "Some Modern Substitutes for Christianity."

STUBB, J. A. O.: "Verbal Inspiration" (1913).

STURGE, M. C.: "Theosophy and Christianity" (1918).

SWEET, L. M.: "The Birth and Infancy of Jesus Christ" (1907).

THORBURN, T. J.: "The Virgin Birth: A Critical Examination."

TISDALL, W. ST. C.: "Christianity and Other Faiths."

TORREY, R. A.: "Difficulties in the Bible."

TORREY, R. A.: "The Fundamental Doctrines of the Christian Faith" (1918).

TOWNSEND, L. T.: Article on Jonah in *The Bible Champion* (September, 1913).

TOWNSEND, L. T.: "Adam and Eve: History or Myth?" "The Deluge: History or Myth?"

TUCK, ROBERT: "A Handbook of Biblical Difficulties."

VINE, C. H. (editor): "The Old Faith and the New Theology" (1907).

WACE, HENRY: "Christianity and Agnosticism."

WENDLAND, J.: "Miracles and Christianity."

WINNINGTON-INGRAM, A. F.: "Old Testament Difficulties" (1909); "New Testament Difficulties" (two vols., 1910, 1911); "Popular Objections to Christianity" (1912); "Reasons for Faith."

BIBLICAL CRITICISM

BAXTER, W. L.: "Sanctuary and Sacrifice" (1895).

BEATTIE, F. R.: "Radical Criticism: An Exposition and Examination" (1894).

BEHRENDS, A. J. F.: "The Old Testament Under Fire" (1897).

BETTEX, FR.: "The Bible and Modern Criticism."

BISSELL, E. C.: "The Pentateuch: Its Origin and Structure" (1885).

BODY, C. W. E.: "The Permanent Value of Genesis" (1894).

BURNS, W. H.: "The Higher Critic's Bible or God's Bible" (1904).

BURRELL, D. J.: "The Teaching of Jesus Concerning the Scriptures" (1904).

CAVE, ALFRED: "The Inspiration of the Old Testament: Inductively Considered" (1888).

COOKE, R. J.: "The Incarnation and Recent Criticism" (1907).

DALE, R. W.: "The Living Christ and the Four Gospels" (1905).

DAVIS, J. D.: "A Dictionary of the Bible" (third edition, 1911, see isagogical articles).

EERDMANS: "Composition of Genesis."

FINN: "The Unity of the Pentateuch."

FISHER, G. P.: "Supernatural Origin of Christianity" (new edition).

GIRDLESTONE, R. B.: "The Building Up of the Old Testament" (1912).

GRAEBLIN, A. C.: "The Prophet Daniel."

GREGORY, D. S.: "Why Four Gospels?" (1876).

GREEN, W. H.: "Moses and the Prophets" (1883); "The Higher Criticism of the Pentateuch" (1895); "The Unity of the Book of Genesis" (1895); "General Introduction to the Old Testament" (1898).

GRIFFITHS, J. S.: "The Problem of Deuteronomy" (1911).

HENSTENBERG, E. W.: "Dissertations on the Genuineness of the Pentateuch" (1847).

HITCHCOCK, F. R. M.: "Christ and His Critics: Studies in the Person and Problems of Jesus" (1910).

JOHNSON, FRANKLIN: "The Quotations of the New Testament from the Old" (1895).

JOHNSTON, H. A.: "Biblical Criticism and the Average Man" (1902).

KEIL, K. T.: "Historico-Critical Introduction to the Old Testament."

KENNEDY, J.: "Old Testament Criticism and the Rights of the Unlearned."

KEYSER, L. S.: "Some Specimens of Liberal Biblical Criticism" (*The Lutheran Church Review* for April, 1915).

KNOWLING, R. J.: "Literary Criticism of the New Testament" (1907).

LEATHES, STANLEY: "The Law and the Prophets;" "Claims of the Old Testament."

LIAS, J. J.: "Principles of Biblical Criticism" (1893).

McGARVEY, J. W.: "Jesus and Jonah" (1896); "The Authorship of the Book of Deuteronomy" (1902); "Short Essays on Biblical Criticism" (1910).

M'INTOSH, H.: "Is Christ Infallible and the Bible True?"

McKIM, R. H.: "The Problem of the Pentateuch" (1906).

MOELLER, W.: "Are the Critics Right? Historical and Critical Considerations Against the Graf-Wellhausen Hypothesis" (1899).

MUNHALL, L. W.: "The Highest Critics *Versus* the Higher Critics" (1896).

MUNROE, J. I.: "The Samaritan Pentateuch and Modern Criticism" (1911).

NICOLL, W. R.: "The Church's One Foundation: Christ and Recent Criticism" (1905).

NOESGEN, C. A.: "The New Testament and the Pentateuch."

ORR, JAMES: "The Problem of the Old Testament" (1905).

ORR, JAMES (editor): "The International Standard Bible Encyclopedia" (1915; the critical articles are of great value).

REDPATH, H. A.: "Modern Criticism of the Book of Genesis" (second edition, 1906).

REICH, EMIL: "The Failure of the Higher Criticism of the Bible" (1905).

Riley, W. B.: "The Finality of the Higher Criticism" (1909).

Robertson, James: "The Early Religion of Israel" (1892).

Robinson, G. L.: "The Book of Isaiah" (1911).

Ropes, J. H.: "The Apostolic Age in the Light of Criticism" (1906).

Rouse, C. H.: "Old Testament Criticism in New Testament Light."

Schmauk, T. E.: "The Negative Criticism and the Old Testament" (1894).

Smith, John: "The Integrity of Scripture: Plain Reasons for Rejecting the Critical Hypothesis" (1902).

Stewart, T. McK.: "Divine Inspiration Versus the Documentary Theory of the Higher Criticism" (1904).

Thorburn, T. J.: "The Mythical Interpretation of the Gospels" (1916).

Thurtle, J. W.: "Old Testament Problems."

Torrey, R. A. (editor): "The Higher Criticism and the New Theology" (1911).

Troelstra, A.: "Organic Unity of the Old Testament;" "The Name of God in the Pentateuch" (1912).

Urquhart, J.: "The Inspiration and Accuracy of the Holy Scriptures" (1895).

Various Authors: "Lex Mosaica."

Vedder, H. C.: "The Johannine Writings and the Johannine Problem" (1917).

Von Orelli, C.: "The Old Testament Prophecy of the Consummation of God's Kingdom" (1885); "The Twelve Minor Prophets" (1893).

Wace, Henry: "The Bible and Modern Investigation;" "Prophecy, Jewish and Christian" (1911).

Waller: "Moses and the Prophets."

Warfield, B. B.: "An Introduction to the Textual Criticism of the New Testament" (1886; old, but still valuable).

Watson, F.: "The Book of Genesis: A True History" (1894).

Whitelaw, T.: "The Old Testament Problem."

Wiener, H. M.: "Studies in Biblical Law;" "Essays in Pentateuchal Criticism" (1909); "The Origin of the Pentateuch" (1910); "Pentateuchal Studies" (1912); "Contributions to a New Theory of the Composition of the Pentateuch" (*Bibliotheca Sacra*, 1918, 1919).

WILKINSON, W. C.: "Paul and the Revolt Against Him" (1914).

WILSON, R. D.: "Studies in the Book of Daniel" (1917); "The Authenticity of Jonah" (*Princeton Theological Review*, April and July, 1918); "Scientific Biblical Criticism" (Ditto, April, 1919); "Present Status of the Daniel Controversy" (*The Biblical Review*, April, 1919).

ZAHN, THEODORE: "Introduction to the New Testament" (second revised edition, translated by Jacobus, 1917).

ZERBE, A. S.: "The Antiquity of Hebrew Writing and Literature" (1911).

SCIENCE AND PHILOSOPHY

AZBILL, W. K.: "Science and Faith: The Spiritual Law in the Physical World" (1914).

BETTEX, F.: "Science and Christianity;" "The First Page of the Bible;" "The Six Days of Creation in the Light of Modern Science."

DAWSON, J. W.: "Eden Lost and Won;" "Modern Ideas of Evolution as Related to Revelation and Science" (sixth edition); "The Historical Deluge;" "Modern Science in Bible Lands."

DENNERT, E.: "At the Deathbed of Darwinism" (1904).

DE PRESSENSE, E.: "A Study of Origins."

DRUMMOND, H.: "Natural Law in the Spiritual World."

EVERETT, C. C.: "Theism and the Christian Faith" (1909).

FAIRHURST, A.: "Organic Evolution Considered" (1897, new issue, 1911).

FISHER, G. P.: "The Nature and Method of Revelation" (1890).

GIBSON, J. M.: "The Ages Before Moses;" "The Mosaic Era."

GRIDLEY, A. L.: "The First Chapter of Genesis as the Foundation for Science and Religion."

GRUBER, L. F.: "Creation Ex Nihilo: The Physical Universe a Finite and Temporal Entity" (1918).

HAAS, J. A. W.: "Trends of Thought and Christian Truth" (1915).

HALL, J. A.: "Glimpses of Great Fields;" "The Nature of God" (1910).

HEAGLE, DAVID: "The Lord God of Elijah" (criticism of evolution, 1916).

HOLBROOK, D. G.: "The Panorama of Creation" (1908).

HUELSTER, A.: "Miracles in the Light of Science and History" (1915).

JOHNSTON, H. A.: "Scientific Faith" (1904).

JOHNSON, W. H.: "The Christian Faith Under Modern Searchlights" (1916).

KELLY, A. D.: "Rational Necessity of Theism" (1909).

LEE, J. W.: "The Religion of Science" (1912).

MERCER, J. E.: "Some Wonders of Matter" (1919).

MICOU, R. W.: "Basic Ideas in Religion: Apologetic Theism" (1916).

PATTERSON, A.: "The Other Side of Evolution" (1903).

REMENSNYDER, J. B.: "Six Days of Creation."

SHEBBEARE, C. J.: "The Challenge of the Universe" (1918).

SHELDON, H. C.: "Unbelief in the Nineteenth Century" (1907); "Pantheistic Dilemmas and Other Essays in Philosophy and Religion" (1920).

SHIELDS, C. W.: "Scientific Evidences of Revealed Religion" (1900).

SMITH, T. H.: "Christ and Science" (1906).

STIRLING, J. H.: "Philosophy and Theology."

TOWNSEND, L. T.: "Evolution and Creation;" "The Collapse of Evolution;" also racy articles in recent numbers of *The Bible Champion*.

WOBBERMIN, G.: "Christian Belief in God: A German Criticism of German Materialistic Philosophy" (translated by Robinson, 1918).

WRIGHT, G. F.: "The Ice Age in North America, and Its Bearing on the Antiquity of Man" (fifth edition); "Scientific Confirmations of Old Testament History" (1906); "Origin and Antiquity of Man" (1912).

DEFENSES OF SPECIAL BIBLICAL DOCTRINES

BARRY, G. D.: "The Inspiration and Authority of the Holy Scripture: A Study in the Literature of the First Five Centuries" (1919).

COOKE, R. J.: "Outlines of the Doctrine of the Resurrection: Biblical, Historical and Scientific."

FAIRBAIRN, A. M.: "The Place of Christ in Modern Theology."

FORSYTH, P. T.: "The Cruciality of the Cross" (1908); "The Person and Place of Jesus Christ" (1909); "The Justification of God" (1917).

GORE, CANON: "The Incarnation of the Son of God."

HEAGLE, D.: "Do the Dead Still Live? The Testimony of Science Respecting the Future Life" (1920).

HITCHCOCK, F. R. M.: "The Mystery of the Cross."

HUNT, J. B.: "Existence After Death Implied by Science" (1910).

KEYSER, L. S.: "The Rational Test: Bible Doctrine in the Light of Reason" (1908).

LIDDON, CANON: "The Divinity of Our Lord."

MABIE, H. C.: "The Divine Reason of the Cross: A Study of the Atonement as the Rationale of the Universe" (1911).

MOORE, A. W.: "The Rational Basis of Orthodoxy" (1901).

MOZLEY, J. K.: "The Doctrine of the Atonement" (1916).

MYLNE, L. G.: "The Holy Trinity: A Study of the Self-Revelation of God" (1916).

ORR, JAMES: "The Problem of Sin."

PRATT, S. W.: "The Deity of Jesus Christ: According to the Gospel of John" (1907).

QUICK, O. C.: "Essays in Orthodoxy" (1916); "Modern Philosophy and the Incarnation" (fifth edition, 1917).

RELTON, H. M.: "A Study in Christology: The Problem of the Two Natures in the Person of Christ" (1917).

REMENSNYDER, J. B.: "The Atonement and Modern Thought" (1905).

ROBERTSON, A. T.: "The Divinity of Christ in the Gospel of John" (1916).

SCHAFF, PH.: "The Person of Christ."

SNOWDEN, J. H.: "Can We Believe in Immortality?" (1918).

STALKER, JAMES: "Imago Christi" (1889); "The Christology of Jesus" (1899); "The Atonement" (1909).

STEARNS, L. F.: "Present Day Theology" (fourth edition, 1898).

STREATFIELD, G. S.: "The Incarnation" (1910).

STREETER, B. H. (and Others): "Immortality: An Essay in Discovery" (1917).

TOWNSEND, L. T.: "Bible Inspiration: The Orthodox Point of View;" "Discussions on the Trinity."

WARFIELD, B. B.: "The Lord of Glory" (1907); "Counterfeit Miracles" (1918).

WHITTEKER, J. E.: "The Separated Life: A Biblical Defense of the Divinity of Christ" (1909).

THE BIBLE AND ARCHEOLOGY

BANKS, E. J.: "The Bible and the Spade" (1913).

BARTON, G. A.: "Archeology and the Bible" (1916).

BISSELL, E. C.: "Biblical Antiquities: A Handbook."

BRUGSCH, H. K.: "History of Egypt Under the Pharoahs."

CLAY, A. T.: "Light on the Old Testament from Babel" (1906); "Amurru" (1909).

COBERN, C. M.: "The New Archeological Discoveries and Their Bearing upon the New Testament" (1917); also valuable articles in *The Biblical Review* for January, 1918, and January, 1919.

CONDER, C. R.: "The Tell Amarna Tablets" (1893); "The Bible and the East" (1896); "The Hittites and Their Language" (1898); "The Hebrew Tragedy" (1900).

DAVIES, W. W.: "The Codes of Hammurabi and Moses" (1905).

DAWSON, J. W.: "Egypt and Syria: Their Physical Features in Relation to Bible History."

GRIMME, H.: "The Law of Hammurabi and Moses" (translated by Pilter).

HILPRECHT, H. V.: "Explorations in Bible Lands During the Nineteenth Century" (1903).

HOMMEL, F.: "The Ancient Hebrew Tradition as Illustrated by the Monuments" (1897).

HOSKINS, F. E.: "From the Nile to Nebo: A Discussion of the Problem and Route of the Exodus" (1912).

JEREMIAS, A.: "The Old Testament in the Light of the Ancient East."

KOENIG, E.: "The Bible and Babylon" (an analysis of Delitzsch's "Babel und Bibel").

KYLE, M. G.: "The Deciding Voice of the Monuments in Biblical Criticism" (1912); "Moses and the Monuments: Light from Archeology on Pentateuchal Times" (1920); also many articles of great value in recent numbers of *Bibliotheca Sacra* and *The Sunday School Times;* "The Problem of the Pentateuch: A New Solution by Archeological Methods" (to be issued soon).

MACALISTER, R. A. S.: "Bible Sidelights from the Mound of Gezer."

NAVILLE, E.: "The Book of the Law Under King Josiah;" "Archeology of the Old Testament" (1913).

PETRIE, F.: "Researches in Sinai;" "Ten Years' Digging;" "Tanis;" "Hyksos and Israelite Cities;" "Egypt and Israel;" "Personal Religion in Egypt Before Christianity."

PINCHES, T. C.: "The Old Testament in the Light of Historical Records" (1902).

PRICE, I. M.: "The Monuments and the Old Testament."

RAMSAY, W.: "Was Christ Born at Bethlehem?" "Luke the Physician and Other Studies;" "Cities and Bishopricks of Phrygia;" "Historical Geography of Asia Minor;" "The Cities of St. Paul;" "St. Paul the Traveler;" "Pauline and Other Studies;" "The Teaching of Paul in the Terms of the Present Day;" "The Epistle to the Galatians;" "Letters to the Seven Churches of Asia;" "The Church and the Roman Empire;" "The Bearing of Recent Discoveries on the Trustworthiness of the New Testament" (1915).

SAYCE, A. H.: "The Higher Criticism and the Monuments;" "Monument Facts and Higher Critical Theories;" "The Early History of Israel;" "The Hittites, or, The Story of a Forgotten Empire;" "The Times of Isaiah;" "Races of

the Old Testament;" "Patriarchal Palestine;" "Fresh Light
from the Ancient Monuments."

TOMKINS, H. G.: "The Life and Times of Joseph in the Light
of Egyptian Lore."

URQUHART, J.: "Archeology's Solution of Old Testament Problems" (1906).

WINCKLER, H.: "The Tell el Amarna Letters."

OLDER APOLOGIES

The older Apologies, dealing with English Deism, French Atheism and General Infidelity, though out of date in some respects,
may still be read with much profit. They prove how God raised
up valiant defenders of the faith in those trying days. In order
to economize space, we give the names of the writers only, with
the titles only in special cases.

Halyburton, Cudworth, Bentley, Samuel Clarke, Conebeare,
Lardner, Bishop Horne ("Introduction to the Holy Scriptures");
Butler ("The Analogy"); Paley, Whateley, M'Ilvaine, Watson
("An Apology" in reply to Paine's "The Age of Reason");
Nelson ("The Cause and Cure of Infidelity"); Gaussen
("Theopneustia: The Plenary Inspiration of the Holy Scrip-
tures," recently reprinted); William Lee ("The Inspiration of
Holy Scripture: Its Nature and Proof"); Rawlinson ("The His-
torical Evidences of the Truth of the Scripture Records");
Gleig ("The Most Wonderful Book in the World," reprinted,
1915); "Lectures on the Evidences of Christianity," delivered
at the University of Virginia by various eminent scholars (1850-
51); Mark Hopkins ("Evidences of Christianity").

INDEX